FRIENDS of DOROTHY

FRIENDS of DOROTHY

Why Gay Boys and Gay Men Love *The Wizard of Oz* · DEE MICHEL

with a foreword by Gregory Maguire

Text copyright © 2018 Dee Michel
All rights reserved

No part of this book may be reproduced, stored in a retrieval system, or transmitted in any form or by any means, electronic, mechanical, photocopying, recording, or otherwise, without express written permission of the publisher.

Portions of this book have appeared in somewhat different form in "Not in Kansas Anymore: The Appeal of *The Wizard of Oz* for Gay Males," *Baum Bugle* 46, no. 1 (Spring 2002): 31–38.

www.deemichel.info

First print edition 2018 Dark Ink Press

ISBN13: 978-0-9997016-0-7   ISBN10: 0-9997016-0-6

Cover and interior design by Michael Starkman

Printed in the United States of America

DARK INK PRESS
www.darkink-press.com

To my father, **MARTIN MICHEL**,
who began the whole thing.

And to **DAVID MAXINE**,
who showed me you could
be out and be an Oz fan,

and **WILL FELLOWS**,
who encouraged and stimulated me
while working on a parallel project.

WHEN I WAS A LITTLE KID my favourite outfit was this little apron that I used to dance around in, pretending to be Dorothy, with a little lamb called Toto. I was like, "Let's go to Oz!" . . . On good days I was Dorothy, on bad days I was the Wicked Witch.

    RUFUS WAINWRIGHT gay singer and composer
    quoted in *The Times* (London) and *Time Out New York*

THE SEEDS OF WHY I DO what I do are in my childhood. I wouldn't let Narnia and Never-Never Land and Oz go. . . . Why would I lose these wonderlands? They were the ways I best understood myself.

    CLIVE BARKER gay writer and filmmaker
    quoted in *Cassell's Encyclopedia of Queer Myth, Symbol and Spirit*

THE WORDS "LET'S PRETEND" are a key that opens the door to a world where fantasies throng. Children whisk in and out of the personalities that inhabit this well-known yet surprisingly unfamiliar country where anything may happen. Here, on the threshold of this magic land, the child may choose the fantasy that will companion him on his journey and the choice of this companion may give us a clue to the child's own innate nature, to the problem, inner or outer, that he is facing and to the deep-buried but centrally impelling attitude toward these problems, even to the problem of life itself. . . . Surprising and revealing things happen in this magic land of "let's pretend."

    FRANCES WICKES psychologist and writer
    The Inner World of Childhood

THE GAY JOURNEY is everybody's journey. . . . It's not a unique story.

    DAVID MIXNER gay political activist
    The Trip (DVD), extra features

CONTENTS

Foreword by Gregory Maguire **xiii**
Acknowledgments **xvii**

Introduction **3**

PART ONE GAY FANS OF OZ
1. Gay Men and Oz **17**
2. Surface Explanations **41**
3. Gay Boys **55**

PART TWO INDIVIDUAL REASONS AND RESPONSES
4. Escaping to Oz **73**
5. Gender Roles in Oz **97**
6. Difference in Oz **117**
7. Messages and Uses of Oz **127**

PART THREE SOCIAL AND CULTURAL CONTEXTS
8. The Subcultural Phenomenon **143**
9. Oz and Judy in Gay Folklore **161**
10. The Oz–Gay Connection Now and in the Future **179**

APPENDIXES
A. The Questionnaire **199**
B. Methodology **207**
C. Was Baum Gay? **219**
D. Cross-Dressing in Oz Performances **223**
E. Early Allusions to Oz in Gay Contexts **227**
F. The Origin of "Friend of Dorothy" **229**

Notes **235**
Index **283**

CHARTS

1.1 The disproportionate number of gay Oz fans **31**
1.2 Versions of Oz stories **38**
2.1 Overlap between fans of the MGM movie and fans of the Oz books **48**
9.1 Folkloric beliefs about Judy Garland and the MGM *Wizard of Oz* **173**

FIGURES

I.1 Me (Dee) with my father's books (ca. 1955) **4**
1.1 *New Yorker* cartoon by Nick Downes (March 16, 1998) **19**
1.2 Ad for sing-along and dance party, Axis, Columbus, OH (1999) **21**
1.3 "Surrender to The Eagle," ad for The Eagle, Boston (2001) **21**
1.4 Ad for "No Place Like Home" show, Chez Est, Hartford, CT (2005) **21**
1.5 Ad for L.A. Shanti's costume ball fundraiser (2002) **23**
1.6 Ad for AIDS Walk Wisconsin (ca. 2000–2016) **23**
1.7 Europride Parade, Manchester, England (2003) **24**
1.8 Ad for Ozzo Unlimited's Oz poppers (1978) **25**
1.9 Illustration by W. W. Denslow from *The Wonderful Wizard of Oz* (1900) **33**
1.10 Illustration by John R. Neill from *Tik-Tok of Oz* (1914) **33**
4.1 Tom Atwood with Dorothy in *The Wiz* (mid- to late 1980s) **81**
4.2 An early Oz drawing by Howard Cruse (1952) **82**
4.3 Fred Barton playing Miss Gulch (and the piano) in *Miss Gulch Returns* (2004) **83**
4.4 Brian Ferrari as the Cowardly Lion (1991) **83**
4.5 Costume designs by John Maddox (1991) **84-85**
4.6 Erick Neher with Margaret Hamilton (1979) **87**

5.1	Princess Dorothy, from *The Lost Princess of Oz* (1917)	**100**
5.2	Chris Garland as Glinda, party at Butterworth Farm, Royalston, MA (2003)	**101**
5.3	Princess Ozma, from *Ozma of Oz* (1913)	**103**
5.4	Scraps, the Patchwork Girl, from *The Patchwork Girl of Oz* (1913)	**104**
5.5	Polychrome, the Rainbow's Daughter, from *The Tin Woodman of Oz* (1918)	**104**
5.6	Ojo and Button-Bright, from *The Patchwork Girl of Oz* (1913)	**112**
5.7	H.M. Wogglebug, T.E., from *The Magic of Oz* (1919)	**113**
5.8	The Frogman, from *The Lost Princess of Oz* (1917)	**113**
6.1	The Tin Woodman and the Scarecrow, from *The Marvelous Land of Oz* (1904)	**118**
6.2	Trot, Ozma, Dorothy, and Betsy, from *The Magic of Oz* (1919)	**121**
6.3	Endpapers of *The Royal Book of Oz* (1921)	**123**
8.1	Scott Robinson as Dorothy on the set of *Miss Gulch Returns* (2000)	**147**
8.2	Friends watching the movie before the pride march, Madison, WI (2001)	**148**
8.3	Rockshots card: "Toto, I don't think we're in Kansas anymore!" (1982)	**150**
8.4	Patrick Quigley with *The Wizard of Oz* (1973)	**155**
9.1	Rainbow flag in Twin Cities Gay Pride Parade (2013)	**170**
9.2	*Once in a Lullaby* by Michael Breyette (2010)	**175**
10.1	Poster for Emerald City Hoedown (2013)	**180**
10.2	Defense of Marriage Act graphic (2013)	**181**
10.3	UConn's homecoming float banner (2007)	**182**
10.4	Cover of Brian Andersen's *Friend of Dorothy*, issue no. 1 (2010)	**183**

DECORATIVE IMAGES

INTRODUCTION (beginning): Dedication image, from
The Patchwork Girl of Oz (1913) **2**

INTRODUCTION (end): Map of the Land of Oz, from
the personal collection of Justin G. Schiller **13**

PART ONE (beginning): The Scarecrow declaiming, from
The Scarecrow of Oz (1915) **14**

PART TWO (beginning): The Tin Woodman, hands on heart,
from *The Wonderful Wizard of Oz* (1900) **70**

PART THREE (beginning): The Cowardly Lion with crown,
from *The Wonderful Wizard of Oz* (1900) **140**

PART THREE (end): Dorothy parting curtains, from
The Lost Princess of Oz (1917) **195**

NOTES (beginning): Dorothy reading Glinda's Book
of Records, from *Glinda of Oz* (1920) **234**

Foreword by
Gregory Maguire

Anything that makes a mark in the air—a mark in time—is open to an evolution of meaning. The striking crucifix against the sky means one thing in the pages of the New Testament, another thing in the windows at Chartres, another to oppressed people hoping for transcendence, and still another to colonialists intending to use it to subdue and dominate.

What is less obvious, it seems to me, is that while irony is the clearest mode in which symbols are reinterpreted, it isn't the only one. We can note a more subtle if imprecise capacity of symbols to reframe and encapsulate a new or revised meaning, just as genuine in nature as the original.

For the exercise of it, think of that very word "Stonewall." For the sake of argument, I am prohibiting myself access to the web for confirmation of these apprehensions. I come up with the concept of "Stonewall" Jackson, first. A public figure with a life much open to interpretation, he always comes to my mind primarily as the first American president to arise from the common people rather than from the landed gentry of the original colonies.

The name itself, built of two strong words ("stone," "wall"), suggests strength, immovability, foundation. The word has gone on to build meaning: truculence, impermeability, obstructionism. To stonewall something is to stop it in its tracks. Sometimes for ill, sometimes for good.

When it comes to the history of liberation, the Stonewall Inn and the riots that took place there in the week following the death of Judy Garland have begun to take on a greater historical meaning than simply identity politics and gay liberation. At the time, the Stonewall riots might have seemed silly, offensive. Disagreeable. An occasion for late-night comics to rip into the spectacle of effeminacy both under and on the attack. (I would love to spend a day in TV archives and see what Johnny Carson and that lot made of Stonewall that week.)

Fifty years later, when gay marriage has become legal in the United States and is slowly becoming recognized as a civil right globally, the street riots in Greenwich Village can be seen without apology as akin to race riots, to uprisings in revolutionary France, to fervor for political rights all across the globe. *Selma, Seneca Falls, Stonewall,* said President Obama. The word grows in meaning and significance, and not only in irony.

. . .

I start with the ability of words and concepts to grow in significance because it seems to me that Dee Michel's thesis about the interpretation and the meaning of L. Frank Baum's magic land, Oz, as a metaphor and a kind of simulacrum of gay identity, has undergone a similar transformation. As history unfolds, older ideas about cultural ikons are also revised, take on added significance.

As the person who set out to rehabilitate the Wicked Witch of the West—designed by L. Frank Baum both to resemble and to deviate from the standard tropes of European fairy-tale witches, and intensified in the public consciousness by Margaret Hamilton's 1939 star turn in the role of the witch in MGM's *The Wizard of Oz*—I feel I ought to know more about how symbols work, especially symbolic iterations of the magic country of Oz. The first thing I did was give the witch a name, Elphaba Thropp—an intentionally ugly name, with the same number of syllables as Almira Gulch (though my intended pronunciation stresses the first syllable, *El*-phaba, much as the first syllable is stressed in the word *Dor*-othy, and also, for that matter, in the words *Mar*-garet and *Ham*-ilton).

But a name alone doesn't recreate or resignify a character. Stonewall is only a name until there is an event it is attached to. And Elphaba doesn't become a person of history until she learns to fly. What is this terrain over which she swerves?

. . .

I'm in the exact demographic to have gotten the annual TV broadcast of *The Wizard of Oz* at the most impressionable age. I was about five when it was first shown. As my parents were strict about TV watching, dubious about its value and concerned about its possible negative effects on the development of childhood character and intellect, I saw much less TV than others of my generation. The annual broadcast of *The Wizard of Oz*, a break in the rules of the household, therefore took on a nearly sacramental aspect, and had in my creative imagination an outsize influence.

However, as a gay kid (who like most of my generation had no idea of the concept, and filtered experience through the usual cloud of unknowing that attends all innocence), I can't say I watched or read *The Wizard of Oz* for cues on how to be—how to be what? Gay? (Tra-la, tra-la.) No, not that, but I am sure I noted something about how to be strong, brave, loving, smart. And a good friend. And how those who don't tell the truth are wicked, no matter what curtain they are standing behind.

A generation ago, when my novel *Wicked* first appeared, the gay press began, initially, to interview me about my attraction to Oz as a paradigm of a gay paradise. I was thought disingenuous when I said I had not recognized the story for its meaning to the young gay or lesbian kid, or to an older knowing homosexual audience. (Never, dear Munchkins, never underestimate the power of cluelessness.) Even well-read and articulate kids sometimes grow up in social and intellectual bubbles, away from the currents of knowing conversation on the coasts. The Internet had not yet flooded universal interpretation across every stone wall. For good as well as for ill, innocence was not yet annihilated.

It is for this reason that I admire the work in hand. Dee Michel has gathered up a lifetime's worth of observations about the meaning of the legend of Dorothy in Oz and considered it with sober affection and keen insight. He provides the kind of analysis and regard that a myth, still growing in meaning, deserves.

Meanings don't stand still. They evolve, they fly. Even Elphaba Thropp means something different to me twelve years after she landed on Broadway than she did when I named her as the first attempt to claim the rights to tell a new story about Oz. I now see Oz itself as a great metaphor, as broad as it is deep, not only for the world in which gay kids and teens and adults can imaginatively plant themselves, but also as a place in which other campaigns of liberation and tolerance and social evolution might occur. My version of Oz, published in 1995, was not as a gay paradise; it was as much about race, gender, and economic inequity as it was about sexual identification and expression. To stand up on a stone wall and posit a thesis for you, I will say that I think L. Frank Baum's original concept of Oz is still rich and strong enough that it will continue to provide a template against which other populations, as yet unborn, will be able to unscroll their own maps of the future, plot their coordinates for change and challenge. I sure hope so.

Acknowledgments

Having worked on this project for almost twenty years, I am extremely grateful for the encouragement and support of many friends and colleagues. Will Fellows and Mark Griffin created and published whole books while I took my sweet time. They were role models for me in their accomplishments, and both have been enthusiastic about my project from very early on. My academic colleagues Michele Besant and Pat Lawton were there at the beginning when I lived in Wisconsin. Ryan Bunch, Angelica Carpenter, David Maxine, and Eric Shanower—friends from the International Wizard of Oz Club—all encouraged me before the book stage. The novelists Gregory Maguire and Geoff Ryman inspired me through their writing and their friendship. Beverly Lyon Clark and Alison Lurie honored me by citing my research.

Several people helped me shape the ideas found in the book. In his writing, conferences, conversations, and email exchanges, Will Fellows helped me clarify my thoughts about gender-atypical boys. Ryan Bunch shared his knowledge of Oz and music. Jim Whitcomb was my co-conspirator, giving me tips about the Oz connection in gay culture. Will Fellows, Nancy Garden, Craig Harbison, Scott McDaniel, Edgardo Menvielle, Alberto Sandoval, and David Wulff read various drafts, chapters, or proposals. Bee Beuhring, Emily Fox, Leslea Newman,

David Pritchard, Athena Stylos, Mary Vazquez, and Ellen Wittlinger sat through practice sessions for talks I was giving.

I have also benefited from advice and logistical help of various kinds. When I was working on my dissertation in library and information science, Elaine Svenonius advised me to pick a narrow topic and explore it for all it is worth. Several friends helped make my questionnaire happen. Ryan Bunch, Will Fellows, Peter Hanff, Neal Rogness, and Jim Whitcomb all gave me feedback on the questionnaire; Jay Blotcher, Will Fellows, and Joe Yranski helped distribute it. A handful of librarians and library staff people did work above and beyond the call of duty by providing relevant books, articles, and information. Liz Amundson of the Madison Public Library and Liz Maguire from Forbes Library in Northampton cheerfully put up with innumerable interlibrary loan requests. Nancy McClements at the University of Wisconsin–Madison was instrumental in early research, and Steve Klein was my king of copies and clippings. My longtime friends Michael Bronski and Don Shewey shared ideas about agents and publishing. Doug Mitchell at the University of Chicago Press and the agent Eric Myers did their best to help me find a way to get my book out there.

I could not have done this project without the cooperation of all of my respondents. Those who shared their Oz-related images with me are doubly thanked. Will Fellows and David Wulff examined the page proofs and offered many spot-on suggestions. Naila Moreira, Nate Jasper, Kate Anderson, and Toby Johnson helped with various aspects of production and marketing

Michael Starkman is a sensitive and talented designer. Katarina Rice is a sensitive and talented editor. Deep, deep thanks to both of them for risking their friendship with me by being involved in a professional way.

FRIENDS of DOROTHY

Introduction

I was first drawn into the Marvelous Land of Oz when my father, who was gay, read the Oz books at bedtime to my brother and me (fig. I.1). Some of these books had belonged to my father and his siblings when they were young. I soon became the Oz fan in the family, and on my birthday I received a new book in the Oz series. Along with much of America in the late fifties, my family watched *The Wizard of Oz* on our black-and-white television. In 1960, at the age of eight, I saw the *Shirley Temple Show*'s TV production of *The Land of Oz*. I remember thinking it odd that the grown-up Temple played the young boy Tip. It wasn't the gender anomaly that bothered me; it was the age difference.

We moved the next year, and I used the list of titles on the jacket flap of new Oz books to put my collection in order in my new room. When I was ten, I read all of the Oz books I owned and went to the local library to find others. By the time I was in high school, I had become a serious collector, visiting the secondhand bookstores in Lower Manhattan. I was surprised to discover that L. Frank Baum also wrote non-Oz books under many pseudonyms. Trying to find reasonably priced books by Baum, Floyd Akers, Laura Bancroft, Captain Hugh Fitzgerald, Suzanne Metcalf, Schuyler Staunton, or Edith Van Dyne became an enjoyable treasure hunt. During this hunt, a bookseller showed me the catalog from a 1956 Columbia University Library exhibit on Baum. The addenda page stated

I.1 Me (Dee) with my father's books, ca. 1955. His Oz collection is on the bottom shelf, to the left of my shoulder.

that the twelve-year-old Justin Schiller had offered some unique items to the exhibit. This blew me away: a young boy was taken seriously as an Oz expert! I remember feeling that this kid was just like me.

In the early 1970s, when I was an undergraduate at Brown University, I briefly joined the International Wizard of Oz Club. It was also at Brown that I finally saw the Metro-Goldwyn-Mayer movie on the big screen of a movie theater, and I took notes on what I didn't remember from my earlier viewings on television. I was delighted, too, to find some early Oz editions in the Brown University Library's rare books collection; from them I made photocopies of some of my favorite illustrations.

In 1992 I moved to Madison to begin teaching at the graduate library school at the University of Wisconsin. On the first day of classes I wore a T-shirt that some friends had given me, with the Scarecrow on the front and "IF I ONLY HAD A BRAIN" on the back. *The Wizard* was such a well-known story that I assumed my students would understand the examples I used from the book and the movie.[a] When a friend on the faculty asked me to give the lecture on *The Wizard* in her children's literature class, I brought along books and other artifacts from my collection.

In 1998 I discovered that the Oz Club's annual Ozmapolitan convention was being held in Delavan, Wisconsin, an hour away, and I knew I had to attend. Meeting other Oz experts and enthusiasts was like coming home. From 1973 to 1992 I had a used bicycle, the parts of which I replaced one after another over the years: seat, brakes, wheels, gears, everything but the frame. I would joke with friends that my bike was like the Tin Woodman, but they rarely understood what I meant. I had to explain what the movie left out: how bit by bit the tin parts replaced the Tin Woodman's flesh until he was a different creature. At the Oz convention, people knew. What joy to be able to make obscure Oz references like these and know that people would get them!

The other delightful thing for me about meeting Oz Club members was seeing what appeared to be a large proportion of gay men. The way they were integrated into the history and functioning of the club was

---

a   As it turned out, this was not the case. One student who grew up in Japan came to see me in office hours to explain that she wasn't familiar with the story and that I shouldn't assume everyone in the class knew it.

unusual and moving. The MGM *Wizard of Oz* was a big deal in gay culture, I knew, but I hadn't realized that gay men were into the Oz books as well. Until that day, if someone had asked me why I was into Oz, I would have said simply that I was drawn to the Oz books because I liked fantasy and through the books I had a special connection with my father. Then, too, I was a born collector and it was fun to become an expert. But now I wondered if it was more than a coincidence that I was the one who had taken up my father's collection of Oz books, not my heterosexual brother, who read a lot of science fiction.

When I mentioned to someone at the convention that Oz seemed to have a particular appeal to gay men and that it would be interesting to publish something on the subject in the club's journal, he said, "That would raise a few eyebrows." I took that as a challenge and decided to write about Oz and gay men.

Early Research

My initial idea was to tell a story that hadn't been told, to fill the gap in the literature for its own sake. And by adding an explicitly gay point of view to Oz criticism, I could also help increase gay visibility. As I read and thought about it, I found the project compelling because the process involved figuring out what Oz meant to me, and perhaps what being gay meant to me as well.

It turned out that quite a few people had written or talked about the MGM movie and its connection to gay culture, but most of the discussion was reductive and simplistic.[b] Except for a thesis on the music of Oz and gay men, writers didn't acknowledge the possibility that it might be the story of Oz—irrespective of version—that appealed to gay males; they all assumed it was the MGM movie in particular that mattered. Some gay men, too, had written or talked about their own love of Oz. Although a few were analytic, the authors of most of these accounts simply described their relationship to Oz at an early age.[c]

---

b   One exception was Robert Hopcke's *Jung, Jungians and Homosexuality* (Boston: Shambala, 1989), which devoted most of one chapter to the Jungian meaning of the MGM film for gay men.

c   In general, citations of sources are listed in the "Notes" section, beginning

I also began to look at writings on the appeal and meaning of Oz in general. Some of the themes that I found in this general Oz literature, such as "home" or "diversity and uniqueness," seemed to me to be especially pertinent to gay males. These observations made me think that any issue in the lives of gay men that shows up in stories set in Oz could be a potential reason for Oz's appeal to gay men and boys. To learn more about issues of importance in gay men's lives that might parallel issues in Oz, I read articles and books in the areas of gay men's identity, culture, and spirituality. One nice affirmation of this line of thinking appeared in the collection *Hometowns: Gay Men Write About Where They Belong*, which documents the importance of home for gay men. Imagine my delight upon discovering that, of the three contributors who used literary metaphors for their feelings about home, two referred to Oz!

In 2000, on the centenary of L. Frank Baum's birth, the Oz Club put on a huge celebration in Bloomington, Indiana. The occasion was the perfect opportunity to give a talk pulling together my reading and thinking so far. I was worried, however, that some heterosexual Oz fans might get defensive or possessive about "their" Oz. When you interpret something from a gay point of view or demonstrate that gay folks have a special affinity for something, there is always the possibility that cranky heterosexuals will think you're stealing something from them. But before my presentation, which I had entitled "If We're Not in Kansas Anymore, Then Where Are We? The Appeal of Oz for Gay Men," many conference goers came up to me to say they saw the listing in the program and were looking forward to my talk; others told me they were disappointed that they couldn't attend.

The session itself was standing room only, about sixty people, with some peering in from the hallway. The gay attendees, who probably made up between a third and half of the audience, came to have their long-standing feelings confirmed and articulated. Some of the straight folks

---

on p. 235. In each case, a page number, the first words of the paragraph, and a key phrase serve to identify the passage in the text for which the source is provided. (For example, for this paragraph—beginning with the words "It turned out"—sources are provided in the Notes for the key phrases "a thesis on the music" and "a few were analytic.")

knew that Oz held a special place in the hearts of gay men and came to find out why. Others, who apparently had no idea there was a special connection between Oz and gay men, came out of sheer curiosity. I think the session was the beginning of a dialog about these matters, for there is no simple answer to the question "Why do gay men have a particular affinity for Oz?" But the talk did more than satisfy curiosity; it also created a sense of community.

During the question period, a gay man of about fifty said that he liked Ruth Plumly Thompson's Oz books better than the earlier ones by Baum, because Thompson's books usually had male protagonists. Then he added with great conviction, "*Speedy in Oz* was my favorite. Speedy was hot!" A woman in the audience responded that she had been attracted to Speedy, too, when she first read the books. At this point, I mimed Phil Donahue, offering a microphone to anyone else who might want to testify about their relationship to an Oz character.

For the rest of the convention, people came up to me to say how much they appreciated my talk. A gay teenager who hadn't particularly been an Oz fan, but attended the event with an older mentor, told me he could see himself becoming a real Oz enthusiast, and would attend other Oz get-togethers in the future. Perhaps my favorite response came from Alison Lurie, whose 1974 piece about Oz for the *New York Review of Books* was in my files. As a token of appreciation for my talk, she gave me an Oz centennial T-shirt of the Cowardly Lion.

Driving home after the conference, I realized that the joyous acceptance of the topic by the Oz Club made me happy indeed. Although both of my parents had died years before, I had felt them looking over my shoulder in Bloomington: my mother was an author of children's poetry, and my father was gay. Talking publicly about being gay and loving Oz, two acutely personal and important aspects of myself, had been a highly integrating experience.

Questionnaire and Model

Since I was writing about what gay men get out of Oz, I soon realized it was presumptuous not to talk to gay Oz fans directly, so after my talk in Bloomington I created a questionnaire. (Appendix A, "The Questionnaire," provides the full text; Appendix B, "Methodology," details other aspects of the research.) To get at the sources of their fandom, I asked gay male Oz fans open-ended questions from many different angles. The first few questions had to do with their initial exposure to the Oz story and the beginnings of their interest and fandom. I asked what they thought *The Wizard of Oz* was about and what it offered them as a child, as an adult, as a man, and as a gay man. Other questions probed their favorite and least favorite characters, the characters they identified with, and aspects of Kansas and Oz that appealed or did not appeal to them. A section on fandom raised such topics as how they currently express their enthusiasm for Oz, how friends and family react to it, and how they benefit from being a fan. Items on the gay connection asked how old they were when they came out, what they knew about the Oz–gay connection, what special meanings they thought Oz has for gay males as a whole, and what contact they had, if any, with other gay Oz fans. Final questions asked them to identify their favorite books and movies.

The present volume is based, in large part, on the responses of the 109 gay Oz fans—ranging in age from nineteen to seventy-one—who filled out the questionnaire. I have also drawn upon what gay men have written about what Oz means to them or about the Oz–gay connection, as well as general writings about Oz and others about gay life, gay psychology, gay spirituality, and gay culture.

At the beginning I wasn't sure how to talk about the meaning of a literary work for a reader or the meaning of a film for a viewer, or about what it means to be a fan. As my research proceeded, however, I developed my own model of interactive meaning, resonance, and fandom. It may be helpful to summarize the model here.

A narrative work of art, whether a film or a novel, places particular characters in particular situations. The responses of the characters to those situations give rise to the themes of the work. The narrative also often contains symbols and images that are open to interpretation. The meaning of a work does not simply reside within it; rather, it emerges from readers' or viewers' interactions with the work, both at the time that they initially experience it in a particular setting and afterward. What readers and viewers bring to the interaction will crucially affect the meaning of the work for them. If there are themes that are similar to issues in their lives, whether they consciously recognize those issues or not, the work will likely have special significance. This paralleling, this matching of what's within the reader/viewer and what's within the work, is what I am calling resonance.

Effects of the interaction between the reader/viewer and the work can occur right away or after the fact. Immediate effects may be positive, such as giving comfort or inspiration, or they may be disturbing or unsettling, perhaps bringing up issues hidden in the unconscious. In either case, readers or viewers get something they need. That resonance—the special significance of the work or its ability to meet the needs of a reader/viewer—is an important part of the appeal of a work, and it may lead to repeat encounters. Longer-term effects of the interaction include sharing one's interest in the work with others, using elements of the work in one's personal or professional life, and recreating the work on one's own. If this engagement with the work is intense and sustained, the reader/viewer qualifies as a fan. As readers or viewers change over time, so too may their responses to the work; that is, they may get different things out of it at different points in their lives.

My Point of View

Because any work is colored by the author's beliefs and background, I would like to state mine at the outset. I have been a gay activist since I came out in 1975. I think public discussion of gay issues, both by gay and non-gay people, is an important way to advance gay liberation and equality. I am Jewish, white, middle class, progressive, urban, well educated, literary, analytic, and part of the Baby Boomer generation. These aspects of my history and disposition influence my conclusions.

I love both the Oz books and the MGM movie; to me they are all of a piece. And although I appreciate Judy Garland's talent, I do not consider myself a Garland fan in particular.

I believe there is such a thing as homosexuality. It makes sense to say that the *concept* or *category* of homosexuality is socially constructed, because categories are learned. Still, there is a *phenomenon* out there in the real world that is the referent of the terms "homosexuality" or "same-sex desire" or "gay sexual orientation." This phenomenon itself is not socially constructed; it has probably existed in all cultures and at all times.[d] I do not take sides on the origins of sexual orientation, and my argument does not rest on whether homosexuality or the particular traits I discuss are innate or might be developed at a very early age.[e]

I believe there is such a thing as a gay identity. That is, gay men who call themselves gay typically feel that their sexual orientation is an important and often defining part of who they are. The concept of being gay is learned from one's social environment, and a gay identity, then, is something one takes on and articulates. So it makes sense to think of gay identity as socially constructed.

Perhaps more controversially, I believe there is such a thing as a gay sensibility. That is, gay men differ from heterosexuals in how they experience the world. Gay men share certain characteristics and have common concerns. They tend to feel different or that they are outsiders; they appreciate, create, and restore both esthetic objects and functional ones; and they have a heightened sense of imagination, fantasy, and play. These characteristics are not unique to gay men, of course; rather, they are more salient or more common among gay men.

I also think that in the United States gay men have created and share a set of beliefs, values, practices, artifacts, and the like that can be summed up as "gay culture." This, too, is a social construct. The appeal of Oz for gay men can be discussed using these concepts of gay identity, gay sensibility, and gay culture.

Let me say briefly, too, why I believe this book matters. Gay fans of the Oz story in one or all of its various forms—the Oz books, the 1939 movie *The Wizard of Oz*, the Broadway musicals *The Wiz* (1975)

---

[d] The difference here—between a concept or category and the real thing or phenomenon it refers to—is perhaps easier to see with a concrete example. We have a concept of "tree," which (roughly speaking) is the idea of a large thing from the plant kingdom that is not the same as a bush or a forest. Some languages might not distinguish between trees and bushes, and people speaking those languages might not have a concept of "tree" as such. All the same, actual trees—the physical things in the real world—exist for them as well.

[e] There is, however, much scientific evidence that sexual orientation itself is inborn. See Glenn Wilson and Qazi Rahman, *Born Gay: The Psychobiology of Sex Orientation* (London: Peter Owen, 2005).

and *Wicked* (2003)—mention themes such as acceptance, home, non-traditional gender roles, utopia, escape, and self-knowledge as reasons for their love of Oz. Looking at why these issues matter to gay men can tell us something about what it means to be gay. And examining how the MGM movie is enshrined in gay culture and gay folklore can reveal important truths about the needs of adult gay men, including the need for a shared culture and history.

To my surprise, practically everyone who responded to my questionnaire was very young when he became enamored of a story set in the Land of Oz—three, four, or five years old. This discovery led me to wonder what it means to be a gay boy. Do young boys who identify as gay later in life share certain sensibilities with adult gay men? Gay middle schoolers and teens have been in the news because of bullying that, in some cases, has led to suicide. Do gay kids kill themselves simply because of a few weeks of taunting, or do they have negative thoughts about themselves, or about their place in the world, long before these final insults? We would do well to look more closely at what it means to be a gay boy and at how gay boys react to the harsh world around them. Given that some gay boys love Oz in a particularly intense way, an examination of their love promises to shed light on their inner worlds.

My argument about gay men and Oz doesn't depend on whether homosexuality exists in other cultures and eras, or on whether it is innate or learned. I am exploring the appeal of Oz and looking to see if such an exploration can teach us anything about what it has meant to be gay from the 1950s onward in North American Anglo culture. When I began my investigation, I didn't have an agenda about gay sensibility or culture, or a strong investment in either side of the nature/nurture debate with respect to homosexuality. I hope that readers, especially those who believe strongly in the social construction of sexual orientation, will keep an open mind and heart. The stories and experiences of very young boys who grow up to be gay speak for themselves.

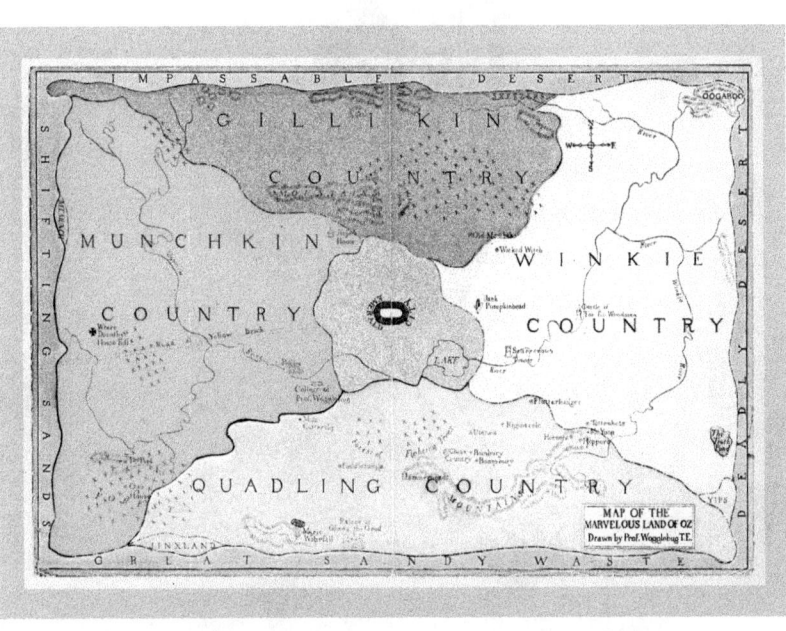

PART ONE GAY FANS OF OZ

1

Gay Men and Oz

"I always wanted to be Dorothy from *The Wizard of Oz*," Rufus Wainwright, the Canadian American singer and composer, told an interviewer, adding, "It's kind of a giveaway."[a] He is not alone in his wish and not wrong in believing that his love of Oz may mark him as gay. But what's the story with gay men and *The Wizard of Oz*? What explains the extraordinary hold of Oz on generations of gay men?

It's not just the appeal of Judy Garland or the spell of movie magic, since other versions of the Oz story can affect gay men in much the same way as the 1939 MGM movie. Greg Louganis, for example, sang "Believe in Yourself" from the Broadway musical *The Wiz* to himself during his Olympic medal-winning diving. The Oz books inspired the English author and visual artist Clive Barker when he was a child. Indeed, gay love for Oz often starts early. One gay man told me that as a three-year-old

---

[a] Most of my sources are listed in the "Notes" section, which begins on p. 235. (Additionally, a few sources appear in footnotes.) In the Notes section, a page number, the first words of the paragraph, and a key phrase serve to identify the passage in the text for which the source is provided. (For this paragraph, for example, beginning with "I always wanted to be Dorothy," a source is provided in the Notes for the Wainwright quotation, and for the next paragraph, "It's not just the appeal of Judy Garland," sources are given for the key phrases "Greg Louganis" and "Clive Barker.")

he was "totally infatuated" with the MGM film. Some gay boys read L. Frank Baum's original Oz story; others watch the movie version of *The Wiz* over and over again.

So what is it about Oz that resonates so powerfully for gay males, young and old? Is the appeal more or less the same for the Oz books, the MGM movie, and other versions of the story? Is there anything about being gay, especially in our society, that gives rise to a particular appreciation of Oz? These are the questions that I tackle in this book.

Evidence for the Oz–Gay Connection

The connection between gay men and *The Wizard of Oz* is widely acknowledged. Ben Brantley of the *New York Times* called Oz "a cornerstone in gay mythology." The authors of a 1999 biography of Judy Garland declared the 1939 MGM movie "a gay landmark." The MGM Oz–gay connection is discussed in a wide range of written material—from speeches, newspaper articles in the national and local gay press, and entries in dictionaries and encyclopedias to a master's thesis, academic journal articles, and book chapters. The view that gay men love *The Wizard of Oz* is so prevalent, in fact, that it has become part of the received wisdom about homosexuals. "What kind of stereotypes are there about gay people?" asks the novelist and essayist Michael Ford. "How about: lesbians hate men, gay men love *The Wizard of Oz*." Even the gay congressman Barney Frank found occasion to refer to the Oz–gay connection on the floor of the House of Representatives.[b] A subcultural example of the stereotype comes from *Love Bites* (1988), a gay vampire movie set in West Hollywood. When asked if he's ever seen any movies, one gay character replies, "Well, I've seen *The Wizard of Oz* sixty-two times."

---

b "Some of my colleagues, some of my friends, I say to my colleagues in the gay community, maybe I will do a little stereotyping, maybe they have seen *The Wizard of Oz* too often. They seem to have Speaker Pelosi, a wonderful dedicated, committed supporter of human rights, confused with Glenda [*sic*] the good witch. They think if she waved her magic wand she could somehow change things." Full text of Rep. Barney Frank's statement on ENDA, Oct. 11, 2007, *Bay Windows* online. http://www.baywindows.com/index.php?ch=news&sc=glbt&sc2=news&sc3=&id=58546.

The stereotype is used to humorous effect in mainstream venues such as a 1996 Hollywood movie, *My Fellow Americans*, in which an "All Dorothy Marching Band" appears in a gay pride parade, and in a *New Yorker* cartoon from 1998 (fig. 1.1). What is striking in all of these cases is the key assumption that non-gay readers or viewers already know of the Oz–gay connection. If they didn't, they wouldn't get the joke.

"And, please, sir, would it be too much to ask for a large and devoted gay following?"

1.1 *New Yorker* cartoon by Nick Downes, March 16, 1998 (used with permission)

Some gay men have also written about how the MGM movie spoke to them as gay boys growing up. These descriptions do not say anything about the phenomenon as a whole, of course, but they provide evidence for the connection on a personal level. After the MGM movie was restored in 1998, the *Atlanta Constitution* asked its readers why Oz held such a special place in their hearts. "In the mid-60s," one wrote, "there were no gay role models. I was around 11 or 12, and I just knew the Lion was my role model. He sings that he was born to be a sissy, he says he's just a dandy-lion and he uses a limp wrist. The movie told me it was OK to be gay."

In his book *Sissyphobia*, Tim Bergling recalls his own sissylike behavior: "I was even a big Barbra Streisand fan, for Christ's sake, and I loved *The Wizard of Oz*." Also testifying that they loved the MGM movie as kids are the gay performers Fred Barton and Rufus Wainwright; the gay writers Patrick Horrigan, Gregory Maguire, Ian Young, and Tomie dePaola; and the gay moviemakers Derek Jarman and John Waters. Gore Vidal and Clive Barker have both mentioned the effect of Baum's Oz books on them.

One direct piece of evidence for a special connection between Oz and gay men is the consistent appearance of the MGM movie on lists of favorite gay movies. The Oz–gay connection is also evident in references to the MGM *Wizard* in gay contexts of all sorts.[c] Gay bars and dance clubs, long a focal point of gay communities, frequently use Oz in their

---

c   The idea that an allusion to Oz in a gay context demonstrates that gay men have a special affinity for the MGM movie brings up the degree of use in the culture at large and conscious targeting. First, the MGM movie is well-known in the general culture. Writers and organizations that aren't particularly targeted at gay men also use Oz references and general gift shops sell Oz items. Couldn't gay writers and organizations and businesses simply refer to Oz as often as other writers and businesses do? I think not. Rather than comparing the gay male subculture with the culture at large, a more proper comparison would be with other minority subcultures. We would then ask: Do stores marketing products to African Americans predictably contain Oz materials? Do the headlines in newspapers for the deaf community often use lines from the MGM film? Do Asian American groups often have Oz-themed events? I don't think they do.

names. There are bars and clubs called Oz in Seattle; New Orleans; Wausau, Wisconsin; Fort Lauderdale; and Toronto. Surrender Dorothy is a gay bar in Auckland, New Zealand. St. Paul, Minnesota, has a bar called Over the Rainbow. Springfield, Massachusetts, used to have two establishments that referred to Oz, Auntie Em's Lounge and the Emerald City cyber café. Other bars create specific Oz-themed events and advertising (figs. 1.2–1.4).

Other gay-oriented businesses also use Oz terminology in their names. The Magical Land of Oz is a gay bed-and-breakfast in Livingston Manor, New York. Oz Creations is a gay gift business in Springfield, Massachusetts, that specializes in items with rainbows on them. A Canadian company named This Ain't Kansas makes T-shirts marketed to the gay community with advertising that reads: "As the Good Witch proclaimed in that fair tale, 'Click your heels and always choose the snappiest clothes Dorothy dear . . . you never know who you'll meet along the road.'" Businesses using the name Dorothy abound. A women's clothing store for men in New York City is called

1.2

1.3

1.4

1.2 Ad for sing-along and dance party, Axis, Columbus, OH, 1999
1.3 "Surrender to The Eagle," ad for The Eagle, Boston, 2001
1.4 Ad for "No Place Like Home" show, Chez Est, Hartford, CT, 2005

Dorothy's Closet; Dorothy's Surrender was a gay souvenir store in West Hollywood, California; there is an Australian gay travel agency called Friends of Dorothy Travel; A Friend of Dorothy's is an online store for gay clothing and accessories based in Vancouver, with the motto "There's no place like home . . . to go shopping"; and a cruise line in San Francisco is called Friends of Dorothy® Cruises. Likewise, Dorothy's dog is a popular choice for names. Toto Apartments is listed in a gay business directory in Madison, Wisconsin, with "Why choose *middle of the road* when you can *follow the yellow brick road*?" in its advertisement. Toto's Revenge is a gay gift shop in Long Beach, California, and Toto Tours, based in Chicago, is an online travel service for gay men. And businesses—both mainstream and gay—use Oz in their advertising to signal events of special interest to gay men. The Time Hotel in New York City, for example, did a travel promo mailing tied to gay circuit party events in February and March 2001, saying, "Toto, this ain't Kansas . . . it's New York City!" and "Ask for Toto's rate." For Pride Month in Boston, June 2001, the sex phone line called The Number was free on weekends; the ads said, "Who needs to go somewhere over the Rainbow? Use The Number."

Businesses are not the only ones using Oz in their names and advertising; nonprofit organizations and services do also. GLENDA [sic] is a gay and lesbian neighborhood development association in Pittsburgh. Surrender Dorothy is an investment group organized by gay men in Chicago. Rainbow Oz Dating & Friendship Emporium is an online network. And gay organizations often hold Oz-themed events. Baltimore's Health Education Resource Organization (HERO), an AIDS group, gave the name "Hey Everybody, Return to Oz" to its annual spring fundraiser in 2004. "A Night in the Emerald City" was a costume ball to benefit L.A. Shanti, an AIDS group, in 2002, with advertisements for the event featuring a sexy Dorothy with three hunky companions walking on the Yellow Brick Road toward the MGM version of the Emerald City (fig. 1.5). Oz imagery and nomenclature also show up in gay marketing. "Follow the Yellow Drip Road," for instance, was a gonorrhea workshop at a gay health conference circa 2000, and the AIDS Walk Wisconsin has used ruby slippers in its publicity materials for years (fig. 1.6).

Oz imagery is frequently seen in LGBT pride parades. Individuals dress as characters, floats use Oz as a unifying theme, and organizers

1.5 Ad for L.A. Shanti's costume ball fundraiser, 2002
1.6 Ad for AIDS Walk Wisconsin, ca. 2000–2016 (used by permission of the AIDS Resource Center of Wisconsin)

choose Oz for the theme of the parade as a whole. The Boston LGBT Youth Pride celebration had Oz as its theme in 2006. The T-shirts said, "There's no place like youth pride"; the event hall was christened Rainbow City; and there were speakers on wisdom, heart, and courage. Members of the planning committee who were dressed as the Scarecrow, the Tin Woodman, and the Lion gave wisdom, heart, and courage awards to individuals and groups. One of the chants in the parade was "Dingdong, homophobia's dead! / Get it through your straw-brained head!" The 2003 Europride Parade, held in Manchester, England, included gay men dressed as characters from *The Wizard of Oz* (fig. 1.7). The 2002 gay pride parade in Chicago contained two floats with Oz themes. The float by Outreach Zone (OZ), an AIDS awareness program, featured Dorothy and Glinda; their many sidekicks, wearing blue-and-white gingham sarongs, handed out safer-sex kits with a picture of Dorothy and Toto on them. The group Queer to the Left had as its theme "There's no place like home" to protest the lack of affordable housing in Chicago; its flyers, saying, "There is no place like home (if you can afford one)," featured

1.7 Europride Parade, Manchester, England (© 2003 Dave Harris)

icons from the MGM movie. The theme of the 2001 Rhode Island LGBT pride celebration was "Over the rainbow and under the stars," and many participants dressed up as Oz characters. Highlights were members of the Providence Gay Men's Chorus, who dressed as characters from the MGM film and rode in an oversize ruby slipper, and a Mr. Potato Head dressed up as Dorothy.

With its recognizable characters, the MGM movie is also a popular theme for gay dances and parties such as Over the Rainbow and Back (Butterworth Farm, Orange, Massachusetts, 2003), Emerald City Ball (Spectrum Center of Marin, California, an AIDS group, 2002), Wizard of Oz Costume Ball (Cape Cod Gay Pride, 2001), and "Under the Rainbow" (Stonewall Prom, Center of Contemporary Arts, University City, Missouri, 1996).

Some campy merchandise created with the gay market in mind plays with Oz imagery. Dorothy's Surrender in West Hollywood carried a T-shirt with an image of Glinda and the legend "Come out, come out, wherever you are." A bumper sticker has the same message. A refrigerator magnet depicts Dorothy/Judy on the Yellow Brick Road with a stylized San Francisco instead of the Emerald City in the background.

1.8 Ad for Ozzo Unlimited's Oz poppers, 1978

Another magnet says, "Sequins, Feathers, & Leather. Oh my!" A commonly seen button bears the message "We are so over the rainbow." In 1978—in the earliest use of Oz in a gay context that I've come across—a Houston company named Ozzo Unlimited marketed "Oz" poppers to gay men (fig. 1.8).

There are, of course, hundreds of non-gay-oriented greeting cards, refrigerator magnets, T-shirts, and ornaments featuring Oz characters and quotes. I have found them in almost every gay bookstore and gift shop I have visited in the United States and Canada, despite their not being created with a gay market in mind. Chances are extremely good that if a gay store carries greeting cards, it will have at least one Oz card, and more likely several. The odds are much lower of finding an Oz-themed card or trinket in a Hallmark store or other non-gay shop that carries greeting cards. Similarly, Oz-related refrigerator magnets and buttons can be found in almost every gay souvenir or gift shop, while not every "mainstream" gift shop that carries refrigerator magnets will have Oz ones.

Oz shows up in a gay context in the fine and performing arts as well, and in literature and nonfiction. Some examples from film will show the prevalence of Oz in one field. An angel in the show-within-a-show in *The Big Gay Musical* (2009) wears ruby slippers and announces his/her name is Dorothy, then says that the gay men he/she is talking to are all friends of Dorothy. "Over the Rainbow" is on the soundtrack during a sequence of the 1978 San Francisco Freedom Day Parade (a.k.a. gay pride parade) in *Milk* (2008). In *Nightmare on Castro Street* (2002), the villain Squeaky Blonde laughs an evil Wicked Witch laugh and says something to the effect of "Going so soon?" as she chases her victim. Meanwhile, we hear Mussorgsky's *Night on Bald Mountain*, which was used in the scenes around the Witch's Castle in the MGM *Wizard*. In *The Rape of Ganymede*

(2001), Ganymede describes Olympus, saying, "I don't think we are in Kansas anymore." When a newly arrived drag queen gets mugged outside the New York City bus terminal in *The Velocity of Gary* (1999), the gay hustler Gary carries him to safety. The queen asks him, "Where are you takin' me?" to which Gary replies, "Where do you think I'm takin' you? Over the rainbow, Dorothy." Characters in *Homo Heights* (1998) refer to Dorothy, Toto, and a broomstick. *Surrender Dorothy* (1998) depicts the relationship between two men, one of whom forces the other to dress as a woman. The short film *Dead Boys' Club* (1992) is about a young man who is given the shoes of his cousin's dead lover. Whenever he puts the shoes on, he is magically more attractive to men and has visions of the disco/free-sex era. Reviewers have noted that the film pays homage to Oz.

Documentaries on gay topics often contain allusions to Oz as well. *Lance Loud! A Death in an American Family* (2003), about the gay member of the Loud family, includes footage of Loud's memorial service. Victoria Galves, a good friend of Loud's, reminisces about how Loud used to click his red Beatle boots as Dorothy, and the camera pulls back to show his boots on display. The film ends with Rufus Wainwright, another friend of Loud's, singing "Over the Rainbow." In "The Castro," an episode of *Neighborhoods: The Hidden Cities of San Francisco* (1997), the historian Allan Bérubé recounts the first time he came to San Francisco, in 1973. He went to a party in the Castro and ended up sleeping with one of the hosts. "He took me up to his balcony, and it overlooked the entire city. The lights were glittering all over the City and the Bay. And he said, 'Welcome to Oz.'" *Over the Rainbow* (1995) is a British television series on the modern gay movement. Marlon Riggs created *Tongues Untied* (1990), a "semi-documentary" about black gay identity. In a voiceover Riggs talks about his experience of being invisible in white San Francisco: "Something in Oz, in me, was amiss, but I tried not to notice."

Gay filmmakers make use of the structure of the film itself. *Queer Today, Gone Tomorrow* (2008) is a short film that begins in color and turns to black-and-white during a fantasy sequence induced by a bump on the head in which all gay people are removed from the world. *Of Oz the Wizard* (2003) is a database version of the MGM film created by a gay film editor who chopped up the film word by word and put each film segment in alphabetical order. *Isle of Lesbos* (1997) is described in publicity materials as a cross between *The Wizard of Oz* and *The Rocky Horror Picture Show*. It seems to be a camp effort by a gay man, and includes a lesbian pagan ceremony on the Isle of Lesbos patterned on the MGM movie.

Still more examples can be found in other communications and performance media. Oz appears in several novels and short stories written by gay men about gay men. Journalism and other forms of nonfiction also afford many opportunities to refer to the connection. Advertising, cartoons, and other visual media created by or for gay men are a rich source of Oz allusions as well.[d] Gay events have featured a *Wizard of Oz* sing-along or a stage version of the MGM movie. And showings of the film on television are advertised in the gay press. In November 2000, Turner Broadcasting took out huge full-color ads in many gay newspapers announcing the November 19 airing of *The Wizard of Oz* on the Turner cable station. The ad exhorted readers to "Grab those Ruby Slippers and follow the Yellow Brick Road."

Who, Where, and When

Discussions of the Oz–gay connection are usually about Oz as part of gay male culture, or the individual love of Oz by gay males. There are a few times, however, when the greater LGBT culture or community is explicitly invoked. In 2001, for example, the Billy DeFrank Lesbian and Gay Community Center of San Jose began a "Yellow Brick Road" fundraising campaign. A kickoff dinner was timed to follow a screening of the MGM movie, which, according to an article about the campaign, "serves as a social allegory for the LGBT community."

---

d   Two pieces of the movie in particular also appear often in gay contexts. "I've a feeling we're not in Kansas anymore" is a favorite camp line. See Lisa Keen, "On the Trail: All Things Gay from Campaign 2008," *Bay Windows*, Mar. 15–21, 2007, pp. 1, 14, and Leigh Rutledge, *The Gay Fireside Companion* (Boston: Alyson, 1989). And "Over the Rainbow" is often considered a theme song for the gay community. See Philip Brett and Elizabeth Wood, "Gay and Lesbian Music," in *The New Grove Dictionary of Music and Musicians*, vol. 9, ed. Stanley Sadie (London: Macmillan, 2001), p. 603. See Chapter 9, "Oz and Judy in Gay Folklore," for the relationship between the song and the rainbow flag.

But does Oz appeal to lesbians, bisexuals, and transgender or questioning folks as much as it does to gay males? Although Oz is not as visible in the lesbian subculture as it is in gay male arena, I have found references to Oz in a few lesbian literary creations.[e] In his *Bisexual Characters in Film: From Anaïs to Zee*, Wayne Bryant notes that for bisexuals the MGM *Wizard* "is cherished for the line in which the Scarecrow informs Dorothy that some people go both ways." I don't have any evidence that Oz is a special favorite for transgender individuals, but many critics have commented on how odd it is that Tip, the male protagonist of *The Marvelous Land of Oz* (1904), turns into a girl, and there is a long tradition of cross-gender casting in stage and film versions of Oz stories. (See Appendix D, "Cross-Dressing in Oz Performances.") But while Oz may appeal to lesbians, male and female bisexuals, and trans folks, the gay male

---

e   Gay men and lesbians are different in many ways, so one wouldn't necessarily expect Oz to appeal to lesbians. See Glenn Wilson and Qazi Rahman, *Born Gay: The Psychobiology of Sex Orientation* (London: Peter Owen, 2005), and Gerard Sullivan and Robert Reynolds, "Homosexuality in Midlife: Narrative and Identity," in *Getting It! Gay Men's Sexual Stories*, ed. Robert Reynolds and Gerard Sullivan (New York: Harrington Park/Haworth Press, 2003). Sullivan and Reynolds cite James Wahler and Sarah Gabbay, "Gay Male Aging: A Review of the Literature," *Journal of Gay and Lesbian Social Services* 6, no. 3 (1997): 2. But Mary Duggan, in her humorous *The History of Lesbian Hair, and Other Tales of Bent Life in a Straight World* (New York: Doubleday/Main Street Books, 1996), describes the "Cult of Dorothy" in the gay community and its eerie parallels to the evangelical Christian movement (p. 56). It's unclear if her reference to "gay community" is to men and women or to men only. There are other literary examples of an Oz–lesbian connection. "First Date with the D.J." is a poem by Gerry Gomez Pearlberg in *The Arc of Love: An Anthology of Lesbian Love Poems*, ed. Clare Coss (New York: Scribner, 1996): "We pulled up to my house / There was a ruby slipper between my thighs, / a poppy field in the back of my brain / though Kansas might as well have been a globe away" (p. 43). Karen A. Snider's "Dorothy Poems," from *Aunty Em Is a Prisoner in Kansas* (Milwaukee, WI: Wicked Witch of the Midwest, 198?), examine Oz from a lesbian feminist perspective. Stephanie Reif's play *Left of Oz: A Lesbian Musical Comedy Extravaganza* was presented in 1995 in Petaluma, California.

connection is the most visible and certainly the most widespread. I am confining myself to that.

The phenomenon of the Oz–gay connection also needs qualifying in relation to ethnicity, geography, and time period. Gay love of Oz is largely a white phenomenon, like much of urban gay culture generally.[f] Because Oz is such a big deal to some white gay men, the African American performer Billy Porter felt the need to explicitly distance himself from it in an interview. The MGM movie didn't appeal to him, but he drew on the film and Dorothy as metaphors for something that did touch him. *Paris Is Burning*, the 1990 documentary about voguing, was "like my *Wizard of Oz*. You know, a lot of gay men have this sort of like connection to the *Wizard of Oz*. *The Wizard of Oz* didn't mean anything to me. *The Wizard of Oz* [is] a bunch of white people runnin' around, lookin' for something that I didn't care about. When I saw *Paris Is Burning*, I said, 'I now—I have found Dorothy. That's my Dorothy.'"[g]

Oz's appeal transcends national boundaries. The first Oz book has been translated into more than forty languages. Evidence of the Oz–gay connection can be found in English-speaking countries such as Great Britain, Canada, and Australia. I have been in touch with individual gay Oz fans from Canada, England, Ireland, New Zealand, Australia, Italy, and Russia, but in this book I focus on gay males in the United States. (The demographic breakdown of my respondents is discussed in more detail in Appendix B, "Methodology.")

---

f   Perhaps *The Wiz* is a version of the story that resonates especially with gay African Americans. According to the promotional materials for the 5th International Black LGBT Film Festival, "What the classic *The Wizard of Oz* is for many in the white gay community, the classic *The Wiz* is for the black LGBT community" ("Stanley Bennett Clay to Receive Lifetime Achievement Award," Aug. 7, 2007, Tribe.com, accessed Mar. 2008). But the ways in which race and ethnicity play into the Oz–gay connection are beyond the scope of this book.

g   Porter also called Jennifer Holliday his Dorothy when he described seeing her perform on the 1982 Tony Awards on television: "I didn't have a *Wizard of Oz*—there are no black people in that show.... Jennifer Holliday was my Dorothy!" (Gerard Raymond, "Billy Belts It Out," *The Advocate*, Feb. 15, 2005, p. 53).

I am looking at the connection between gay men and Oz primarily from 1939 to the present. Generalizing about gay adults across generations may be problematic.[h] It is hard to say how long the Oz–gay connection has been around. We may never know if gay males were especially drawn to the stories by Baum when they first were published, or whether gay fans had a particular part to play in making the 1902 musical version of *The Wizard of Oz* such a big hit in Chicago and New York. The reactions of gay boys and gay male adults when the MGM movie first appeared in 1939 are likewise hard to track down. Only a few of my respondents are old enough to have experienced the movie in 1939. Chapter 9, "Oz and Judy in Gay Folklore," includes a discussion of some historical aspects of the phenomenon, but overall, my study is not historical. And while the future of gay Oz fandom is unknown, I offer some speculations in Chapter 10, "The Oz–Gay Connection Now and in the Future."

Furthermore, I am not claiming that *all* gay men and boys are entranced by Baum's *Wonderful Wizard of Oz* or the MGM movie (or both). Some of my gay friends say they don't understand the appeal of Oz or they never particularly liked the movie. Neither am I claiming that *only* gay males are drawn to Oz. Some heterosexual boys and men, as well as girls and women of all orientations, also respond to Oz.

Chart 1.1 lays out the possibilities. The quadrant in the lower left represents gay men who are not Oz fans. The quadrant in the upper right represents Oz fans who are not gay males. But Oz does seem to hold a *particular* appeal for gay boys and men. To put it another way, within Oz fandom there is a greater proportion of gay males than can be explained by their numbers in the general population. The curved extension of the upper left quadrant into the quadrant below it (the darker section below the dotted line) represents those "extra" gay male fans, the ones you would not expect simply from the proportion of gay males in the population as a whole. Explaining where those "extras" come from is an important goal of this book. There are, as I will show, many themes in

---

h   See, for example, Sullivan and Reynolds, "Homosexuality in Midlife." They point out that the social environment of men coming to terms with their homosexuality in the 1950s is very different from that of men coming out in the 1980s.

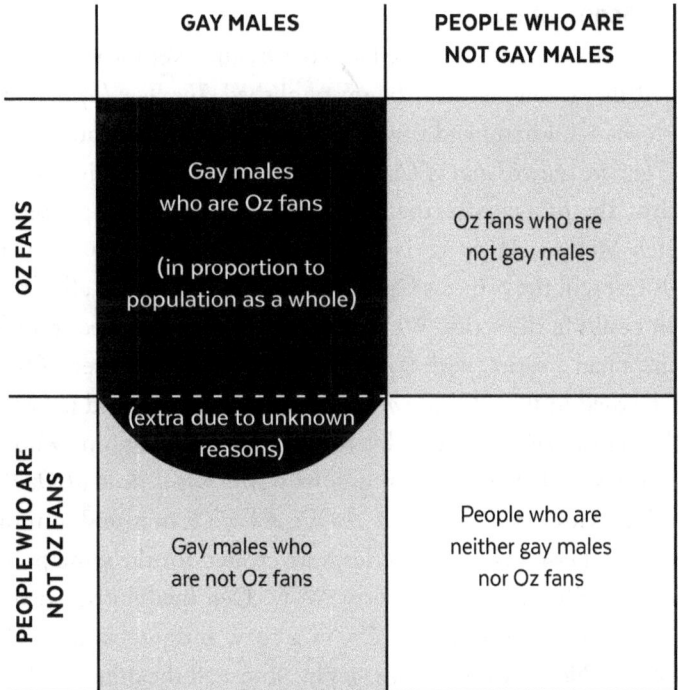

Chart 1.1 The disproportionate number of gay Oz fans

the Oz stories that appeal to gay men and boys at different times in their lives. Some of the reasons that gay men are drawn to Oz may be unique to them; others are probably shared by fans who are not gay.

A given gay fan's responses to stories set in Oz, whatever the format, may differ from the reasons for the embrace of the 1939 MGM film by the gay subculture as a whole. This book describes and explains the attraction at both the individual and subcultural levels. Much of my argument is based on a detailed analysis of questionnaire responses from more than one hundred gay Oz fans. I asked a few questions about the gay community's embrace of Oz, but most of the questionnaire probed respondents' personal reactions to characters, settings, and meanings. The chapters in Part Two, "Individual Reasons and Responses," address themes in the stories that resonate with individual fans. The chapters in Part Three, "Social and Cultural Contexts," deal with the gay subculture as a whole.

The Scope of Oz

There are many stories set in the Land of Oz, and over the years they have appeared in various formats. Baum published *The Wonderful Wizard of Oz* in 1900. Children liked this story so much that he wrote a sequel in 1904, *The Marvelous Land of Oz*, set wholly in Oz, which did not include Dorothy.[i] The protagonist, the boy Tip, escapes from being a servant to the witch Mombi. At the end of his adventures Tip is transformed back into his real self, the princess Ozma of Oz, who rules Oz in all of the subsequent books in the series. When a third Oz novel appeared in 1907, the publishers had a series, with Baum writing a total of fourteen Oz books before he died in 1919. *Glinda of Oz*, his last, was published in 1920.

The series was continued by Ruth Plumly Thompson, who wrote nineteen more Oz books, beginning with *The Royal Book of Oz* in 1921 and ending with *Ozoplaning with the Wizard of Oz* in 1939. From 1940 to 1963 seven other books in the series were created for the same publisher, bringing the official canon to forty. W. W. Denslow illustrated the first book, *The Wonderful Wizard of Oz*, in a cozy, antique (to us) style (fig. 1.9); John R. Neill created the images in almost all the other books in the canon, with longer, more elegant lines (fig. 1.10).

Many other lovers of Oz have written their own Oz stories, both book length and shorter. Some of these have been published by small presses or fan organizations, such as the International Wizard of Oz Club, and others are available in digital form. Most of these stories continue in the tradition of being written for children. But a few, such as Philip José Farmer's *A Barnstormer in Oz* (1982), are written with adults in mind, having more complicated themes and sometimes including sex or violence. Geoff Ryman's 1992 novel *Was* is not set in Oz but weaves together many Oz-related strands. In the novel, Baum, a substitute teacher, meets a young girl named Dorothy who inspires him to write *The Wonderful Wizard*, and we see the resonance Oz has a century later for Jonathan, a gay actor and Judy Garland fan who searches for this long-ago "real" Dorothy. *Wicked: The Life and Times of the Wicked Witch of the West*,

---

i   Subsequent editions of the first two Oz books dropped the adjectives from the titles. Most people refer to the books simply as *The Wizard of Oz* and *The Land of Oz*.

1.9 Illustration by W. W. Denslow, "The Lion ate some of the porridge," from *The Wonderful Wizard of Oz*, 1900
1.10 Illustration by John R. Neill of Betsy Bobbin and Erma, Queen of Night, from *Tik-Tok of Oz*, 1914

written in 1995 by Gregory Maguire, tells the story of the Wicked Witch from her point of view. Including aspects of both the movie and the books, the story deals with the serious themes of fascism and discrimination, among others.

Other narrative formats have lent themselves to Oz stories as well. Some original graphic Oz stories include Eric Shanower's *The Enchanted Apples of Oz* in book form (1986) and two violent comic-book series, *Oz Squad* (1990s) and *Oz/Dark Oz* (1990s). Perhaps the strangest Oz tale I've seen is found on the web. "Friends of Dorothy" by Bob Kanefsky, a software researcher, is a beautifully written short story about a very intense set of sexual activities between the two good friends. First the Scarecrow uses oil from the oil can to give the Tin Woodman a hand job, and then the Tin Woodman has his way with the Scarecrow by taking out all of his straw.

There have also been scores of abridgments of *The Wonderful Wizard* and other stories from the canon, such as Golden Books and coloring books, as well as novelizations and retellings of the MGM movie. Robert Sabuda's pop-up *Wonderful Wizard of Oz* was a surprise best seller in 2001.

Oz has also been depicted on the theatrical stage. Baum himself helped create a musical version of his children's book, which opened in Chicago in 1902 and in New York in 1903, and was involved in other stage productions of Oz adventures in an effort to reproduce the huge success of the stage version of the book. There have been many more recent dramatic versions, with and without music, of previously published and new Oz stories, performed by both children and adults. *The Wiz*, an "all-black, jazzed-up rock-music edition" of the Oz story, opened on Broadway in 1975, winning seven Tony awards. (Although the plot and the placement of songs are very similar to those of the MGM movie, *The Wiz* also contains elements found only in the book, such as the field mice, poppies, and Kalidahs.) *The Wizard of A.I.D.S.* is a musical parody created by Chicago's AIDS Educational Theatre in 1989, with the motto "There's no sex like safe sex." In 2003 a musical version of Gregory Maguire's *Wicked* began a long and successful Broadway run, and a musical based on Geoff Ryman's *Was* appeared in workshops and regional theaters from 2000 to 2005. Various stage versions of the MGM movie have appeared over the years.[j] Puppet and marionette versions began as early as 1928. A $9 million *Wizard of Oz on Ice* appeared in 1995 with Bobby McFerrin singing most of the parts. And a multimedia program based on *The Patchwork Girl of Oz* (1913), Baum's seventh Oz book, was performed in Los Angeles in 2002.

Film versions of the Oz story have the potential for a much wider audience than stage productions. Baum had a hand in early silent movies made by his Oz Film Manufacturing Company. And a 1925 silent *Wizard* featured Oliver Hardy as the Tin Woodman. But the most famous and widely distributed film version of an Oz story is undoubtedly the 1939 MGM *Wizard of Oz*. It starred Judy Garland as Dorothy, with Ray Bolger as the Scarecrow, Jack Haley as the Tin Man, and Bert Lahr as the Cowardly Lion. Also memorable are Margaret Hamilton as the Wicked Witch of the West, Frank Morgan as the Wizard, and Billie Burke as Glinda. The score by Yip Harburg and Harold Arlen includes "Over the Rainbow," one of filmdom's most beloved songs. This MGM *Wizard* was re-released in 1949 and 1955, followed by a second life on television beginning in 1956. The movie was televised almost annually from 1959 to 1976.

---

j   A stage version of the film written by John Kane for the Royal Shakespeare Company was first seen in London in 1987 and recorded in 1989; it has been performed throughout the United States as well.

The Land of Oz, a television version of the second Oz book, was broadcast in 1960, starring Shirley Temple as the boy Tip. *The Wiz* became a Hollywood movie in 1978. It was set in a strange version of New York City, with Diana Ross as an older schoolteacher version of Dorothy and Michael Jackson as the Scarecrow. A highly anticipated sequel to the MGM *Wizard* appeared in 1985, *Return to Oz*. It was based not only on *The Marvelous Land of Oz* but also on the third Oz book, *Ozma of Oz* (1907). But it had no music and was considered by some to be much darker than the 1939 fantasy. It begins with Aunt Em and Uncle Henry sending Dorothy off to a mental institution for electroshock therapy because she insists she really went to Oz. The year 2013 saw the release of Disney's immensely successful *Oz the Great and Powerful*, with James Franco as the Wizard. It tells the story of the Wizard's arrival in Oz, his accession to the throne, and the Wicked Witch's becoming wicked.

Animated versions of Oz began in 1933 with a nine-minute *Wizard of Oz*. The 1972 *Journey Back to Oz* is loosely based on *The Marvelous Land of Oz*, featuring the voices of Judy Garland's daughter, Liza Minnelli, as Dorothy and Margaret Hamilton as Aunt Em. *Oz Kids*, created by Willard Carroll, is a recent series of animated movies about the children (!) of the familiar characters. Individual episodes aired on Japanese television and were released as videos for sale in the United States.

Most of the Oz stage productions and films have been recorded in one form or another. Videos and DVDs are available of the MGM *Wizard*, *The Wiz*, and the early animated and silent movies. You can hear the soundtrack of the MGM movie with songs only, or including dialog and sound effects. Recordings of the stage and screen *Wiz*, the Royal Shakespeare Company version of the MGM movie, and songs from the early Oz musicals are available on CD, as well as readings of the books in both complete and abridged versions. Dozens of artists have recorded their renditions of "Over the Rainbow." In 1973, the gay icon Bette Midler recorded her version of "Optimistic Voices," the song inviting Dorothy and her companions to come out of the woods and step up to the Emerald City.

Oz is also kept alive by fan clubs, museums devoted to memorabilia, conventions, annual festivals, websites, and online discussion groups. And Oz has generated numerous decorative objects and collectibles. Fans can buy T-shirts, greeting cards, stickers, refrigerator magnets, party plates, clocks, cookie jars, music boxes, tree ornaments, and coloring books. Most of the widely available objects contain images from the MGM version of the story, but fans and collectors have also produced objects with images and quotes from the Oz books. In a manner similar to fairy tales, *The Wizard of Oz* has been annexed by the folk and is no longer the work of one author. Oz is, in fact, the perfect example of transmedia storytelling.

Of course, an analysis of the story as it appears in one medium may or may not be valid for other versions of the story, so a summary of the differences between Baum's *Wonderful Wizard* and the MGM film based on it may be particularly useful.[k] The shoes Dorothy takes from the feet of the Wicked Witch of the East are silver in the original book, so the symbolism of the color red cannot be used as a reason for the appeal of the book. The MGM Dorothy is older and less assertive than Baum and Denslow's. But the story is more Dorothy's in the movie, because viewers see her as "flesh and blood." Several episodes from the book did not make it into the movie: Baum's Dorothy and her companions travel through many smaller countries, such as the China Country and the land of the Hammerheads, and they deal with more obstacles on their journey, such as a large ditch, a river, and a fight with the ferocious Kalidahs. But the most obvious aspect of the movie that is not in the book is the dream as a framing device. People familiar with the movie may be surprised to learn that the characters from Kansas who appear in the "dream"—the farmhands, Professor Marvel, and Miss Gulch—do not appear in Baum's original story at all. While purists may not like the story's being turned into a dream, the new characters serve to connect Dorothy's life in Kansas to her adventures in Oz.

The changes from printed page to screen also affected the overall tone of the story. Which is felt to be scarier, the book or the movie, depends in part on the features one focuses on. The many bloody events

---

k   A longer analysis of the differences between the book and the movie is given in chapter 7 of Suzanne Rahn, *"The Wizard of Oz": Shaping an Imaginary World* (New York: Twayne, 1998).

depicted in the book would surely seem to make it more frightening. And Baum's Kansas lacks the hominess and comfort that the film depicts, with its three jolly farmhands. But because the Witch is a much more significant character in the movie, and because we actually see the tornado, and Aunt Em inside the Witch's crystal ball, others think the movie is more terrifying.

The illustrations in *The Wonderful Wizard* and succeeding Oz books give readers memorable images of objects, characters, and scenes, such as the eyeglasses used to counteract the dazzle of the emeralds in the Emerald City, and the different forms that the Wizard takes for Dorothy and each of her companions. But readers are still invited to create their own mental images of the often-dramatic actions that punctuate these stories, which cannot help but enlarge the imagination. In contrast, film presents the viewer with ready-made images, which, tapping directly into the viewer's subconscious, generate visceral reactions. But if the medium of film can make the scary parts of the story more frightening, it can also make the gorgeous parts of Oz even more fabulous. Oz in general and the Emerald City in particular are more breathtaking, more stunning, in the MGM movie than in the imaginations of most readers. It's hard for any prose description to match the sparkle of Dorothy's slippers, the shine of the MGM Emerald City, or the phosphorescence of Glinda's bubble. The visual aspects of the Hollywood *Wiz*, too, are most impressive.

While the MGM screenwriters simplified Baum's original story considerably and enlarged what happens in Kansas at both ends of the story, the main narrative remains the same. As one critic summarizes it:

> A little girl falls asleep and dreams she is lost and cannot find her way home. She is harassed by a Witch she must kill, and the solution to this problem is easier than she imagined (perhaps something as simple as throwing a bucket of water at her). Then she travels to a Wiseman only to learn that he can provide her with no solutions, though he gives her a hint when he tells her three companions that they already possess what they believe they lack. Finally, a Fairy Godmother tells the girl she has always had the power to solve her own problems, and the child finds her way back home . . .

In this book I use the terms "*The Wizard of Oz*" and "the main story" interchangeably to refer to the core story of the original book by L. Frank Baum, and also to that core story as it has been represented in various stage and screen versions. To refer to the first book in the series, I use the original title, *The Wonderful Wizard of Oz,* or a shortened version, *The Wonderful Wizard,* or simply "the book." The terms "the MGM movie (or film)," "the movie," and "the MGM *Wizard*" all refer to MGM production #1060, released in 1939, starring Judy Garland. "The Oz books" refers to the canon of forty books by Baum and others, published by Reilly & Britton and later by Reilly & Lee. Chart 1.2 shows the versions and my terms for them.

	"THE OZ BOOKS"		
"THE WIZARD OF OZ" or "THE MAIN STORY"	"The Wonderful Wizard of Oz" "The Wonderful Wizard" "the first book" "the book" (1900)	"the MGM movie" "the movie" (1939)	other versions (*The Wiz,* etc.)
	13 other books by Baum (1904-1920)		
	19 books by Ruth Plumly Thompson (1921-1939)		
	7 books by additional authors (1940-1963)		

Chart 1.2 Versions of Oz stories

Oz stories in any medium take place completely or primarily in the Land of Oz. While Oz—or, more formally, the Land of Oz—is the name of a place, I will generally use "Oz" as shorthand for all versions of all stories in all media set in the Land of Oz, as well as related phenomena such as organizations and collectibles.[1] Thus an "Oz fan" can be a fan of the movie, the books, the place, or some combination.

. . .

The many pieces of evidence explored in this chapter for an Oz–gay connection combine to create a compelling picture of gay love of Oz at the subcultural level. Various explanations have been offered to account for this subcultural phenomenon. It is to those explanations that I turn in the following chapter.

---

1   Justin Knowles, the publisher of *The World of Oz*, by Allen Eyles (Tucson, AZ: HP Books, 1985), calls this "the whole Oz phenomenon."

Surface Explanations

"JUDY GARLAND." When people hear about my research into Oz's appeal for gay men, many of them, both gay and straight, reply dismissively, "Oh, it's the cult of Judy." Their logic goes something like this: Judy Garland starred in the movie; gay men love Judy; therefore, it is Judy's performance that makes the movie a gay favorite. Judy Garland's role as Dorothy Gale of Kansas is certainly an unforgettable aspect of the MGM movie, and her performance is a good reason for liking the movie. But what is it about Judy Garland that makes her a gay icon?

Loving Judy Garland because of her performance in the MGM movie does happen, and it sometimes happens early. After watching the film for the first time when he was four, one Oz fan told his mother he was going to marry Dorothy. Another "immediately fell in love" with her when he saw the movie on television at age five. Many adults appreciate Judy Garland as a performer as well. Fans often say that in the MGM movie and her concert career Garland showed strong emotions and great vulnerability, which allowed her to establish a special relationship with her audience. Aspects of Garland's appearance and performing that resonate with gay men in particular include her lack of conventional beauty, her androgynous costumes, her self-awareness, and her playfulness with regard to her own failings.[a]

---

a   Using empirical data, Richard Dyer has made a detailed analysis of Judy

Other reasons for loving Judy Garland stem from her life story. Garland was a talented, creative, sensitive person who was manipulated by society. She had problems with drugs and alcohol. Her money was mismanaged in later years. Soon after she was fired from MGM in 1950, she tried to kill herself. It is probably around that time that her appeal to gay men began. Many gay men related to her struggles specifically, or to the idea of a hard life in general. Judy's resilience—she always seemed to bounce back—was also greatly admired. Perhaps because they saw aspects of Judy in themselves, gay men placed her at the top of their list of idols. Gatherings of gay men at Judy Garland concerts enabled them to feel like part of a community. This "gay space" phenomenon—covert in those early days—mirrors the sense of community felt decades later by gay fans at showings of the MGM movie at the Castro Theatre in San Francisco.

But there are several reasons why love of Judy cannot completely explain the MGM movie's special status with gay men. First, the number of movie fans citing Judy Garland as the reason for their fandom is small. Of the sixty questionnaire respondents who said that *The Wizard of Oz* was their favorite version of an Oz story, only five mentioned Judy Garland's performance as a reason for their loving the movie as kids; six others said their favorite character was Dorothy and/or that they identified with her in part because of Garland's performance.

Second, other Oz fans say Judy does nothing for them. One of my respondents wasn't keen on having her as an icon because he had seen her emceeing on television's *Hollywood Palace* (1964–70) in a drunken state. Another said that he doesn't approve of self-destruction and isn't crazy about camp. For an older fan, Judy was a child entertainer only. He noted that he was fed up with "the whole Judy Garland thing." Most

> Garland as a gay icon. His conclusions are based on letters from gay men in response to queries he put in the gay press, writings in gay publications (after her death and after the emergence of the modern gay movement), and his own knowledge of Garland's film, concert, and TV performances and on record albums. See Dyer's "Judy Garland and Gay Men," chap. 3 in *Heavenly Bodies: Film Stars and Society* (New York: St. Martin's Press, 1986), reprinted in *Rainbow: A Star-Studded Tribute to Judy Garland*, ed. Ethlie Ann Vare (New York: Boulevard Books, 1998).

of the anti-Judy respondents were fans of the Oz books more than the movie, but one movie fan was just as adamantly anti-Judy, saying he was a fan of the film but not of Judy Garland. (Positive and negative feelings about Judy and the Oz connection will come up again in Chapter 8, "The Subcultural Phenomenon.")

Third, gay diva worship was declared over in the new millennium: supposedly, it was a phenomenon of the pre-Stonewall life of the closet. Since we are free to be out in these enlightened times, the argument goes, we can have out gay men as role models rather than emotional or strong women. As one journalist put it in 2000, "Young gay men have ditched diva worship."[b] He applied that observation to Judy Garland in particular, who was a tragic and pathetic example for gay men before Stonewall. Whatever one makes of the argument that diva worship is dying among gay men, it is noteworthy that there do not seem to be comparable statements about *The Wizard of Oz*. In books about gay culture published in the last few years, the MGM *Wizard* is still often listed as a gay favorite.

Fourth, Oz fans rarely cite other Garland movies. In response to my question "Do you have any other favorite movies?" only five gay Oz fans mentioned Judy or her movies. Three respondents listed *A Star Is Born* (1954), one said *Meet Me in St. Louis* (1944), and one person who makes his living as a Judy Garland expert said "everything by Judy." That only two Judy films were mentioned out of the two hundred favorite titles given by over one hundred respondents is telling. If Judy transforms the MGM *Wizard* into a gay favorite, why doesn't she transform all her movies into gay favorites? Both *A Star Is Born* and *Meet Me in St. Louis* could easily lend themselves to gay appropriation. Why are there no bars named after the songs "The Man That Got Away" or "The Boy Next Door," no T-shirts bearing those words? *Meet Me in St. Louise* is a gay parody crying to be made.

One could argue that Judy Garland's roles in these movies aren't as poignant, and the stories aren't as affecting. But that is precisely my

---

b   *Wicked* is an Oz story without Dorothy, and the musical version of *Wicked* can help exorcise gay male embarrassment over Judy Garland as a gay icon. See Peter Chattaway, "Friends of Dorothy: *The Boy from Oz* and *Wicked*," *New Criterion*, Dec. 2003.

point: the story is what matters. It's not that Judy has nothing to do with the gay appeal of *The Wizard of Oz*; it's that she isn't the main reason. As we will see, aspects of her performance in the movie will tie in with other issues. Garland's rendition of "Over the Rainbow" makes the song the epitome of a longing for escape. Fans see Judy's Dorothy as an alienated adolescent, and her emotional line readings bring out the love and friendship her character feels for her companions. Escape, alienation, and caring, issues that appear in the Oz books as well, are some of the deeper reasons gay men and boys respond to Oz.[c]

Another reason that the cult of Judy Garland cannot account for Oz's appeal is that many gay fans respond positively to other specific aspects of the 1939 film. Some men focus on improvements the movie made over Baum's original book. The movie is simpler and more direct, it corrects the book's excesses, it is less fantastic—more limited, in a good way—than the series. Even the fact that Dorothy's journey to Oz is cast as a dream in the movie is a plus to one movie lover. One important aspect of the MGM movie for gay Oz fans is what it looks and feels like. The music and visuals have made Oz special. When he was five and first saw the MGM Oz, one fan was intrigued by the "candy land appeal" of horses that change color and of the wildly outfitted Munchkins, as well as the voice of Glinda and the music. The glorious appearance of the film—the sepia of the Kansas scenes, the intensity and richness of the colors in Oz—are beguiling to fans. The bright hues of Munchkinland, the Yellow Brick Road, the Ruby Slippers, and the Emerald City all make a big impression.[d] There is even "glamour" in the castle of the Wicked Witch of the West and the forest approaching it.[e]

---

[c] In fact, the argument that Judy causes love of Oz can be reversed: perhaps it is her association with Oz that causes Judy Garland's fame. See Martin Gardner, preface to *The Annotated Wizard of Oz*, ed. Michael Patrick Hearn (New York: Norton, 2000), p. xi. When I mentioned this possibility at the Centennial Oz convention in 2000, the audience of Oz aficionados, unsurprisingly, roared its approval.

[d] In the late fifties and early sixties, some families had black-and-white televisions, so not everyone grew up seeing Oz in color.

[e] Some fans note that they found the MGM esthetics very attractive when

Explanations Other Than Judy

If love of Judy Garland does not explain why gay men love *The Wizard of Oz*, what other reasons might there be? Three other superficial explanations of film's gay appeal—that is, explanations unrelated to the exact content or execution of the movie—are worth examining:

"IT'S A MUSICAL." *The Wizard of Oz* is a musical, and gay men love musicals.[f] Perhaps this can explain the gay appeal. But the MGM *Wizard* is not a typical musical. There is no boy-meets-girl story in the plot (in fact, one or two gay fans mentioned this as a positive aspect of the movie). The movie contains very little dancing, and the second half of the movie has no songs at all. Admittedly, the production values are high, and the spectacle and fabulousness we associate with MGM musicals are there in abundance. But most gay fans of the MGM movie do not think of it as a musical. Only two respondents talked about the genre of the movie explicitly, one who loved musicals and one who said the fact that it was a musical was a reason to dislike it. Musicals in general did not rank high when respondents listed other favorite movies.[g] Not thinking of the

---

they were young, especially the vivid colors, but color in itself isn't a plus to everyone. Other aspects of moviemaking may be important. Some fans appreciate the performances of Bert Lahr and Margaret Hamilton. For one fan, *The Wizard of Oz* is about making films, the movie giving him his first glimpse of "movie magic." The pre-Oz scenes grip another; he finds the Kansas sequences "hauntingly beautiful" and the scene with Professor Marvel and Dorothy the "most beautifully acted." Knowing about the film and film history also adds to some fans' appreciation.

f In fact, the idea that gay men love musicals applies mostly to *stage* musicals; gay men's love of *movie* musicals is less well documented. But for works addressing both topics, see the Notes section at the key phrase "gay men love musicals."

g Other musicals mentioned were *The Sound of Music* (1965), six respondents; *Gentlemen Prefer Blondes* (1953) and *Singin' in the Rain* (1952), three each; and *The Rocky Horror Picture Show* (1975), *Gigi* (1958), and *Cabaret* (1972), two each. A few fans did mention the music as a reason for liking the film, and some have recordings and sheet music among their favorite objects. One adult fan often listens to the deluxe Rhino Records edition of the soundtrack and has memorized "every orchestral moment of Herbert Stothart's Oscar winning

film as a musical is consistent with how others view it. In lists of movies, the film is usually considered a children's fantasy, not a musical.

"Gay people created the movie." The fact that gay people helped create the MGM *Wizard* is another potential explanation for its gay appeal. The movie was a product of gay designers, who may have contributed their gay sensibility to the film. One of the screenwriters, Edgar Allan Woolf, was gay, as were George Cukor, who was replaced as director and didn't receive screen credit, and Roger Edens, Judy Garland's voice coach, who was the rehearsal pianist for the movie and helped write and arrange some of the music. Billie Burke and Judy Garland both had affairs with women. Presumably if people with a gay sensibility participated in and made the film, people with a gay sensibility would respond to it. The visual fabulousness of the set, costumes, and choreography may very well be things gay men like. But evoking a gay sensibility really begs the question. What is there in particular about the sets and costumes, Cukor's direction, or Woolf's contributions to the screenplay that makes it appealing to gay men and boys?[h]

"It's a gay thing to do." When I began this project, I assumed that a large proportion of gay Oz fans became enamored of Oz because being a *Wizard of Oz* fan was a gay thing to do. After coming out and embracing a gay identity, these men would discover the movie was a gay favorite and look at it through new gay eyes. Or perhaps it was simply

score." Of the many colorful songs by Harold Arlen and E. Y. Harburg in the film, only "Over the Rainbow" was mentioned at all, in more than one hundred questionnaires. This song's significance is explored in Chapter 9, "Oz and Judy in Gay Folklore."

h If having a lot of gay people involved in a movie behind the scenes guaranteed strong gay appeal, we should find *West Side Story* (1961) at the top of the gay pantheon. Many of the creators of both the stage musical and the film adaptation were gay. The original stage version boasted the composer Leonard Bernstein, the book writer Arthur Laurents, the lyricist Stephen Sondheim, and Larry Kert as Tony; it was conceived, directed, and choreographed by Jerome Robbins. The film version kept the songs by Bernstein and Sondheim, and Robbins choreographed and co-directed it. But there don't seem to be any bars named *West Side Story* and characters from the film don't appear in pride parades.

a matter of hearing so many other gay men talk about Oz that they got into it in order to fit in. But for several reasons the "keeping up with the Bruces" explanation cannot explain the gay appeal of Oz.

First, while it is possible to become enamored of Oz as an adult, this timing is extremely unusual. Gay fans are almost always hooked on Oz before adolescence, with fandom striking most often between four and nine years old. Many become enamored of some version of an Oz story as young as two or three. Their discovery that the MGM film is a gay favorite tends to come long after they become Oz fans themselves. Furthermore, a small percentage of gay Oz fans don't know about the Oz–gay connection, so it is doubtful that they were influenced by it. Of the two respondents who knew when they became fans that the MGM movie is a gay favorite, one said it didn't have anything to do with his own fandom. For only one respondent out of 109, then, did knowledge of the Oz–gay connection lead to his becoming a fan.

Many of the gay fans who do know about the Oz–gay connection insist that their love of the movie has nothing to do with its status as a gay favorite. In fact, they distance themselves from what they see as superficial gay fans of the film, contrasting their individual personal relationship with the movie with the general cultural position of the movie. (The relationship between knowing that the movie is a gay favorite and personal fandom will be discussed in more detail in Chapter 8, "The Subcultural Phenomenon.") Finally, even if the fact that many gay men love the MGM movie did have a ripple effect, creating new generations of fans who simply adopted the movie as a favorite, this doesn't answer the question of how the movie became a gay favorite in the first place, nor does it explain why so many men would remain such devoted fans without having any special feelings for the content or form of the story.

It's Not Just the Movie

Of all the versions of Oz stories, the MGM *Wizard* was mentioned most often by my respondents as their favorite. This is not surprising, since it is the movie that looms largest in the popular imagination, and many more people have been exposed to the movie than to any other version. However, as chart 2.1 shows, the favorite version for about one-third of

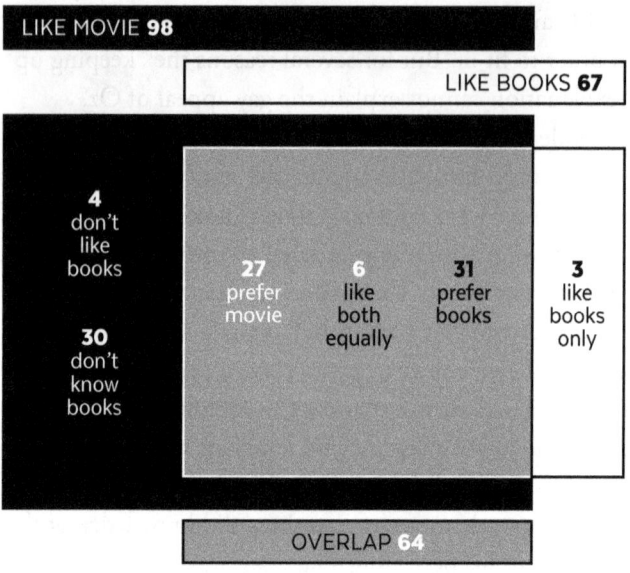

Chart 2.1 Overlap between fans of the MGM movie and fans of the Oz books

my respondents was Baum's *Wonderful Wizard* or one or more of the other books in the official series. There were also a few fans who liked the books and the movie equally.[i]

The respondents who preferred the books usually mentioned specific books in the series. *The Wonderful Wizard* was the most frequently mentioned favorite, followed closely by *The Patchwork Girl of Oz*. Others mentioned by more than one fan were *The Marvelous Land of Oz*, *Ozma of Oz*, and *The Magic of Oz* (1919). Three non-Baum books considered

---

i   In their questionnaire responses, surprisingly few book lovers objected to what Hollywood did to Baum, but some did feel that Baum's version is "the real Oz." Some fans of the books also reported going through an anti-movie stage, since the widespread assumption that the movie is all there is to Oz means that they have found themselves constantly explaining that Baum's *Wonderful Wizard* came first. Many gay fans took exception particularly to the fact that the MGM screenwriters made Dorothy's journey to Oz a dream. The ramifications of turning it into a dream are discussed further in Chapter 4, "Escaping to Oz."

favorites by one fan each were written by Ruth Plumly Thompson, Baum's successor as "Royal Historian of Oz": *The Gnome King of Oz* (1927), *Pirates in Oz* (1931), and *Ojo in Oz* (1933). *Merry Go Round in Oz* (1963), by Eloise Jarvis McGraw and Lauren McGraw, was also the favorite of one respondent.

One intriguing set of responses includes visual aspects of the Oz books. The illustrations of the Oz books appealed to fans both as children and as adults, perhaps in ways analogous to viewers' responses to the visual splendor of the MGM film and the Hollywood *Wiz*. One fan had a more complicated relationship with the visuals from both the movie and the books. When he was six, he was obsessed by the MGM movie and drew its characters. Then he switched over to creating his version of the John R. Neill illustrations in the Oz books.

Despite its street language and other modernizations, the 1975 stage version of *The Wiz* was well liked by a handful of respondents. The stage rendering of *The Wiz* was one fan's favorite version of Oz; he saw it over fifteen times. Like the Royal Shakespeare Company stage version of the film, the stage *Wiz* combined aspects of the movie and the original book, which may be part of its appeal as well.[j] The black gay activist Keith Boykin has described how, as an adolescent, he identified with Dorothy/Diana Ross in the 1978 movie version of *The Wiz*. The same movie helped form the white writer Patrick Horrigan's identity. Some questionnaire respondents related to themes in the movie version of *The Wiz*—citing the themes of feeling different, home, and self-discovery—in exactly the same ways as others writing about the MGM *Wizard* or the Oz books.

Some gay book fans cited the 1985 *Return to Oz* as their favorite movie version because of the realistic detail with which Oz was created, the special effects, Faizura Balk's portrayal of Dorothy, the lack of songs, and how close it was to Baum's spirit. But for every person who liked *Return* for being faithful to Baum's books, someone else felt it wasn't.

Two novels, Geoff Ryman's *Was* and Gregory Maguire's *Wicked*,

---

[j] Some people associated with various versions of *The Wiz* were gay: Andre De Shields, who created the character of the Wiz on Broadway, and Joel Schumacher, the screenwriter of the film version.

engage with aspects of both the MGM film and the Oz books.^k While opinions about these stories and their stage incarnations vary among gay Oz fans, many respondents loved *Was* and *Wicked* for adding breadth to Oz. The novel *Wicked* was rated favorably by many. The few respondents who had seen the musical version of *Wicked* or heard the music also felt positive about it. One adored the musical, finding the music inspired. Another rated its music as highly as that of the MGM story, finding the songs as personally significant as "Over the Rainbow."

Some respondents appreciated the darker aspects of Ryman's novel. They liked how Dorothy's harsh life, explored in the novel, inspired the fictional Baum to imagine a better life for her. A fan who called *Was* brilliant commented that it drew on everything he loved about the MGM film, making use of the negative picture of Kansas and exploring the secret stories behind the way things appear. Fans related to the story of a gay outsider, as well as the political aspects of Ryman's tale, which keeps the wonder of the film amid the dark issues of sexual abuse.

The appearance of the MGM film on lists of favorite gay movies and the numerous uses of and allusions to the MGM Oz in a gay context demonstrate that the movie is an important part of gay culture. But it is not just the MGM movie that is embraced by individual fans; Oz stories in other media, as well as other Oz movies, are also embraced.^l Gay love of Oz is remarkably diverse and complex, and gay fans have a variety of responses to the many different versions of Oz stories that they love. Often the reasons a particular Oz story is beloved by a gay fan relate to what is different or unique about that version and don't address deeper aspects of the stories themselves, or the qualities of the Land of Oz itself that matter to gay fans. What is telling is that answers to questions about favorite characters, first exposure, feelings about Oz and Kansas, gay meaning, and the like are surprisingly similar, regardless of what the fan's favorite version is. For example, a theme such as growing up or an

---

k   Both Ryman and Maguire are gay, and in the years since their publication (*Was* in 1992, *Wicked* in 1995), both novels have become musicals.

l   Writers looking at the Oz–gay connection do occasionally mention versions other than the MGM movie. See, for instance, Chris Carpenter, "Return to Oz," Arts and Culture, *Blade California*, Nov. 2011, p. 35.

ambivalent relationship to home and family is given as a reason for liking both the film version of *The Wiz* and the MGM movie. Dorothy is appreciated for her spunk in both the movie and the Oz books.

Another piece of evidence that the gay appeal of Oz isn't limited to the MGM movie is the larger number of gay men associated with more general Oz activities. The International Wizard of Oz Club was founded in 1957 to celebrate Oz as depicted in the books by L. Frank Baum and other official "Royal Historians of Oz." And while the club has since come to embrace fans of the MGM movie and all versions of Oz stories, the most active members still tend to be book fans. I first realized that the appeal of Oz to gay men is not just a matter of the MGM movie when I saw how many gay men there were at the club's conventions. In fact, in the six decades since its founding, gay men have been active in all aspects of the club in disproportionate numbers. Of the men who have received awards from the club, been officers, or served as editors of club publications, somewhere between one-quarter and one-half have been gay.[m] A handful of club members are also acknowledged experts on Oz, publishing books on Oz topics and speaking at Oz events around the world.

In addition to Oz Club members, there are other gay men who are devoted experts, collectors, and writers on Oz. While this is hard to quantify, the percentage of gay men within the group of Oz experts is much more than 10 percent. Let me give just two examples. On May 15, 1998, in honor of Baum's birthday, the Boston radio show called *The Connection* was devoted to the meanings of *The Wizard of Oz*. Of the six guests, three were gay men, although only one identified as such. (That was Michael Bronski, who was picked specifically to talk about the gay angle.) At the Ozmapolitan Convention, the Midwestern gathering of the Oz Club in 2004, at least three of the five presenters were gay. Of the two performers, one was a heterosexual woman and the other a gay man.

Finally, there is the fact that gay gift shops sometimes offer Oz products that are not based on images or lines from the MGM film.[n] One

---

m The imprecision arises from the fact that some were not, or are not, officially out.

n Uncle Mame, at the edge of the Castro neighborhood in San Francisco, sold two Oz games. Pulp, a stationery and toy store near the Castro, offered

could argue that these non-MGM Oz items are simply spillover from the movie: a buyer thought "Oz!" and got these items because he or she knew that Oz items sell. But that is exactly my point. The draw is Oz in general, not just MGM's *Wizard*.

. . .

So how do the reasons commonly given for the gay appeal of the movie hold up? Not well, as I have shown in this chapter. Garland's performance does not explain it; for one thing, her other movies are not uniformly beloved of the gay men who love Oz. And fans mention other aspects of the movie, such as its visual design and cinematography, as part of its appeal. While the movie is a musical, the genre per se does not seem to have much to do with its gay appeal. One might say that gay people associated with the movie contributed their gay sensibilities, thus making it speak to others with similar sensibilities, but that does not shed light on the question of what exactly in the movie springs from or speaks to those sensibilities. And the fact that the MGM movie is a gay favorite cannot explain its appeal to gay men.

Furthermore, Oz is more than the MGM movie; stories set in this magical land appear in other movies, in book form, and in other media.

two postcards of illustrations from the Oz books by John R. Neill. Pride and Joy, a gay bookstore and gift shop in Northampton, Massachusetts, displayed an Oz postcard, the cover of *The Wonderful Wizard*, with Denslow illustrations. The manager also encouraged a local collage postcard artist to make an Oz postcard. In addition, the shop stocked Robert Sabuda's pop-up *Wizard of Oz* (2001) and Gregory Maguire's *Son of a Witch* (2006), the sequel to *Wicked*. The Stamping Ground is a stationery and gift shop run by a gay man in Woodstock, Vermont, with a rainbow flag outside to attract gay customers. It sells four or five Oz-themed rubber stamps that are not images from the MGM movie. For the Christmas 2000 season, We Think the World of You, a gay bookstore in Boston, carried two books published that year, *Oz: The Hundredth Anniversary Celebration* and the second edition of *The Annotated Wizard*. According to the owner, both sold well. In the spring of 2001 the store carried *Was*, *Wicked*, and two Oz magnets. Calamus Bookstore of Boston carried *Oz Before the Rainbow* (2000) and two Oz magnets.

Many Oz fans consider the Oz books or more modern retellings their favorite version, and they respond to the same themes in all versions of the stories. This leads gay fans to be active in larger Oz fandom; they are also a ready market for Oz items not related to the MGM film.

What is most important, the reasons related to fans' enthusiasm for a particular version of an Oz story just skim the surface of Oz's gay appeal. They don't address the deeper question of what the gay Oz fan gets from the story. Oz's values, relationships, characters, and geography have been elaborated in succeeding Oz books and have appeared in other stories set in the Land of Oz in non-book media. Research has shown that the values embodied by all stories set in Oz, regardless of medium, are what matter most.

But before we take a look at the deeper reasons for the Oz–gay connection, it is worth exploring early Oz fandom. What, one might wonder, can we make of boys who became fans when they were three or four or five years old, long before they were gay adults?

3 Gay Boys

Oz stories often resonate with young boys, even boys as young as three or four. Most of these boys will grow up to identify as gay. Can we call them gay at such a young age? Gay men do not appear on earth as grownups, fully formed, like Athena; they must be boys before they are men. Some people use the term "pre-gay" to refer to such boys. But might we call these pre-gay boys gay? To put it another way, do gay boys exist?

Kids are aware of their sexual orientation at earlier ages and coming out earlier than ever before. Gay–straight alliances have formed in high schools and recently in middle schools. Thus the general public has been exposed to the fact that lesbian, gay, bisexual, and transgender teens exist. But the literature on gay identity and gay psychology is silent on the topic of gay children younger than teens. Gay activists are also surprisingly quiet on the topic of gay youngsters.

There are at least two reasons for this silence. First, many people believe kids can't be gay. They think sexual orientation is a matter of sexual activity, and they assume that children don't have sex. In fact, however, homosexuality is a constellation of feelings and desires that often appear long before sexual expression per se. Second, many gay adults are afraid of feeding into the stereotype of gay men as child molesters. They fear that showing an interest in gay children, in the form of advocacy or research, would be misinterpreted as sexual predation. This fear, while perhaps not unfounded, is unfortunate. It keeps gay adults from learning about and providing services for a vulnerable and largely invisible segment of the population, as well as keeping them from broadening their horizons across generations.

Writings by and interviews with gay adults and teens often include accounts of early feelings and behaviors, as do interviews with gay celebrities. When a person tells his own story, it can include otherwise unobservable feelings. And the story is specific, concrete, and often quite moving. But retrospective accounts of this sort may not be accurate. Another source of information about gay children is parents' descriptions of their sons' behavior, usually somewhat later than when it is observed.[a]

The best information would come from accounts of gay boys' lives at the time they are lived. But it is hard to identify young gay boys, because desire and inclination themselves are abstract concepts and cannot be observed unless they are acted upon. However, gender-atypical behavior—that is, activities and preferences not considered typical for males—is often observed, and researchers have found that a high proportion of boys who act in gender-atypical ways later identify as gay. Observation of young boys who are gender-atypical can be a window into at least some young gay boyhoods.

In the 1970s and 80s the psychiatrist Richard Green collected a group of boys who were identified by their parents as manifesting problematic gender-role behavior. He tested and interviewed them and their parents over fifteen years. In this chapter I draw on his work,[b] as well as the work

---

a Interestingly, mothers are more likely to tell their tales than fathers, although fathers are represented in a few collections. Additionally, there is a memoir written by a mother and her son. It is worth noting that in more than one account the parents report knowing very early that their sons were gay. For titles of works by mothers, fathers, and the mother-and-son team, see the Notes section for this page and paragraph, at the key phrase "parents' descriptions."

b *The "Sissy Boy Syndrome" and the Development of Homosexuality* (New Haven, CT: Yale University Press, 1987). While Green did have a comparison group—boys who weren't considered "feminine" by their parents—his study was flawed in many ways. To be eligible for participation, parents had to want to change their son's sissy behavior; thus Green's sample is not

of Edgardo Menvielle and Catherine Tuerk, who for many years led a support group for the Children's National Medical Center, in Washington, DC. The support group, which was part of the center's Outreach Program for Children with Gender-Variant Behaviors and Their Families, helped parents understand and accept their children. Among other things, the leaders discussed the correlation between childhood behavior and adult orientation, saying that it was likely that the child was gay then (as opposed to becoming gay in the future). Having someone else observe or ask questions, such as Green or Menvielle and Tuerk, adds greatly to our understanding of gay boys' lives by being more objective. Reports by people looking at the children from outside avoid the pitfalls of faulty memory and embellishments or bias that we might see in reports by a person looking back.

If young children don't yet identify as gay, how do we know that gay boys exist? The strongest argument for the existence of gay boys is a matter of logic: one's sexual orientation does not begin magically with the onset of puberty. Heterosexual little boys have crushes and show romantic and even sexual interest in little girls well before puberty. Boys who grow up to be gay have similar interest in or desire for other boys. This early same-sex desire can manifest itself as strong affection, watching and being excited by other males, fantasizing about them, and engaging in actual physical activity.

Many gay adults report having had special affection for other boys when they were young. In fact, clinicians report gay boys having same-sex attractions well before puberty, between the ages of nine and eleven. The affection is often manifested as wanting to spend time together and feeling that time spent with another boy is special. Bryce McDougall, the editor of the anthology *My Child Is Gay*, remembers "being attracted to another kid":

> I must have been three or four years of age. It certainly was not a sexual feeling, because I did not know what a sexual feeling was.

representative of all gender-atypical kids, only those whose parents felt that their sons' behavior was problematic. But it is the only longitudinal study I know of that sheds light on the actual lives of gay boys.

I liked being with him, and I enjoyed going around to his house to play. We would climb trees together, have morning tea on our own special little table and just enjoy each other's company.

Saul, one of the boys included in Green's study, wanted to be with his next-door neighbor, Gary, forever. Craig, who tells his story in Adam Mastoon's *The Shared Heart*, fell in love with his best friend in fourth grade; this love lasted eight years.

Being excited by seeing another male, often without clothes, is another way early same-sex desire can manifest itself. Four gay men who are quoted in the collection *Born Gay* talk about those early feelings. Looking back, Vernon knew he was gay when taking a shower with his dad felt strange to him, even at three years old. At age four, Clark watched the lifeguard at his parents' country club use the bathroom and take a shower. Otto knew he was interested in men at age five, creating a scheme to stay in the locker room to watch the men get dressed. Cyril liked to look at naked cadets in the locker room at age nine. Ken Haller, a questionnaire respondent, liked to see male skin, and connects these feelings to seeing a clothed actor on television:

> I grew up on Long Island, and we used to go to Jones Beach in the summer. I remember feeling funny and excited by the sight of young, usually Italian guys taking their shirts off, and knowing somehow that those feelings were "wrong." Second, I very vividly remember having very similar feelings for Bill Bixby on *My Favorite Martian* [a TV show of the mid-1960s].

The psychologist Don Clark had a spiritual connection with a young man in a shower at a beach when he was four:

> He was a young man probably in his early twenties, tanned and fit, cheerful, smiling and laughing. . . . I was drawn to him as if to a magnet, yet I knew I must not go into the shower to touch him though I had a strong urge to do so. I wanted to be close to him. . . . He gave me a dazzling smile and winked at me. It was strange. I felt connected to him—as if I knew him. It was

a sudden bond, stronger than I felt with anyone in my family. I looked into his eyes. He seemed to understand what was happening though I did not. . . . He could and did welcome me to my tribe with that wink and smile.

When adults and teens experience feelings of a sudden bond, of being instantly understood, it is called infatuation. Looking back, I realize I had just such a crush on John Hill, my best friend in fourth grade.

Young boys can also fantasize about the objects of their desire. Dean Jones's dimples in *The Love Bug* (1968) made a deep impression on the seven-year-old Mike McGinty, and two years later Mike masturbated to the image of his landlord, Mr. Matheson. At age nine, Michael McAllister, a contributor to the collection *From Boys to Men*, wanted to look under the towel of a grown-up visitor named Steve. He later saw Steve asleep in the family car:

> I looked down at Steve as his chest rose and fell. Something about his soft eyelashes, coupled with his strong, stubbled jaw, relaxed in sleep, stunned me. . . . I wanted to run my fingertips over the rough shadow of his beard, and feel his Adam's apple bobbing at his throat. I wanted to curl against him, lay my head on his chest, and inhale the warm, clean scent he'd carried with him that morning, wrapped in that towel, a scent worn and deepened by now. And the things I wanted tangled and intertwined with another feeling, envy: . . . I wanted to be like him, to resemble him, to have Steve's angelic face for mine; my face softening the people who glimpsed it, compelling them to look at me, admire me, and guard me from danger.

One of Richard Green's subjects, called simply "Son" in a chapter on parents and sons, recounts his fantasies about being held by an older man when he was young:

> SON: I remember when I was very young, like six, seven, eight years old, I used to fantasize about me and a strong he-man. . . .

RG: Do you remember in that fantasy whether there was any kind of physical touching or caressing or holding?

SON: Yes. . . . Maybe just holding hands. No kissing or anything like that. Basically just holding hands or the person was holding me in his arms.

RG: Up until what age did you have that fantasy?

SON: Maybe twelve or eleven.

We certainly crave same-sex affection and physical contact even before we can conjure up sexual imagery. Our fantasies become concretely sexual as we learn about sex.

Because affection and fantasy are not observable, it is easier for others to say that such things don't exist. But early same-sex desire can lead to actions that are observable by others. Such actions are mentioned in the personal accounts in Michael Zambotti's *Born Gay*, Bennett Singer's *Growing Up Gay*, and other collections, as well as in the reports of my respondents. In early grade school John Selig tried to find ways to be near the object of his affection, "to gain his attention and his friendship." As a first grader Horehound Stillpoint followed a sixth grader around so often that the older boy got gay-bashed. When he was about eight, Wayne put his hand down his best friend's swim trunks. Mark played with the long hair of his sister's boyfriend, also at age eight. At ten Harry wrote "love letters to Andrew and Chuck and Glenn . . . [that] were as graphic as a ten year old could be about sex." The filmmaker Jonathan Caouette snuck into a gay club when he was eleven.

When the radical priest Malcolm Boyd was about ten, he had a very intense relationship with Jamie, a boy he met at a vacation resort in the Adirondacks. Direct looks and smiles were followed by physical longing, heart-to-heart talks, and a week of being inseparable. This culminated in swimming naked, wrestling, and more:

> I stretched full length on top of him, our heads touching. . . . I felt my penis grow hard against his body, and, pressed against mine, I felt his grow hard too. I raised my head and looked at his face. He was looking at me. After a long moment I lowered my head till our lips touched. And held.

Then I moved over on my side next to him, and my hand reached down, slowly, until I touched the flesh of his cock. It stiffened still more and Jamie's hips stirred. I felt a wonder. I had caused this to happen in someone else. Someone else felt as I did. I wasn't alone. There was Jamie. And now we had *our* secret.

Some boys who grow up to be heterosexual learn about sex through touching other boys, so it could be argued that a same-sex-oriented phase doesn't "mean" anything. But the emotional component is different with young boys who grow up to be gay. They are acting on feelings of desire and attraction that are not merely a matter of experimentation.

Many adults and teens say they were always gay; there was never a time when they didn't have some same-sex desire or feel different somehow; they just "grew up that way." Most heterosexual people would agree that *their* sexual orientation was simply there from a very early age; it did not emerge out of nowhere, fully developed, at the onset of puberty. It's a gradual process. Think, too, of celibate or isolated adults: they can fall in love or be aroused by others or have fantasies about others; without actually having sex, they have a sexual orientation, whether hetero-, homo- or bi-. So, it seems, can children. Boys who have crushes on boys, who take pleasure in gazing at naked men and boys, who fantasize about being with other boys, or who put their hands down their best friend's swim trunks—why not call these boys gay?

■ ■ ■

What are the lives of gay boys like? Are their concerns, interests, and issues different from those of boys who aren't gay? For one thing, homophobic and heterocentric social attitudes and conditions can affect the development of the young gay boy.[c] Gay boys may experience societal attitudes as an impersonal media barrage of stereotypes. Or they might get a subtle negative message through silence, a lack of any discussion or information about their feelings or identity. Elementary school teachers,

---

c Homophobia is the hatred or disparagement of homosexuality; heterocentrism is the assumption that everyone is heterosexual.

for instance, rarely mention same-sex relationships in class.[d] The effects of this lack of information can be damaging. Gay kids know less about what life can offer them, which can result in feelings of isolation and confusion, depression, and worse.

Kids perceived as gay are often teased and bullied. Richard Goldstein, a columnist for the *Village Voice*, notes how common the experience is: "Lucky is the gay man who doesn't remember being marked and manhandled as a faggot." One young man who tells his story in *The Shared Heart* reports, "As I got older, the name-calling began. From fifth until probably ninth grade, I was always known as the fag." Several respondents mentioned their rough childhoods in their questionnaires. Dave Gott was called "pussy" in fifth grade. Patrick Horrigan, Tim Tucker, Mark Griffin, and Earl Storm were all taunted and called "faggot" in grade school or junior high. Seth Bookey was "deemed the class faggot at an early age." Eric Rofes and Mark McClellan were bullied for being effeminate. Joe Yranski was taunted by friends and family alike. And teachers told "fag" jokes in Warren Blumenfeld's presence.

Parents often disapprove of their gay sons, especially if they are sissy boys. The director Adam Shankman's parents brought him to a child psychologist when he was only three. When Chris, of *The Shared Heart*, was barely six, his father would often scream about "killing faggots" as part of his general abuse of Chris's mother and siblings. Parents who now support their gay sons often write about earlier disapproval. In the face of that disapproval or outright harassment, some young gay kids learn to conceal their true feelings and leanings, and others repress them entirely. As psychologists and many others have noted, there are lasting effects on the child. Being ridiculed can result in being withdrawn. Repression can slow down the development of identity and relationships. Acknowledging but concealing one's desires can interfere "with the development of self-consistency, self-concept, and self-esteem."

Why are gay boys perceived as gay? Most of the time it's not because

---

d   In an effort to address the problem, Debra Chasnoff created *It's Elementary: Talking About Gay Issues in School* (San Francisco: Women's Educational Media, 1996).

they are openly expressing same-sex desire, but rather because they manifest behavior not typical for a male in our society: they are sissies. Among gender-atypical behaviors are being fascinated by or obsessed with activities and objects traditionally associated with girls, disliking rough-and-tumble play and contact sports, and stating the wish to be the opposite sex.[e] Some respondents mentioned their own gender atypicality or sissiness.[f] Seth Bookey was unathletic. Eric Rofes was "girlish, non-athletic, studious, [and] emotional." Ralph A.'s sexuality was "constantly identified as feminine." Lew, a contributor to Zambotti's collection, thought his mother should have known he was gay: "I discovered Mother's jewelry box and high heels. . . . I was playing with my sister's Barbies, watching *Wizard of Oz* without knowing how campy it was, and wanting, but not getting, an Easy-Bake Oven."

Do gay boys have a different way of being, a gay sensibility, as it were?[g] Today the idea of a gay sensibility is controversial because it often

---

e   Statements about wanting to be a girl appear very early and usually disappear as the boy grows older. See Edgardo Menvielle and Catherine Tuerk, "An Outreach Program for Children with Gender-Variant Behaviors," handout from a PowerPoint presentation by the Children's National Medical Center (n.d.).

f   "Gender-atypical boys" is a mouthful. While "sissy" is often used as an insult, some writers are reclaiming it in the term "sissyboy." See Kevin Sessums, *Mississippi Sissy* (New York: St. Martin's Press, 2007), and Tim Bergling, *Sissyphobia: Gay Men and Effeminate Behavior* (New York: Harrington Park Press, 2001).

g   A gay sensibility might be socially constructed, or it might be innate; most probably it is some combination of the two. For example, liking Broadway musicals is almost certainly not innate in itself. But one might be born with a propensity for the theatrical, and an appreciation for opera and musicals, with their heightened drama, might come from this more general leaning. Some might argue that even the more general leaning is a response to oppression, such as Daniel Harris in *The Rise and Fall of Gay Culture* (New York: Hyperion, 1997) and Brian Pronger in *The Arena of Masculinity: Sports, Homosexuality, and the Meaning of Sex* (New York: St. Martin's Press, 1990), but what of the tales of boys who love musicals at a very early

draws on negative stereotypes of gay men. But there is anecdotal evidence that gay boys are likely to be both gentle and imaginative. Many gay men were more tender and less aggressive than their peers when they were young, as contributors to Zambotti's book testify. Samuel hated hunting as a boy and by age twelve refused to hunt with his father. Justin hunted and fished as a young boy but objected to such killing when he was twelve. Alan wouldn't use a gun as a boy, and as a teenager he wouldn't go fishing. That gay men might be less inclined to violence is backed up by empirical research.

Imagination and creativity seem to be hallmarks of gay male adults and often manifest themselves quite early in gay boys' fantasy play, as does interest in the performing arts. Many of the sissy boys in the Gender-Variant Behaviors support groups retreat into fantasy. They pretend they are female characters, sometimes with magical powers. When the boys become aware of the social stigma of acting like a girl, they may limit such gender-atypical behavior to unobservable fantasy and private play. Eric Karl Anderson, a contributor to *From Boys to Men*, staged elaborate scenarios using his sister's Barbies, who committed suicide because Ken ignored them. Oz-related fantasy play is not uncommon. (Specific examples are discussed in Chapter 4, "Escaping to Oz.")

There is also anecdotal evidence that gay boys manifest an early interest in design. Adam Shankman designed costumes when he was only three. Zambotti's *Born Gay* contains many other examples. From age three until he was thirteen, Justin did his family's Christmas decorations and cookie making, and at fifteen he drew up plans for re-landscaping the yard. Earl and Luke both rearranged the furniture when they were ten.

Similarly, many gay adults report—in *Born Gay* and other works—

age? It makes more sense to think that behavior causes oppression: young gay boys are teased because they like musicals. It is quite unlikely that a three- or four-year-old would somehow experience gay oppression before manifesting any particular behavior and then develop these interests; see Will Fellows, *A Passion to Preserve: Gay Men as Keepers of Culture* (Madison: University of Wisconsin Press, 2004).

having been interested in the performing arts at an early age. As a four-year-old Clint loved listening to *Madama Butterfly*, making his relatives read him the liner notes on the record album. At age seven Nick amazed his relatives by singing the complete "Que Sera, Sera" at his grandmother's eightieth-birthday party and felt like he became Doris Day. Austin was a fan of musicals at seven or eight. Kerry, also at seven or eight, sang his younger brothers to sleep by lip-synching to a Julie Andrews album and then used the rest of the songs as a lullaby for the family dog. At age eight or so, Brad made clothes for his GI Joe doll and created a puppet show with costumes, and by age ten he was doing musicals. Timothy, at age ten, used to fight to watch Judy Garland on TV when everyone else wanted to watch *Bonanza* (1959–73). In *Sissy Boy Syndrome*, Richard Green, too, noted the propensity of his subjects to gravitate to careers in the theater.

Even before they label themselves as gay or feel any explicitly sexual attraction, many gay kids have an uneasy sense of being different, of being outside the mainstream.[h] Describing their boyhood, many adult gay men say that from an early age they felt they were seen as "different," "deviant," or "other." More formal research has corroborated these anecdotes. Gender-variant boys will most certainly feel different, even if they do not understand what makes them so. It is not limited to the United States; subjects from Canada, Australia, New Zealand, England, and Ireland also cited a sense of being different when they were young. Even gay teens who considered their same-sex desires normal felt different by virtue of their attraction to other males.

---

h   Gregory Maguire puts it well: "When you grow up gay, you're marching to the beat of a different drum without even hearing the sound of the drum" (quoted on pp. 58–59 of Peter Galvin, "A Wizard with Words," *The Advocate*, Oct. 17, 1995, pp. 56–59). It is probably true, as A. O. Scott says with respect to the Harry Potter books, that all kids have "the sense of being misunderstood, different, special," but Scott himself acknowledges that this feeling is more acute for gay kids: "You grow up in a hostile world governed by codes and norms that seem nonsensical to you." See A. O. Scott, "Harry in the New World," The Book Club, *Slate*, Aug. 25, 1999, http://www.slate.com/id/2000111/entry/1003490/.

Once you believe you are different from your peers, it is a quick step to feeling that there is nobody in the world like you. When you sense you don't fit in, you feel alone and isolated. This sense of not belonging is a common experience of gay boys, and feelings of isolation are a common theme of gay teens and adults looking back at their younger years. Young gay boys can also become emotionally isolated because of the lack of support from their parents. Some gay boys isolate themselves as a way to avoid being teased or bullied, and some gravitate toward solitary pursuits, such as reading, and individual sports, such as tennis, swimming, or figure skating. As they begin to recognize their feelings toward other males, gay kids may come to see themselves as not understood by their parents or siblings or peers. Feeling different, alone, and not understood gives rise to the common fantasy of the "special friend" who will understand and value you.

Gay youth themselves experience—or hear about other gay people who experience—physical violence, harassment, and bullying. Whenever religious leaders, politicians, school officials, and parents say that gay marriage is a bad thing, the message is likely delivered that being gay itself is bad. If you realize you have an attraction to or desire for other males, you take these negative messages to heart. You internalize society's homophobia and become ashamed of yourself. Eight-year-old Carlos, for example, whose parents were members of Menvielle and Tuerk's support group, wrote in his secret diary, "I hate myself, I think I am a fag!"

When kids (and adults) are ashamed of being different or of having desires directed at males, they often hide their feelings, hoping that people won't discover their secret. Along with the fear of being found out, keeping the secret often leads to a feeling of being a phony.[i] Some

---

i The first chapter in a self-help book by Alan Downs, *The Velvet Rage: Overcoming the Pain of Growing Up Gay in a Straight Man's World* (Cambridge, MA: Da Capo Press, 2005), is titled "The Little Boy with the Big Secret." And Andrew Tobias, in his memoir *The Best Little Boy in the World* (New York: Ballantine, 1973), which was published under the pseudonym John Reid, writes eloquently and with great humor about hiding his secret, being cosmically depressed over it, and feeling like a phony.

gay kids just want to escape. Another response is the development of a strong drive to be validated, the "best little boy in the world" syndrome. Some people offer this need for approval as a reason gay men seem to demonstrate higher-than-average academic achievement or decorating and design ability.[j]

Of course, not every gay boy has negative feelings about himself or is in an unsympathetic environment; many grow up in loving, supportive homes. Morris Kight grew up in Texas in the 1920s and felt different "almost from the beginning." His father, a blue-collar worker, sensed his son's difference, wanted to make life easier for him, and bought him an embroidery set. Increasingly, gay boys grow up in gay-positive homes like Kight's, and a lack of trauma is much more common now than it used to be. Being different doesn't have to make you unhappy. It can also make you feel special. Many gay boys revel in their talents and gifts.[k]

∎ ∎ ∎

While gay boys may not exist in the literature on homosexuality, they do exist in the real world. Long before puberty, some boys have strong feelings for other boys. They may have sexual and romantic fantasies about other males, and in some cases they may even act upon their fantasies. Many gay boys manifest gender-atypical behavior, which may mark them as gay to others. They may display what is called in adults a gay sensibility, being less aggressive and more creative than average. They may feel different, alone, misunderstood, or ashamed.

j   Downs ascribes gay design expertise to wanting to "decorate our worlds to cover up seamy truths" (*The Velvet Rage*, p. 3).
k   Will Fellows has compiled a checklist of traits that he calls "The fabulous gifts of gay men," which he hands out when he speaks on the topic. And times are changing. Homosexuality is now so much more out in the open that kids hear discussion of gay issues and know about gay parents, gay teachers, and gay celebrities. Some kids report being always out, never feeling ashamed or having the need to hide. How this might affect gay Oz fandom is discussed in Chapter 10, "The Oz–Gay Connection Now and in the Future."

There are, then, clusters of feelings and experiences that gay boys are more likely to have. Aspects of adult gay sensibility and desire are often apparent in boys before puberty. Not every gay boy has the same feelings and experiences at the same age or in the same order, of course. A sexually precocious boy is on a different developmental trajectory than a late bloomer; a self-aware and self-accepting boy has a different internal life than one who is repressed. And of course non-gay boys may manifest similar behavior or have similar experiences. But the logic is the same as in the case of Oz fandom and its relationship to gay males: not all gay boys have these qualities, and gay boys are not the only ones to manifest them, but it is fair to say that gay boys have an increased likelihood of possessing these qualities.

Understanding what gay boys are like in general helps us understand why individual gay boys (and men) are drawn to stories set in the Land of Oz, the topic to which I turn in Part Two.

PART TWO INDIVIDUAL REASONS AND RESPONSES

4 Escaping to Oz

When gay fans talk about what Oz means to them, the words "fantasy" and "escape" often come up. "Fantasy" can refer to a daydream, a sexual scenario, or a literary genre; the core meaning shared by all these senses is a mental act of escape, getting away from the here and now. Oz stories belong to the literary genre of fantasy, and many of these stories are about escaping to a fantasy land. Fans use "escape" in the sense of removing themselves, in their mind's eye, from where they are and going somewhere else. Thus, in the context of gay Oz fandom, both words refer to being taken away from your current reality and traveling to the world of Oz in your imagination.

Why would gay fans, young or old, want to escape to Oz? Many gay fans say their childhood was generally unpleasant at the time that they became fans. They often experienced feelings of difference and loneliness, as well as actual abuse by peers and family members. For the editor Mark Thompson and other young gay baby boomers, the need to escape the scrutiny of heterosexual peers and parents was particularly intense:

> The safest place to hide was the town's library. I could lose myself for hours on one of the window seats lining its spacious front room. There I read and reread all fourteen of L. Frank Baum's Oz books; his phantasmagorical land was the farthest point from

Pacific Grove of any yet found. The annual broadcast of *The Wizard of Oz* during the fifties and early sixties was always an eagerly awaited event in our house. . . . Dorothy's departure from Oz resonated with my longing to escape a harsh and unwelcoming world.

But gay Oz fans don't retreat to fantasy and make-believe simply as a way to compensate for something.[a] Fantasy and make-believe can be positive, joyful experiences in their own right. Going to Oz brings gay fans joy, silliness, whimsy, humor, wonder, sweetness, peace, solace, gratitude, hope, optimism, and innocence. For adults, nostalgia is another positive reason to go to Oz.[b]

The meanings each gay fan extracts from stories set in Oz will vary, as will how his fandom manifests itself. And different versions of the story are available in different eras, so boys growing up in the 1930s may have encountered and appreciated a different form of the story from those growing up in the 1980s. Later, they may or may not have been exposed to or sought out other versions. Which version they prefer now, as adults, also varies, as do their favorite characters and the characters they identify with. But there are some commonalities in the onset of fandom and the

---

a You could escape to Oz for one reason, such as avoiding negative circumstances, and then decide to stay or revisit for another, more positive reason, such as joy or spiritual fulfillment. In an interview about his book *Black Gods of the Asphalt* (2016), Onaje X. O. Woodbine made the same point in a different context—that black men and boys first escape to the basketball court for one reason and later return to it for another (NPR's *All Things Considered*, June 5, 2016).

b In fact, *The Wizard of Oz* appeals first and foremost to children. L. Frank Baum wrote *The Wonderful Wizard of Oz* for children and was himself an adult who had stayed a child in many ways. For many Oz fans, Baum's understanding of children is part of his appeal as a writer. The MGM movie based on Baum's book was marketed in 1939 as a family movie. The large number of tickets sold at children's prices is one reason the movie lost money at its original release in 1939. See John Fricke, Jay Scarfone, and William Stillman, *The Wizard of Oz: The Official 50th Anniversary Pictorial History* (New York: Warner Books, 1989), pp. 168–69.

depth of the initial reaction. Almost without exception, the individual young fan's interest is early and intense. Before they are nine, gay boys have fallen in love with the story in one version or another, having identified strongly with one or more characters. They want more Oz, escaping to the magical land for both negative and positive reasons.

Most adult fans love Oz now because they were fans as kids and have remained so as adults. They often reread favorite books from childhood, finding comfort in the familiar stories and characters. The cartoonist Eric Shanower goes back to about one Oz book a year, and the anthropologist Bill Beeman carries one or two books in electronic form on his Palm Pilot to read at odd moments. In his questionnaire Aaron Hamburger noted that he began rereading the Oz books recently:

> I was moving to Prague, and I was really scared. It was a real transitional point in my life and I wasn't sure where I was heading. I was staying in my childhood bedroom for a month before leaving the country and I noticed the books on my shelf. I began reading them and they gave me a real sense of security. . . . I just let the magic take over and become a kid again. When I read one now, I can't put it down, and I read it with the same excitement as I used to when I was younger. In fact, recently I went to Israel on a research trip that I was nervous about and I brought the books with me there too.

Now that the 1939 movie is available as a video or DVD, it is easy to watch it whenever you feel like it. But some adult fans still treat the viewing as a special occasion and choose to view it only once a year.

Gay kids might be attracted to Oz for one reason, and as they mature into teenagers and adults other aspects become apparent or more significant. While some adult fans are still serious lovers of Oz, their current interest may not be as intense as it was earlier. Other fans' interest in Oz has actually increased. Growing up allows for internal reflection, which can lead to a deeper relationship to the story. Coming out may have the same effect (see Chapter 8, "The Subcultural Phenomenon").

For many adult fans, a large part of Oz appreciation is nostalgia for a childhood fantasy. Reading a book you liked as a child helps you remember what it was like to be a child. Beliefs formed in middle childhood often become elaborate fantasies that last a lifetime, and adults looking back may recollect them playfully or reflect on lost innocence. Oz brings some fans back to their childhood immediately—"like a home movie," as one questionnaire respondent described it. During unhappy teenage years Oz can bring back childhood joy. For others, nostalgia offers a chance to contemplate earlier portions of their lives. And still others lament not being able to recapture their childhood reactions, but they find solace in Oz nevertheless.

Ways to Get to Oz

For my respondents, the most common first experience with Oz was seeing the MGM film during its annual showing on television and being entranced by it. Before movies were available on videotape, there were limited opportunities for seeing a movie more than once. The MGM *Wizard of Oz* was one of the few movies shown regularly on television in the 1950s, 60s, and 70s. Families would anticipate the yearly showing, making it a tradition. Those without televisions in the early years of the annual viewing might visit neighbors or relatives. Some young fans had their own private ceremonies. The respondent Jim Whitcomb wrote:

> I used to get very anxious when the movie would air on TV. I'd get the privilege of being allowed to be the only one in the living room. I'd put a rocking chair in front of the TV, turn out the lights, close myself in there . . . and take my journey with Dorothy down the Yellow Brick Road.

Having to wait a year to go to Oz again was difficult for many young fans. Some would consciously summon up the movie in their minds or even draw pictures to help remember it. The annual viewing could become a more significant ritual than Christmas or birthdays. Part of its specialness was knowing that others were also watching. In retrospect, this pre-video sharing can assume mythic proportions. The writer Gregory Maguire says that his generation would "thrill in simultaneous shock and delight" as they "experienced the story at the same time, in a hundred thousand households." The MGM *Wizard* is still shown regularly on television, but now that movies are widely available in recorded form and online, an annual showing is not so special. Younger fans are thus more likely to say that their fandom is not related to when they grew up.

First encounters with Oz in print form can also result in immediate fandom, as it did for those whose parents read to them from the Oz books, or for Jeff Miller, who came across a Golden Book of *The Road to Oz* when he was six. If you own an Oz book or have borrowed it from the library, you can read it once and then read the whole thing again or go back over your favorite parts. Experiencing stories this way allows for a more personal and controllable relationship with Oz. Young fans also like the fact that Oz is depicted in a series of books that extends over time; they want to know what happens to Dorothy from one book to another.[c] In some cases young boys are so captivated by the story that they are willing to struggle their way through it. At least two of my respondents noted that the first book they read entirely by themselves was an Oz book.

When parents buy the young fan a new Oz book each year, for his birthday or Christmas or both, a yearly dose of Oz is administered in a manner analogous to the annual television viewing of the MGM film. Some young fans save up money or use gift certificates to buy books for themselves. Others make good use of libraries. One sixth grader got a library card from the local junior college and was delighted to find a copy of Michael Patrick Hearn's *Annotated Wizard of Oz* (1973), prompting him to explore Oz more fully on his own.

■ ■ ■

---

c   The series of books allows the world of Oz to be depicted in much greater depth. While respondents didn't talk much about the series aspect of the Oz books, the other favorite books most often mentioned were classic fantasy series or multiple titles set in the same world. J. R. R. Tolkien's *The Lord of the Rings* (1954–55) and/or *The Hobbit* (1937) were mentioned by eight gay Oz fans, followed by the Harry Potter books (1997–2007), seven fans; the Earthsea books by Ursula Le Guin (1968–2001), six; C. S. Lewis's Chronicles of Narnia (1950–56), six; and the Alice books by Lewis Carroll (1865 and 1871), five. These numbers also attest to the appeal of fantasy as a genre for the respondents.

Some young gay fans' second encounter with Oz is in a different format from their original exposure. A common pattern is to see the movie first and then discover Baum's Oz in book form. Young fans may pester their parents for more stories about Oz; the parents may then find their own old copies of the Oz books and read them out loud. The young fan might also happen upon an Oz book serendipitously, as the respondent James Milton did:

> When I was aged 7 . . . I happened to stumble across a copy of *The Wizard of Oz* in my school library. I did not actually connect the book to the film right away; I was initially attracted to the book both by its name (I loved fantasy stories at this age) and the picture on the cover. . . . I started reading the book in my lunch hour and by that evening I was several pages in and loving it! For my 8th birthday my mum gave me my own copy, and between then and, say, the age of 11, I must have re-read it many, many times.

Other versions can also feed a young boy's fandom. One two-year-old was told by his brother that an animated Oz story, *Off to See the Wizard* (1967), was going to be on television. He was very excited because he already knew the story from having seen the movie. Another youngster was lucky enough to find *The Wonderful Wizard* in a boxed set of record albums. He checked it out of the library sometimes and listened to it in the basement over and over. And a few days after being a flying monkey in a marionette production of *The Wizard*, Aaron Almanza saw a poster for the 1985 movie *Return to Oz* and became obsessed with it. When he finally saw *Return*, it became the only movie he wanted to see over and over.

Once gay boys experience a story set in the Land of Oz, they take the story to heart. Any one of a number of aspects of Oz might resonate at first. Because of these resonances, they want to experience the story again. They watch the movie every year. They ask for Oz books on each birthday or Christmas. Asking for and initiating repeat encounters with a narrative is what distinguishes true fans from mere readers or viewers.

Gay Oz fans may initially try to hold consciousness at bay and become absorbed in the story in an addictive, escapist way; when they are finished reading, the experience is evanescent, as nourishing as cotton candy. But they soon turn into a different kind of reader or listener. They are imaginatively involved in the story, which awakens deep feelings. They seem to be another person, transported to another place. They are entranced; their experience is enlarged, and they live more intensely. When they are done reading they remember details clearly and savor them.[d]

The fantasy and play that arise from stories allow kids to make sense of the world, affording much cognitive and emotional growth. In fact, people engage in such fantasy and play throughout their lives, although the engagement takes different forms at different times and is more evident in some people than in others. The make-believe play of early childhood (roughly ages two to seven) is a forerunner to the interior fantasy play of middle childhood (ages eight to twelve), which turns into adolescent and adult fantasy and daydreaming.

Many gay boys revel in the words that are built into stories; they love drama and performance. They are sensitive to visual images and pay attention to and get sustenance from popular culture. Their imaginations and creativity give rise to drawings, dress-up, fantasy play, and—when they are a little older—more formal creations such as stories, backyard dramas, and even films. These talents are brought into play when young fans are not content to visit Oz via relatively passive reading or viewing or listening to standard versions. They become more active participants in the story by creating or performing their own versions. They make the stories their own by adding their own touches, amplifying elements they like or find important and ignoring, downplaying, or eliminating what they don't like or find irrelevant.

---

[d] The psychologist Victor Nell, whose work shaped my thinking here, uses the terms "absorption" and "entrancement" to distinguish two distinct physiological states related to two kinds of reading; see *Lost in a Book: The Psychology of Reading for Pleasure* (New Haven, CT: Yale University Press, 1988). See also Will Brooker, "A Sort of Homecoming: Fan Viewing and Symbolic Pilgrimage," in *Fandom: Identities and Communities in a Mediated World*, ed. Jonathan Gray, Cornel Sandvoss, and C. Lee Harrington (New York: New York University Press, 2007).

Having a story read to you again, reading it again yourself, or watching a movie over and over can be considered a kind of play. Creating an imaginary world or participating regularly in a world of someone else's creation can give a young child not only feelings of comfort, pleasure, and well-being but also a sense of safety and mastery. The complex real world can be miniaturized into a more controllable one. All children encounter novelty and incongruity, but perhaps gay boys have an extra helping that stems from their own sense of being different. Repetition of a play scenario breeds familiarity, and new situations become integrated into existing schemas, which allows for mastery and satisfaction.

In early childhood, the very youngest fans can participate more actively in the story by going to their own version of Oz through fantasy play.[e] Fans can also use an Oz character as an imaginary friend. Dressing up as an Oz character is another way to take control of the story when you are young. Andre, a contributor to Zambotti's *Born Gay*, played Oz when he was six or seven, using dresses from his neighbors' toy box and wearing his mother's red high heels. The character of the Wicked Witch in both book and movie versions has captivated young admirers so much that they want to become her for Halloween.[f] Because Oz is a magical

---

e   Fantasy play often takes place at an age too young to remember, but in two contemporary works of fiction by gay writers, young boys who grow up to be gay develop fantasy play after seeing the MGM movie on television. Both episodes share themes of being scared, feeling deeply touched, and wanting to be Dorothy. At seven, Wally, the protagonist of William J. Mann's *All American Boy* (2005), is obsessed with the movie, drawing melted witches, pestering his teachers, and imagining a sequel. Wally acts out all the characters with toy cars, since his father will not allow him to have dolls. Jonathan is one of the main characters in Geoff Ryman's *Was* (1992). When he sees the MGM movie for the first time on television, he is upset by the differences from his beloved abridged book version, and the witch terrifies him. When he wakes up the next day, he imagines that Dorothy and her companions are there on his bed with him. They all brush their teeth with him in the bathroom.

f   After reading *The Wonderful Wizard* with his imaginary companion Epiphany, a very young Kevin Sessums wanted to be a witch; see *Mississippi Sissy* (New York: St. Martin's Press, 2007). Because of his fascination with the land and the stories presuppose magic, young viewers or readers can actually hope to be transported to Oz via this magic. One eight-year-old, mimicking the character Button-Bright from Baum's 1909 *Road to Oz*, would pick up umbrellas—Button-Bright has a magic one—and command them to take him somewhere. Another young fan wrote letters to Princess Ozma in the snow, thinking that she would get them when they evaporated, and burned letters in the fireplace with the same hope. Oz was so real for some young fans that they felt they actually went there. Adult fans may know better, but that doesn't stop some from having the same wishes. Having imaginary friends who are Oz characters is another way to make Oz real.

It is also very common for fans in middle childhood to corral siblings, relatives, or neighbors into participating in shared Oz fantasy play. This backyard play usually involves reenacting scenes from the movie, since it is better known than the books, but fans might act out stories from the books as well. As a child Gregory Maguire directed a large cast of local children and six siblings, playing the Scarecrow because he couldn't be Dorothy. Insistent young boys have also cajoled adults into putting on official productions at their schools and YMCAs. They want to star in them and may be crushed when they don't get to portray their favorite character. The photographer Tom Atwood was lucky to play the Tinman in *The Wiz* in grade school (fig. 4.1). Young fans can also make their own films based on the MGM production. At the age of eleven the intrepid Mark Griffin produced, directed, and starred in a backyard production.

4.1 Tom Atwood with Dorothy in *The Wiz*, mid- to late 1980s

witches in the Oz books, a young William Mann insisted one Halloween on being a witch himself.

Young fans may also write their own Oz play scripts to be enacted by siblings, neighborhood children, or even toys. One eight-year-old managed to play all three of Dorothy's companions, and he and his sister roller-skated down a Yellow Brick Road in their carport. Another enthusiast convinced his teacher in grade school to stage a version of the movie for the rest of the school. He then wrote the abridged script, constructed the costumes, directed the production, and starred as the Cowardly Lion. Some fans create their own Oz stories in middle childhood. These creations might be for family consumption only,

4.2 An early Oz drawing by Howard Cruse, 1952

or they might appear in school newspapers or Oz Club publications. Atticus Gannaway began writing and publishing his own Oz stories at age ten or eleven. He has by now written a dozen Oz books. Oz also lends itself to visual creativity. Many young boys draw their own pictures based on the MGM movie. Howard Cruse, who later became a professional comic artist, drew his own comic versions of the story when he was eight or nine (fig. 4.2). Eric Shanower began writing his own stories when he was seven or eight. He is now a professional cartoonist, known for his Oz graphic novels and illustrations of Oz books.

Adults can play with Oz in a more deliberate way. If they are talented enough, adult Oz fans can participate in amateur or professional productions, sometimes even making a living via Oz-related creation and performance. Gregory Maguire and Geoff Ryman have written popular Oz-related novels. Mark Haas has written and published two Oz novels. Some gay Oz fans have also created their own stories as fan writing. The theater is a potent professional arena for Oz creativity as well. After playing Miss Gulch and the Wicked Witch in a stock production of *The*

4.3 Fred Barton playing Miss Gulch (and the piano) in *Miss Gulch Returns*, 2004

Wizard of Oz and seeing Margaret Hamilton speak, Fred Barton wrote, performed, and recorded *Miss Gulch Returns* (fig. 4.3). Brian Ferrari portrayed the Cowardly Lion in his first professional theater job (fig. 4.4). Alan Turpen was Dorothy in a version of *The Wiz* in a gay bar in the 1970s. Anthony Whitaker has co-written children's theater versions of six Oz books and a one-man show, *I Was a Teenage Judy Garland Fan* (2013). He has also designed costumes for Oz on stage, written some Oz-related songs, and created an Oz-themed album of his songs called *All in Good Time* (2003). John Maddox

4.4 Brian Ferrari as the Cowardly Lion, 1991

4.5 Costume designs by John Maddox (Glinda, Wicked Witch, Munchkins), 1991

found his interest in Oz reinvigorated when he was asked to create costumes for a New York high school stage production (fig. 4.5). Jesse Dolce directed the stage version of the movie in Draper, Utah, in 2002. Brent Terrien has a Munchkin costume that he hopes to use either in a play or at a costume party. Conrad Jarrett is now a television producer, which he attributes to his love of the MGM film. The movie has also inspired gay fans such as Derek Jarman to become filmmakers.

Visual artists also make use of Oz. Fans have created Oz pop-up books, put allusions to Oz on an Internet cartoon strip, and created high-concept Oz-themed costumes for Carnival in New Orleans. Brian Finnegan frequently uses Oz imagery in his paintings. Two fans have put Ozzy art directly on their bodies. Doug McClemont has "Ding Dong" tattooed on his shoulder, handwritten by the Munchkin actor Meinhardt Raabe. Anthony Whitaker has six Oz-related tattoos, representing the Oz books, the MGM movie, and the International Wizard of Oz Club. Publishing and journalism lend themselves to Oz-related work, too. David Maxine and his partner Eric Shanower have created Hungry Tiger Press, a small publishing company devoted to Oz. Fans who write for a living have addressed Oz in articles, book reviews, essays, and interviews. Another has created one of the preeminent websites devoted to Oz.

The gay Oz fan's immersion in and personal enhancement of stories set in Oz can have a spiritual dimension via a process called active imagination. In Jung's original formulation, one relaxes conscious control,

letting words and images surface from the unconscious. The patient concentrates on an image or event, and a series of fantasies develops, becoming more like a story. The narrative then takes on a life of its own. In this actively imagined narrative, you can have a dialog with different parts of yourself and symbolically live another life.[g]

The rich visual symbols of film strike viewers in a visceral way, and the strong emotional reactions that are evoked might suggest a kind of dialog between the conscious mind and the unconscious, a process akin to active imagination. Having contact with the unconscious circumvents the ego, avoiding the contemplation of unpleasant or scary potentials. Encountering repressed and unlived aspects of ourselves can thus turn these aspects into strengths. And after seeing a movie, the viewer might find that his or her active imagination takes over and fuses imagery recollected from the

---

g "Visionary daydreams" (John Beebe's term) can be seen as part of a long, multicultural tradition of "waking dreams" (Mary Watkins), in which events occur on a meeting place between the conscious and unconscious. See John Beebe, "*The Wizard of Oz*: A Vision of Development in the American Political Psyche," chap. 5 in *The Vision Thing: Myth, Politics and Psyche in the World*, ed. Thomas Singer (London: Routledge, 2000); Mary Watkins, *Waking Dreams* (New York: Harper Colophon, 1976); and Robert Johnson, *Inner Work: Using Dreams and Active Imagination for Personal Growth* (New York: Harper & Row, 1986), pp. 139–40.

film with the substance of personal fantasy. This interaction seems particularly applicable to the writings of L. Frank Baum, who encouraged his readers to become actively involved in the story, by, for example, figuring out that the Scarecrow is already smart before he gets his brains.

We all have unfulfilled aspects of ourselves; we fantasize about being more assertive or more sensitive, or having a different career or relationship path. Identifying with various characters allows you to live out or try on different identities. In active imagination you can actually experience these unlived parts of yourself. It is a well-accepted idea that books enable young readers to go to other places and understand other lives: this is the vicarious experience of a culture "out there." But fantasy as a genre in particular lets us see other possible versions of ourselves and society. Fantasy also moves inward, and myths in particular enable us to tap into our truer selves.[h] But saying that active imagination is part of the process of encountering a literary fantasy is an even stronger claim. In active imagination you can *live* another life and *actually experience* all the emotions that you would have experienced if the events were physically lived. This can help explain why reading fantasy is so intense. The reader actually experiences the archetypes and energies that are in the collective unconscious. Going to Oz when reading the book(s) or watching the movie may then be a way to connect your conscious mind with your unconscious, and to have a more fulfilled life in a particular kind of place.

Another way to immerse yourself in Oz is to join a fan organization such as the International Wizard of Oz Club. The primary benefits of belonging to the Oz Club are receiving the club's journal, the *Baum Bugle*, and finding out about regional conventions. Some young enthusiasts become members as early as eight; others join in high school. Erick Neher

---

h In *Men Loving Men: A Gay Sex Guide and Consciousness Book,* rev. ed. (San Francisco: Gay Sunshine Press, 1994), Mitch Walker calls this the "magical spirit-source within" (pp. 150–51). Ann Swinfen makes a distinction between secondary worlds that mirror the "inner mind" and those that represent "metaphysical reality" in her *In Defence of Fantasy: A Study of the Genre in English and American Literature Since 1945* (Boston: Routledge & Kegan Paul, 1984), p. 45.

attended three club conventions with his (gay) best friend when they were twelve, thirteen, and fourteen. During David Maxine's adolescence, the club was his primary social outlet; he has been going to conventions at least once a year since 1977, when he was fourteen.

The adults who form the bulk of the Oz Club's membership take the younger members and their interests seriously, and youth appreciate being treated as equals. Going to a fan gathering is like coming out, in that you find others who share your interests and values. Some fans who become members of the International Wizard of Oz Club in childhood retain their memberships when they get older, while others join as adults. Before the first time he attended a gathering, one fan worried that he would be out of place around kids, but he has been making pilgrimages to conventions ever since. Connecting with others who share your enthusiasm is validating: you can talk about obscure Oz issues and be understood. Sharing values embodied in Oz stories also creates a sense of belonging and pride in being part of the Oz "family."

Young fans can also get a taste of real-life Oz by encountering someone associated with a particular version of the story. A handful of young fans met or got in touch with Margaret Hamilton. When he was fourteen, Erick Neher met Hamilton at an Oz Club meeting and received her autograph (fig. 4.6). When Fred Barton was ten years old, he saw Margaret Hamilton in *Oklahoma!* and wrote her fan letters. She wrote him back, sending postcards and photos, and six years later, when he was sixteen, he met her in her dressing room in Boston. Conrad "Kenny" Jarrett contacted Hamilton at age twelve in 1972. After a six-year correspondence, he flew to New York with a friend and took a taxi to her apartment building in Gramercy Park. They spent hours talking and looking through her scrapbook, and went out to dinner together. Adult fans have also socialized with Margaret Hamilton and remember her

4.6 Erick Neher with Margaret Hamilton, 1979

fondly; often their most prized Oz possessions are Hamilton autographs or Wicked Witch items.[i]

The Wonderful Land of Oz

Many fantasy stories take place in an alternate world, which may be populated by humans or supernatural and magical beings.[j] Oz is one such magical but realistic place. It offers an effective escape because Baum's land is so complete and convincing, so three-dimensional. Young fans appreciate the recreation of an entire world, with its own logic, boundaries, peoples, and cultures.

The four main countries in the Oz of the books are noted for their color coordination. The Winkies dress in yellow, and in some books the people and animals there actually have a yellow tint. Similarly, the Munchkins are devoted to blue, the Quadlings are associated with red, and the Gillikins' color is purple. Many of the small kingdoms within the four main countries are often further organized by a concept. In addition to the small and strange inhabitants of the MGM Munchkinland, there is the China Country in the first Oz book, whose people and buildings are all made out of china. In Utensia, King Kleaver rules over a Spoon Brigade, a Ten Quart Kettle, a High Priest Colender [*sic*], and a Judge Sifter. The colors of the four main countries and the concepts of the smaller places can be thought of as themes, appealing to children for the same reason that theme parties and collections do.[k] Baum's use of color coordination and theming might be especially appealing to gay boys and men.

---

i   Fans were more successful in establishing contact with Hamilton than with any other actors from the movie—perhaps because she was alive, her character was vivid, and she had a reputation for being approachable. Fans' feelings about the character of the Wicked Witch are analyzed in Chapter 5, "Gender Roles in Oz."

j   J. R. R. Tolkien calls the real world "the Primary World" and the alternate land of Faerie "the Secondary World" ("On Fairy Stories," the first part of *Tree and Leaf*, in *The Tolkien Reader* [New York: Ballantine, 1966]).

k   Color theming and theme parties were very much in vogue at the turn of the twentieth century; see Suzanne Rahn, *"The Wizard of Oz": Shaping an Imaginary World* (New York: Twayne, 1998), p. 101. Baum was familiar with color theory and color coordination, and writing about these topics appeared

The Land of Oz is a beautiful place. Taking their cue from Baum, creators of stories set in Oz almost always emphasize its visual splendor. This is most apparent in the 1939 Hollywood version. Once seen, the Technicolor visuals of the MGM film are rarely forgotten. The MGM Oz's beauty contrasts poignantly with the real lives of some young fans. In our society, caring about beautiful things is generally not considered a manly trait, but appreciating the visual splendor of Oz is acceptable.

By and large, the Land of Oz is a benign place. The citizens of Oz do not age and cannot die of natural causes.[1] In fact, humans and animals don't seem to ever be hurt, which appeals to timid gay boys. Violence is avoided at the social level in Oz as well. One of the two laws in Oz is that groups of people are not allowed to fight with each other. In *The Emerald City of Oz* (1910), Princess Ozma refuses to fight an invading army because she doesn't want to hurt anyone, even to save her kingdom; as one critic points out, this is an excellent message for children. The Royal Army of Oz consists of one private, the Soldier with the Green Whiskers, who doesn't seem to count as a real army. Not having to live with the threat of violence is enough of a reason to be drawn to Oz, but there may be an even deeper connection between nonviolence and gay men's natures. Gay men are much less prone to violence than their straight counterparts; for example, physical altercations in gay bars are rare. Gay men, it seems, are much less likely to be violent in all-male public settings than heterosexuals. Even if one doesn't buy the idea of an innate gay sensibility in general or gay gentleness in particular, the appeal of Dorothy's "someplace where there isn't any trouble" is clear: you won't get beaten up for being gay.

---

    in his publication *The Window Trimmer* (Michael Patrick Hearn, interview on *Fresh Air*, Dec. 4, 2000).

1   In the MGM movie there is the Witch's continual threat of violence, and the two animated creatures, the Tin Woodman and the Scarecrow, are badly hurt and dismembered by the Winged Monkeys. In the Oz books, evil people can be killed by good people or die through an accident. See Michael Riley, *Oz and Beyond: The Fantasy World of L. Frank Baum* (Lawrence: University Press of Kansas, 1997).

But Oz is not all utopian goodness and happiness, of course. Any tale set in a fairyland or a secondary world must have a certain amount of conflict to be interesting, and in the main story, Munchkinland and Oz itself are communities under threat. The struggle between good and evil in the main story is important to many gay Oz fans, and may have been especially important when they were children. The bad guys and gals are pretty clear in Oz, and gay fans like the fact that good wins out over evil.

Oz's geographic detail makes it particularly appealing as an object of exploration. As the Oz books developed, one of Baum's standard plot devices was to send his protagonists to explore out-of-the-way places. Gay Oz buffs get a thrill from exploring Oz along with the characters. In Oz, wonderful, unique, and strange things are always about to happen. Gay fans love the fact that anything can happen in Oz; that Oz is a place of infinite possibility gives fans faith that their own lives can be better. For one young fan who wasn't allowed out without supervision, Oz was a place he could explore and do whatever he wanted. To a lesser extent this exploring aspect, where everything is new and exciting, feeds movie fans too.

Luckily for readers of the books and viewers of the movie, most of Oz isn't too orderly or "civilized." In later books, this adventure happens outside the comfy confines of the Emerald City. Characters' adventures contrast with the humdrum, lackluster life of young enthusiasts. They identify with Dorothy and want to be part of her thrilling exploits. The MGM Dorothy also elicits this sense of identification, as does Dorothy in the later film, *Return to Oz*.

One thing that makes a journey adventurous is danger: the possibility of running into scary and evil obstacles. In the preface to *The Wonderful Wizard*, Baum said his aim was to eliminate "blood-curdling incident," but he didn't do so entirely. Dorothy's companions in the book save her from natural dangers in violent ways. The Tin Woodman beheads the great wolves, the Kalidahs are "dashed to pieces" at the bottom of a large gorge, the Scarecrow twists the necks of crows, and a swarm of bees dies after breaking their stingers on the Tin Woodman's body. The MGM Oz is even scarier to some, in part because of the bigger role of the Witch.

Many gay fans enjoy the scary aspects of the MGM version of Oz.

Going through danger can bring adventurers closer together. For adults the scary parts of the film temper the upbeat parts and prevent it from becoming too sweet. But parts of Oz are too scary for some, especially at an early age. While perhaps not as terrifying as the MGM film, the Oz books also contain frightening elements that some fans dislike. Fans can be repelled by and attracted to the darker aspects of Oz at the same time. The MGM Wicked Witch of the West brings out this ambivalence the most. Gay children can find the Witch both terrifying and fascinating. One fan reports that the Wicked Witch scared his two heterosexual brothers, although he himself was delighted by her. (So much for the stereotype of the timid, sissy gay boy!) If young enthusiasts like being frightened, the scary elements add to the appeal of Oz, and boys enjoy the fright, the way they would a funhouse or a roller-coaster ride.[m] To those who tend not to like scary stuff in general, these aspects are off-putting. Either way, the Wicked Witch, her monkeys, the Nome King, and the Scoodlers from the Oz books make the stories in which they appear more nuanced; they are shadows throwing the happiness and joy of Oz into relief.

Adventure and conflict make up a prominent part of children's fantasy activity. Children may choose themes of danger because they are more aware of real-world issues, or simply because such topics are more interesting and allow for exploration. The Oz stories embody these kinds of conflicts, sometimes reflecting the cruel side of play. Scary incidents in stories also allow kids to master their fears and to feel the "thrilling vividness of individuality" that fear evokes.[n] The scariness of the MGM movie can help repeat viewers get over fears of the Witch

---

m   Many horror and noir/detective/suspense movies were mentioned as favorites, especially those of Hitchcock, corroborating fans' interest in being safely scared. Scary books were not mentioned as often, but one fan said that among his favorites are the "scary stories" of Stephen King.

n   According to Jerry Griswold, from whom the "thrilling vividness of individuality" quotation comes, five attributes of children's literature resonate with ways in which kids view the world: scariness, smallness, aliveness, lightness, and snugness. These five qualities abound in Oz stories, and in my view they may also capture feelings and points of view in young gay boys' lives. See

and by extension other people with power over them, including bullies, parents, teachers, and older siblings.

Oz seems to have enough adventure and scariness to satisfy kids' needs. Except for Dorothy's MGM encounter with the Wicked Witch, however, the conflict is on the mild side. And even in the MGM film the conflict isn't really the main point of the story. Many gay kids are teased and bullied; most gay Oz fans, at least, don't seem to want stories to replicate the violence of their real lives. The Land of Oz is thus a place of gentle conflict, and this seems to resonate perfectly with many gay boys' natures. And despite the adventure and scary encounters they offer, Oz stories written for children end joyfully. The happy endings to Oz books and movies are something gay fans appreciate, especially as kids.

One aspect of the alternate worlds of fantasy that distinguishes them from the outer-space realms of science fiction is magic. Magic is part of Oz's marvelousness, and an important part of its appeal for both gay men and boys. Some Oz devotees relate to specific magical objects, such as Glinda's bubble and the Wicked Witch's crystal ball in the movie or the Powder of Life in Baum's books. The Ruby Slippers are perhaps the strongest icon of the MGM movie. Fans appreciate the Slippers for their magic and power in a general sense and for their specific ability to take one somewhere.

Magic gives one power in Oz. The rulers, those in power—the Witches, Ozma, Glinda—all practice magic. When individuals try to use magic for their own good, a conflict is created. Both the power and the comeuppances of these bad folks from the books are savored. The King of the Nomes, in particular, is always frustrated in his attempts at evil, and readers of the books enjoy this.

Small characters mirror the child's powerlessness, and a world populated by small creatures can give the child an alternative to adult importance. The smallness and relative powerlessness of Toto, the Munchkins,

---

Griswold, *Feeling Like a Kid: Childhood and Children's Literature* (Baltimore, MD: Johns Hopkins University Press, 2006), p. 50; see also Glenys Smith, "Inner Reality: The Nature of Fantasy," in *Give Them Wings: The Experience of Children's Literature*, ed. Maurice Saxby and Gordon Winch (South Melbourne/Crows Nest, NSW, Australia: Macmillan, 1987).

and the denizens of the China Country can reflect the young gay boy's feeling of helplessness. Young fans like and/or identify with Dorothy and, to a lesser extent, other characters because of their vulnerability, inadequacy, weakness, or ineffectiveness. Children may be attracted to the power of magic in Oz because they themselves feel inadequate, powerless, or scrawny.º Talking animals, animated toys, and conscious objects also mirror the child's lack of self-importance. When the gay Oz fan takes the talking Cowardly Lion, the animated Sawhorse, or the Patchwork Girl to heart as a beloved character, he is identifying with the powerless "other" and therefore loving himself.

Fantasy in general and myths and fairy tales in particular generate wonder and awe. L. Frank Baum was alert to the wonder of the everyday world and tried to show it to readers. If we use our imaginations, Baum felt, we can discover the marvelous in our everyday lives. Reading or viewing Oz stories enhances our ability to see the wonder and magic in the everyday and allows the gay fan to get a glimpse of another eternal, metaphysical world.ᵖ

Oz as Home

Home is most commonly thought of as the place where the family you grew up in lives. But home can also mean a refuge, a haven, a snug place of safety and familiarity. When you escape to Oz, you can be free of the

---

o   But characters such as Uncle Henry, the Scarecrow, and the Wizard are *disliked* for their weakness, perhaps because the perceived weakness hits too close to home. For more about the Wizard's strength or lack thereof, see Chapter 5, "Gender Roles in Oz."

p   Hard though it is for rational people like me to admit it, there may very well be a plane of existence in addition to the natural one we see around us. People in other cultures and at other times have viewed the spiritual realm as more real than the material world, which one might call the "world of appearances." See Swinfen, *In Defence of Fantasy*, p. 11; Mitch Walker, *Visionary Love: A Spirit Book of Gay Mythology and Trans-mutational Faerie* (Berkeley, CA: Treeroots Press, 1980); C. S. Lewis, "On Three Ways of Writing for Children," in *Only Connect: Readings on Children's Literature*, 1ˢᵗ ed., ed. Sheila Egoff, G. T. Stubbs, and L. F. Ashley (New York: Oxford University Press, 1969).

constraints of your old home and create a new gay home for yourself, with new friends and an adopted gay family.

The arc of Dorothy's feelings in the 1939 movie about home in the first sense—home as the place where her family is—is well-known. She leaves Kansas because nobody understands or appreciates her, and then she runs back home when there's a storm brewing. After being transported to Oz, Dorothy tells everyone that she wants to get back home, and she finally arrives there. The last line is "Oh, Auntie Em, there's no place like home!" Dorothy's acceptance by her aunt at the end of the book, and by everyone from the farm in the movie, strikes a deep chord, in part because of gay men's ambivalent feelings about family and home.

Dorothy's yearning to go home and her final return there at the end of the MGM movie bring out very strong feelings. Some fans cannot understand why Dorothy wants to go back home to Kansas farm life. Dorothy may not be happy at home for long. While *she* may have changed in the course of her dream adventure, the conditions that made her want to leave at the beginning of the story, such as the bleakness of Kansas and Miss Gulch, and the lack of understanding of Em and Henry, have not. In fact, fans rarely have anything good to say about the Kansas of either the MGM movie or the book; it is humdrum, dingy, gray, grim, drab, bleak, and full of sameness. Camo Bortman attended a showing of *The Wizard of Oz* at the Castro Theatre, in the heart of gay San Francisco, and heard a chorus of booing at the point when Judy/Dorothy says that her heart's desire is in her own backyard. For many gay men, this ending is a cop-out. They are with Dorothy in her new home in Oz and don't want her to succumb to her old way of life.q At the end of the movie, it appears that Dorothy didn't "really" go to Oz, because her journey was a dream. Lovers of fantasy, including me, want

---

q   The few fans who identify with Dorothy's fervor to go back to Kansas tend to say that the MGM Kansas is similar to their hometown or that it reminds them of their grandparents' places, places that they visited as kids. The family feeling among Dorothy's aunt, uncle, the farmhands, and Toto are also positive aspects of Dorothy's Kansas home. But many gay fans do identify with Dorothy's longing for home in a general sense.

Dorothy's experiences in Oz to be real; we want Oz to exist, at least within the fiction of the story. We object to the dream ending of the movie because it invalidates the reality of Oz.[r]

In the third, fourth, and fifth Oz books, Dorothy returns to Kansas because that is where she is from and Aunt Em and Uncle Henry are there. But in the sixth volume, *The Emerald City of Oz*, Princess Ozma transports Dorothy's aunt and uncle to Oz and settles them on a cozy new farm. Now Dorothy has no reason to return to Kansas, and Oz is her home. In fact, she lives in Ozma's palace in the Emerald City and is free from the obligations of her old home. Fans who don't understand Dorothy's apparent preference for Kansas are happy with this turn of events. In an essay about the MGM film, Salman Rushdie sees a deeper meaning in Dorothy's settling in Oz. Home is the place we make into our home, not the place where we started out.

When a gay male goes off on his own as a teenager or young adult, he often makes a set of new gay friends who become a new supportive, understanding family.[s] Likewise, newcomers feel at home in Oz; you can build a new family in Oz with friends who embrace you for who you really are. When Dorothy gathers up her three companions along the Yellow Brick Road, she is cobbling together a new family—not in a legal sense, of course, but in an emotional sense. Other characters in Oz also get to form new family bonds. In a later Thompson book the boy protagonist Ojo is kidnapped by Realbad, the bandit chief, who plans to turn him in for a reward. Eventually Ojo discovers that Realbad is his real father. The Tin Woodman finds a brother of sorts in a Baum book, and in another the Scarecrow goes off in search of his family tree.

---

r   One fan suggests a marvelous cinematic way to show that Dorothy's trip to Oz wasn't a dream. At the end of the film the camera should have panned down to the Ruby Slippers still on her feet, "proving to the nay-sayers that she was really in OZ."

s   George Keating, the emcee of the official *Sing-A-Long* [sic] *Wizard of Oz*, is quoted in "Sing Out, Dorothy!" as saying that the movie appeals to the gay community because we "are familiar with the idea of creating your own family—deciding for yourself what and where 'home' is" (*Next Magazine* 10, no. 48 [June 6, 2003]: 12).

In general, Baum represents home and family as things to escape from. In his first six books we encounter nomads, irresponsible parents, children who wander away from their loving parents, orphans, houses and homes that are prisons, disregard for the value of homes, and other themes and characters that undermine our sense of home as a welcoming place.

Like Salman Rushdie, many gay fans want to redefine "home" as Oz; they feel that Baum's message is "Make your own home." Since World War II, large coastal cities, especially New York and San Francisco, have been places of refuge for gay men. These cities have become associated with transformation of identity. The idea that Oz itself is thought of as home, rather than Kansas, is reinforced by the many examples of Oz and the Emerald City being used as metaphors for the places gay men move to.[t] New York and its most famous gay neighborhood, Greenwich Village, have often been associated with Oz, as have San Francisco and its Castro district.

When we come out, we often search for gay space. We want to be safe, in a place where other people are either gay themselves or extremely understanding and accepting. When Judy Garland sings "Over the Rainbow," she is yearning for a place "where there isn't any trouble." For gay boys and men, this is a place where they aren't teased, ostracized, bullied, or abused for being gay, a place where gay boys and men are accepted and feel they belong. In this sense Oz has much in common with traditional gay spaces such as bars or gay organizations and support groups. In Oz you can be yourself—obviously gay, gender-atypical, flamboyant, whatever; it's all OK.

---

[t] The volume *Hometowns: Gay Men Write About Where They Belong*, ed. John Preston (New York: Dutton, 1991), is collective testimony to gay men's strong feelings about home—wanting to leave for someplace better, but also wanting to be accepted in the place where they grew up. Of the twenty-eight writers groping for ways to express their feelings about leaving and returning home, three used literary metaphors. Two were of Oz, standing for New York in one case (Michael Lassell) and San Francisco in the other (Lawrence Tate); the third was of Lewis Carroll's Wonderland.

5 Gender Roles in Oz

Science fiction, with its ray guns, rockets, and hard science, is for boys. Fantasy, or at least the kind with fairy princesses, is usually seen as being for girls.[a] *The Wizard of Oz* falls squarely in the "girl thing" camp. In general, boys seem less inclined to own up to liking Oz and may feel the sting of gender stereotyping if they are found out. Given the stigma, why would a "girls' story," especially one with a female protagonist, attract gay boys?

Gay boys have a lot in common with girls of all stripes. Many have interests more typical of girls; they often have girls as playmates and friends. They seem to be more likely than heterosexual boys to identify with girl characters. Gay boys find males attractive, as heterosexual girls do, and they share with lesbian girls a sense of being different. Being familiar and comfortable with girls, gay readers and viewers can feel at ease experiencing works that have lots of girl characters.[b]

---

a   While the Oz books are more popular with girls than with boys, boys may be stronger fans; see Beverly Lyon Clark, *Kiddie Lit: The Cultural Construction of Children's Literature in America* (Baltimore, MD: Johns Hopkins University Press, 2003). Interestingly, about half of the specific male fans Clark cites are in fact gay men. Certainly not all lifelong male fans are gay, but a disproportionate number—more than 10 percent—are.

b   Almost all of the human protagonists in Baum's fourteen Oz books are

In Oz, adult males are often weak and women strong.[c] Walter Murch, the writer and director of *Return to Oz*, considers Baum's message feminist because the creative and interesting characters are women who see the truth while the men are fools and charlatans. From Dorothy onward, girl characters leave the domestic sphere to have adventures in Oz. In contrast to the many sissyish, weak, and emotional males, the females in Oz accomplish things. In fact, girls and women rule Oz. Gay fans like this aspect of the story, and for some of them this feminist vision is also a gay vision.

Gender-atypical behavior usually begins to manifest itself between ages three and five, the same time that Oz fandom often strikes. A human acting in nontraditional ways would be a good role model, but a young reader or viewer might be put off by a human character who is a sissy or wants to be called by a name that doesn't match the outer gender. But children in the early years can easily identify with animals and other non-human creatures. Toys and automata—machines that move—tend to be nonthreatening; they can indulge in behavior that might be considered unacceptable in humans. In the animals and other nonhuman creatures in Oz stories that reflect his own nontraditional aspects, the gender-atypical boy gets role models for his unique way of being.

In middle childhood, gender-atypical behavior becomes more suspect. The gay child might be told to stop playing with girly things. Acceptance by one's peer group becomes more important, and children are likely to want to impress and seek approval. Gay boys begin to feel different, and perhaps alone. As they become aware of gender norms and are subjected to teasing and bullying, gay boys may internalize society's homophobia and feel bad about themselves. In middle childhood they

---

    girls. Most of the succeeding Oz books by Ruth Plumly Thompson and others have male protagonists. Questionnaire respondents tend to identify with male characters, but their favorite characters tend to be females.

c   Baum probably learned to question gender roles from his mother-in-law, Matilda Gage, a prominent and historically significant suffragist. See Mark West, "The Dorothys of Oz: A Heroine's Unmaking," in *Stories and Society: Children's Literature in Its Social Context*, ed. Dennis Butts (London: Macmillan, 1992), and Alison Lurie, "The Oddness of Oz," *New York Review of Books* 48, no. 20 (Dec. 21, 2000): 16–24.

may have a conscious wish to be a particular Oz character. Van Farrier wrote in his questionnaire:

> I knew I was a fan when I began to fantasize about being Dorothy. I was in elementary school and I would dream I was hit on the head by a window & wake up in Munchkinland.

Fans also appreciate that "feminine" qualities are considered more important in Oz than "masculine" ones. When male and female characters manifest qualities typically associated with the other gender, gender boundaries are blurred and Oz becomes a land of girlish boys and boyish girls.[d] Stories about Oz thus become an implicit feminist critique of standard gender roles. Baum's gender politics are part of Oz's appeal for at least some gay fans, because they are feminists themselves. They realize that the gender expectations of our society are not followed in Oz.[e]

Female Characters

The character gay fans most commonly cite as a favorite, and the character they most often identify with, is Dorothy Gale of Kansas.[f] She is one of

---

d The homophobic critic Osmond Beckwith finds lots of gender confusion in Baum's Oz books and claims that the strong girl characters and gender-related plot devices are bad for both girl and boy readers; only narcissistic girls and boys (or men) with castration anxieties would like them. Like the reactionary Frederic Wertham, who saw homosexuality in Batman comics, Beckwith does seem on the mark in terms of pointing out situations from which gender-atypical kids might get validation. See Osmond Beckwith, "The Oddness of Oz," *Children's Literature* 5 (1976): 74–91, reprinted in *The Wizard of Oz: The Critical Heritage*, ed. Michael Patrick Hearn (New York: Schocken Books, 1983). See also Fredric Wertham, *Seduction of the Innocent* (Port Washington, NY: Kennikat Press, 1972; orig. pub. 1953).

e This gender awareness appears in fans' explanations of why they like movies other than *The Wizard of Oz*. One respondent loves "movies that celebrate the triumph of the feminine spirit." *Women in Love* (1969) challenges gender constructions. *Ma Vie en Rose* (1997) and *Billy Elliot* (2000) are about "gender liberation."

f Dorothy was mentioned almost three times as often as her nearest compet-

the early strong female protagonists in children's literature and movies. Baum's Dorothy is more heroic and forceful than MGM's, in part because she throws the water at the Wicked Witch of the West on purpose. Dorothy also has power and stature in later Oz books. She's made a princess of Oz by Ozma in the third book, and wears a coronet to signify this office (fig. 5.1). She occasionally wields a Magic Belt that can transport anyone anywhere. Fans are drawn to Dorothy's daring, longing, being lonely, wanting more out of life, and getting to go away from everyday life. Her loyalty, her stick-to-it-iveness, and the fact that she is a survivor also endear her to gay fans.[g]

5.1 Princess Dorothy, from *The Lost Princess of Oz*, 1917

Dorothy's companions—the Scarecrow, the Tin Woodman, and the Lion—can be seen as representing aspects of Dorothy herself. And since they are male characters, they can stand for traditionally male qualities (even though a loving heart isn't a particularly male quality). Thus Dorothy's quest is often read as a journey to wholeness, integrating the masculine qualities of making one's way in the world and the feminine qualities of cultivating relationships. In a Jungian analysis by the psychotherapist Robert Hopcke, Dorothy's "inner masculinity" is represented by the

> itors, the Scarecrow and the Wicked Witch of the West, as the favorite, and more than twice as often as her competitors for object of identification, the Scarecrow and the Lion.
>
> g   Fans like Dorothy's positive characteristics, such as being practical, sensitive, loving, and idealistic. Some movie-specific reasons were the Ruby Slippers, and wanting to sing like Judy Garland. But Dorothy is not universally loved. Some fans hate her for being girly, phony, and irritating in later books. Strong negative feelings were also evoked by her "no place like home" pronouncement at the end of the MGM movie.

Wizard, and gay men who see themselves as feminine identify with her journey. The Wicked Witch of the West stands for negative femininity, the "destructive power of society's identification of gay men as feminine." When Dorothy destroys the Witch with water, gay men, through their identification with the heroine, can feel better about both male and female aspects of their psyches. Even if one doesn't accept the psychoanalytic idea that characters in dreams represent aspects of oneself, or the Jungian animus concept of the inner feminine for men, Dorothy shows strength during her quest. As a girl, she also has the typically feminine virtues of empathy and concern for others. By the end of the story, she combines aspects of the feminine and the masculine into an integrated whole. (The idea of Dorothy's journey as a trip toward wholeness is discussed in Chapter 7, "Messages and Uses of Oz.")

In the Oz books two powerful practitioners of magic, the sorceress Glinda and the fairy princess Ozma, use their powers for good. They are beloved of gay Oz fans for what they do and what they look like. In *The Wonderful Wizard*, Glinda is described as beautiful and as appearing young despite being very old. When Dorothy first sees her, Glinda is sitting on a throne of rubies, dressed in pure white. Her rich red hair falls in ringlets; her blue eyes are kind.

The MGM Glinda is often the center of interest for young gay fans for her beauty, voice, and stature. Her voice, gown, and crown all give her "femme allure." Her "cotton candy" outfit makes her immediately recognizable, and some fans love to dress up as the MGM Glinda (fig. 5.2). She also gets to utter one of the handful of lines with special meaning to LGBT folks, "Come out, come out, wherever you are." As

5.2 Chris Garland as Glinda, party at Butterworth Farm, Royalston, MA, 2003

gay adults, fans learn about camp appreciation of exaggeration and artificiality and see the MGM Glinda in a different way. She is a girly girl. The round, glittery pink costume and high voice make her a caricature of femininity, especially in contrast to the Wicked Witch's hard edges, dark colors, and harsh voice. While she isn't on-screen very long, Glinda looms large in the power dynamics of the movie as the main foil to the Wicked Witch of the West. Glinda's wisdom is part of her appeal for gay fans in all her incarnations. She is the one who tells Dorothy that the Wicked Witch of the East's shoes have the power to bring Dorothy back to Kansas. The MGM screenwriters add that Dorothy had to learn this about the slippers "for herself." And in the movie version of *The Wiz*, Dorothy learns about home from Glinda: "Home is not just a place to eat or sleep. If you know yourself, you're at home anywhere."

In her role as Dorothy's helper in the MGM movie and as a powerful sorceress in the Oz books, Glinda can also be thought of as a mother or grandmother figure, and when gay fans identify with Dorothy, Glinda becomes a mother figure for them as well. Kristin Chenoweth, who played Galinda/Glinda in *Wicked* on Broadway, has ascended into the pantheon of gay divadom.

The benevolent Princess Ozma, "the most beautiful girl the world has ever known" (fig. 5.3), is introduced in the sequel to *The Wonderful Wizard* as the fairy ruler of Oz. She first appears after Glinda undoes the enchantment that changed her into a boy:

> From the couch arose the form of a young girl, fresh and beautiful as a May morning. Her eyes sparkled as two diamonds, and her lips were tinted like a tourmaline. All down her back floated tresses of ruddy gold, with a slender jeweled circlet confining them at the brow. Her robes of silken gauze floated around her like a cloud, and dainty satin slippers shod her feet.

Although sometimes appearing quite young, Ozma can be considered a mother figure like Glinda. She lives in the Royal Palace in the Emerald City, surrounding herself with her favorite subjects. Most of these are peculiar Ozian personalities, but some are flesh-and-blood girls from the United States. Dorothy and, later, Trot and Betsy Bobbin have lavish apartments

5.3 Princess Ozma, from *Ozma of Oz*, 1913

in the palace, and Ozma plays along with them like "a merry little girl."

As a fairy, Ozma has magical powers and possesses wonderful objects such as the Magic Picture, which lets you see anyone you want wherever they are, and the Magic Belt, which can transport anyone anywhere. Because Ozma is in charge of Oz and thus is the one who can bring people to this magnificent place, she is the object of fans' longing. Some want to be her, others to meet her. And even if you can't go to Oz and meet Ozma, she can be a spiritual companion.

The Wicked Witch of the West is the most commonly mentioned powerful woman after Dorothy, both because of and in spite of the fact that she is evil and scary. She is the third most favorite character of gay fans, after Dorothy and the Scarecrow.[h] Some fans like the Witch for her evil and her power. Her fervor is so captivating that some fans can't take their eyes off her. Conrad Jarrett wrote in his questionnaire:

> I was mesmerized by her magical powers and the fact that she placed so much fear into everyone. I used to think that she was having so much fun being evil. I grew to love movie villains because of her, and I refer to her character as probably every child's first introduction to wickedness.

Fans also identify with the Witch as an underdog. The most famous sympathetic view of the Witch is that of Gregory Maguire in his novel *Wicked*.[i] Some adults also appreciate the MGM Witch for her camp

---

[h] As far as I can tell, these were all votes for the Margaret Hamilton embodiment of the Witch.

[i] The popularity of Maguire's novel and of the musical version, which opened on Broadway in 2003, shows that there is an audience for revisionist Oz

value. The gay singer/songwriter Fred Barton has created a sympathetic and campy portrait of Miss Gulch, the Witch's alter ego, in his cabaret revue *Miss Gulch Returns*, theorizing that her sexual frustration may resonate with gay fans as well. And as we have seen, several young fans developed a special relationship with Margaret Hamilton.

Four other female characters are noteworthy for their independence or strength. Scraps, the Patchwork Girl, is a silly and adventurous creature who talks in rhyme (fig. 5.4). She is admired for her anarchic spirit, strength, and intelligence. The stunning fairy Polychrome, the Rainbow's Daughter, is the favorite of a handful of fans because of her charming nature and delicate beauty (fig. 5.5). She, too, is a free spirit. She often dances off her home on the rainbow, and when the rainbow dissipates, she is left on the ground to have adventures. Handy Mandy, the title character in a late Thompson book, is also valued for her independence.

5.4 Scraps, the Patchwork Girl, from *The Patchwork Girl of Oz*, 1913

5.5 Polychrome, the Rainbow's Daughter, from *The Tin Woodman of Oz*, 1918

in general and for seeing the Witch in a positive light in particular. At the time of my survey, *Wicked* hadn't been on tour, and only one respondent mentioned seeing it. He strongly related to Elphaba and said that two songs from *Wicked* were as important to him as "Over the Rainbow" had been.

Jinjur is another strong female character. She is the general of an Army of Revolt that Tip encounters in *The Marvelous Land of Oz*. When asked why her army is marching to the Emerald City, Jinjur replies that men have ruled Oz for long enough. Furthermore:

> The City glitters with beautiful gems, which might far better be used for rings, bracelets and necklaces; and there is enough money in the King's treasury to buy every girl in our Army a dozen new gowns. So we intend to conquer the City and run the government to suit ourselves. . . . What man would oppose a girl, or dare to harm her? . . . We are about to begin our great Revolt against the men of Oz! We march to conquer the Emerald City—to dethrone the Scarecrow King—to acquire thousands of gorgeous gems—to rifle the royal treasury—and to obtain power over our former oppressors!

It's not just females generally who matter in Oz, but strong ones specifically. If you are going to identify with or appreciate a female character, a strong one is a good model. Strong females are in a way the opposite of how many sissy boys perceive themselves: as weak males. And gay men, at least in typical urban gay male culture of the baby boomer generation and before, often idolize the strong females of popular culture.[j] But unlike Joan Crawford or Bette Davis or the Wicked Witch of the West, the good and powerful Oz females are not butch. They don't dress for rough-and-tumble action, as, for example, Doris Day does in the film *Calamity Jane* (1953). On the contrary, fans seem to like the female characters for their (feminine) appearance. Perhaps fans are responding to beauty not as a gendered or feminine quality but as an esthetic one. It could be that

---

j More evidence for the appeal of strong women for gay men is that two of the top three other favorite movies of respondents have famously strong and independent female leads: *All About Eve* (1950) and *Auntie Mame* (1958). The third most often cited as a favorite is also the story of a creative and strong-willed female: *The Sound of Music* (1965). As for why gay men like strong women in film, see David Rothenberg, "What Vito Russo Taught Me," *LGNY* (*Lesbian & Gay New York*), April 26, 2001, p. 17.

gay Oz fans like Polychrome and Ozma for the same reason they respond to the turrets of the Emerald City in the books or the art deco design of the MGM movie: these characters are nice to look at, evoking feelings of appreciation that have nothing to do with their gender. In any case, by looking pretty and being active and powerful, these gender-atypical characters embody the best of both genders.

Male Characters

Traditionally, masculinity is associated with strength and power, and many males in Oz are weak, ineffectual losers. Other male characters are effeminate, fey, gentle, and sensitive: the opposite of macho.[k] Men in our society typically prove their strength by besting someone else. Finding one's strength within oneself, on the other hand, is not something traditional men are taught, and this is one of the messages of the MGM movie. In Oz, males are allowed to express emotion, an activity that in our society is typically reserved for females and gay men. In our culture men are supposed to be serious, and fans make the connection between Oz's whimsy and being less of a "real man." Oz offers men imagination, fantasy, and whimsy, all of which allow fans to take themselves less seriously. Some males in Oz even look like girls; boys drawn by John R. Neill, for instance, usually have longish hair and frilly clothing. If a male worries too much in our society about what he looks like, he's a "dandy" with questionable masculinity. In Oz, the males who care about their appearance are never disparaged by either the narrator or other characters. (Baum himself was quite the dandy; see Appendix C, "Was Baum Gay?")

Of the male characters, the Scarecrow, the Tin Woodman, and the Lion appear most often in respondents' comments, both as favorites and as objects of identification. Since they play a major part in the MGM movie and appear in many Oz books, the large number of mentions is not surprising. Gay Oz fans may relate to these characters simply because they are male. But they also see themselves in the characters for more

---

k   While fans appreciate the sensitivity of many male characters, others are despised for their weakness, such as Uncle Henry in the movie, who is called weak, ineffectual, and a pussy whip. Gender atypicality itself does not guarantee that a character will be liked.

specific reasons. Gay men are often seen as deficient males, in that they lack true masculinity. Dorothy's companions are also males with deficiencies, joining her on her journey to the Emerald City because of what they lack.[1]

The Cowardly Lion as portrayed by Bert Lahr in the MGM film has been called all sorts of names. He is "one of filmdom's professional sissies" and "the cinema's best-loved nelly character." The writer of *The Zen of Oz* even urges the Lion to come out.

When Dorothy and her companions encounter the Lion in the scary forest, he is tough, butch. Like a schoolyard bully, he challenges the travelers to a fight. "Hah, put 'em up, put 'em up. Which one of ya first? I'll fight ya both together if ya want." Then he teases them and calls them names. He taunts the Tin Woodman: "How long can ya stay fresh in that can? Come on! Get up and fight, ya shiverin' junkyard." And to the Scarecrow, "Put ya hands up, ya lopsided bag of hay!" But as soon as Dorothy slaps him, he starts to bawl and sob. "Well, ya didn't have to go and hit me, did ya? Is my nose bleedin'?" Then the Lion just has to sing to his new friends about how he feels. "Yeah, it's sad, believe me, missy / When you're born to be a sissy / Without the vim and verve." He actually calls himself a sissy! This is unusual for any character, in a book or movie, directed at kids or adults. Soon after, the Lion sings, "I'm afraid there's no denyin' / I'm just a dandy-lion / A fate I don't deserve . . ."[m]

Later the four travelers are given makeovers at the Wash and Brush Up Company in the Emerald City. When they emerge and ask to see the

---

[1] Lacking intelligence, a heart, and courage can even symbolize being a eunuch (Beckwith, "The Oddness of Oz," p. 236).

[m] The dandelion/dandy-lion pun is notable for two reasons: a dandy is of course a stereotype of and euphemism for a homosexual man, and Lahr makes a "stereotypical limp wrist" gesture as he says "dandy," reinforcing the gay reading, as Richard Smith points out in "Daring to Dream: On the Centenary of the Birth of Yip Harburg," *Gay Times* (London), no. 211 (Apr. 1996), pp. 60–61. Censors have even found the sissy line objectionable. When he was in London, 1976–77, Paul Dana saw the MGM movie three times in three different theaters. In all three viewings the line was dubbed as "It's sad to be admittin' / I'm as timid as a kitten / Without the vim and voive" (Paul Dana, personal correspondence).

Wizard, we notice that the Lion has a blue ribbon in his hair, similar to Dorothy's red one, and his hair has been elaborately curled. When the fab four are told they can't see the Wizard, the Lion complains in a campy Mae West voice, "Aw shucks, and I had a permanent just for the occasion." Here the Lion seems to acknowledge his sissiness and play on it. The Lion's camping and flamboyance demonstrate how silly, how socially constructed, masculinity is. The MGM Lion thus brings gender issues to the fore in a way that other effeminate or non-macho male characters in Oz do not.[n]

Acting effeminate and being a sissy are two different things, and of course neither is the same as being gay. Effeminacy is about surface appearance: lisping, having a limp wrist, having relaxed or loose body language, batting your eyelashes, making extravagant gestures. Sissydom is more about behavior: being timid or cowardly.[o] Both terms are often applied to men and boys who don't act the way males should, and both are part of the gay stereotype. By declaring himself a sissy and acting effeminately, Lahr's Cowardly Lion opens himself up to being

---

n The MGM screenwriters got many of the Lion's sissy aspects from Baum's description of Dorothy meeting the Lion in chapter 6 of *The Wonderful Wizard of Oz* (with my italics):

> "What makes you a coward?" asked Dorothy, looking at the great beast in wonder, for he was as big as a small horse.
> "It's a mystery," replied the Lion. "I suppose *I was born that way*. All the other animals in the forest naturally expect me to be brave, for the Lion is everywhere thought to be the King of Beasts . . ."
> "But that isn't right. The King of Beasts shouldn't be a coward," said the Scarecrow.
> "I know it," returned the Lion, *wiping a tear from his eye with the tip of his tail*. "It is my great sorrow, and makes my life very unhappy. But whenever there is danger, my heart begins to beat fast."

The 2011 stage version of the film, produced by Andrew Lloyd Webber, makes the Lion a little more explicitly gay. He sings, "I am what I am," and says that he is "proud to be a friend of Dorothy."

o *The American Heritage Dictionary*, 4th ed., gives two meanings for "sissy": (1) A boy or man regarded as effeminate, and (2) A person regarded as timid or cowardly.

seen as gay. His sissyness does in fact resonate with some gay fans. The Lion is gay Oz fans' fourth most popular character, and they identify with him more than any other character except Dorothy. Fans say they identified with him when they were younger because they themselves were sissies as kids, and found solace in him. While Baum's Lion is not flamboyant, fans still relate to his being able to face his fear, which is a sign of strength.

Lahr's Cowardly Lion also brings out strongly negative feelings in gay Oz fans. The Lion is the *least* favorite character of a good number of Oz fans for the same reasons that others identify with him. One fan is offended that the character was played for laughs. Other fans don't like the Lion because his sissyness hits too close to home.[p] Fans also object to Lahr's campy humor and exaggerated performance, considering it a "fag joke." Part of the distaste some fans feel for the Lion comes, I suspect, from the fact that these aspects of Lahr's performance are related to the gay stereotype of the flamboyant screaming queen and fans' own discomfort with that aspect of being gay.

Learning about camp after coming out can lead to seeing the Lion differently; his exaggerated mannerisms can now be viewed as humorous rather than embarrassing. And when acceptance of one's own gender atypicality is added to an awareness of camp, the Lion can actually become a positive role model. As an adult, Reid Davis attended a showing of *The Wizard of Oz* at the Castro Theatre in the heart of San Francisco's gayest neighborhood. He notes that the audience cheered and laughed at moments that could be interpreted in a new light. Davis dubs this reconceived Lion a "Sissy Warrior" who deconstructs gender.

---

p   Alexander Doty describes his early negative reaction to the Lion in "'My Beautiful Wickedness': *The Wizard of Oz* as Lesbian Fantasy," in *Flaming Classics: Queering the Film Canon* (New York: Routledge, 2000), p. 50. The Lion was problematic for me, too. As I read what the *Atlanta Constitution* had printed from a reader about the Lion being a sissy role model, I hit my forehead with the palm of my hand. Well into my research I hadn't remembered that the Lion sang about being a sissy and a dandy-lion! Given that I practically know the movie by heart, I suspect I repressed memories of the Lion's effeminacy because they were too threatening for me.

The strong reactions fans have toward the Lion as portrayed by Lahr correspond to how they feel about not conforming to gender roles in general. If they see gender atypicality as something bad, they will find the Lion disturbing and distasteful. But those Oz fans who feel comfortable with their own effeminacy and sissyness can embrace him.

In the MGM film the mannerisms and appearance of Jack Haley's Tin Woodman are considered fey. Because of his voice and makeup, the Tin Woodman actually appears more effeminate than the Lion.[q] In the Oz books the Woodman is extremely concerned with his appearance, but this quality has no negative connotations. He polishes himself not only to keep rust at bay; he wants to sparkle and shine. In *The Marvelous Land of Oz*, the Woodman has become Emperor of the Winkies and keeps his guests waiting:

> "This is his Majesty's day for being polished; and just now his august presence is thickly smeared with putz-pomade."
>
> "Oh, I see!" cried the Scarecrow, greatly reassured. "My friend was ever inclined to be a dandy, and I suppose he is now more proud than ever of his personal appearance."

Even children notice that there is something not quite masculine about the MGM Woodman. At ten, Gregory Maguire found the Woodman "a bit fey in his manner and voice." And as in the case of the Lion, the qualities that mark the Woodman as less than masculine make him seem gay. For some gay fans that association puts the qualities in a positive light, but for others the reverse is true.

The Tin Woodman also stands for sensitivity, empathy, and an open

---

q   A student at a presentation I gave pointed this out. The MGM Woodman's silver skin made his lips seem unusually red in contrast, although they were actually black; see Aljean Harmetz, *The Making of "The Wizard of Oz"* (New York: Dell, 1989). The behavior of a character reminiscent of the Woodman in an unrelated film, the fussy robot C-3PO in *Star Wars* (1977), has sparked discussion as to whether he might be gay (Harry Benshoff and Sean Griffin, *Queer Images: A History of Gay and Lesbian Film in America* (Lanham, MD: Rowman & Littlefield, 2006), p. 149.

heart, and fans who see themselves as sensitive identify with him. In "Song for the Tin Man," the gay duo What Time Is It, Mr. Fox? sing of an emotionally vulnerable gay man: "No one comes round / When the Tin Man's heart starts to rust." Even before he gets his heart from the Wizard, the Woodman does in fact care a lot. In the MGM movie, he often breaks into tears, and in the books, citizens of Oz love him for his courtesy, kindness, and gentleness. Baum's Woodman even empathizes with bugs and flowers. Once, after he killed a beetle by accident, his jaw rusted from his tears of regret and sorrow. Some fans identify with the Woodman's search for a heart, relating it to their own lack of emotion. For young gay men who hide their emotions from others or themselves, he is a potent metaphor.[r] The Woodman can even stand for an inexpressive male to fantasize about.

The MGM Woodman is also overshadowed by the Scarecrow, who is the closest of the three to Dorothy, and the scene-stealing Lion. This may be another aspect of the Woodman's sissyhood. He lets the Scarecrow and the Lion push him around and crowd him out of screen time that is rightfully his.

Four other male characters show weakness by crying. In the MGM film, the Emerald City Guard played by Frank Morgan bursts into tears. When he overhears Dorothy getting sadder and more discouraged, he begins to sob buckets, saying, "I had an Aunt Em myself once." Many of the young boys Baum introduces in the Oz books are also easily moved to tears. Tip is about to cry when he is informed that he must be transformed back into a girl at the end of *The Marvelous Land of Oz*. Button-Bright has almost shoulder-length, Prince Valiant-like hair, and his main talent is wandering off and getting lost. He is introduced in *The Road to Oz*, in which he cries or begins to cry at least four times. Ojo, the protagonist of *The Patchwork Girl of Oz*, is a young Munchkin boy who "definitely isn't butch," as Tim Tucker put it in his questionnaire.[s]

---

r   Blocking out all feeling is a fairly common response to early gay desire. Andrew Tobias explains in *The Best Little Boy in the World* (New York: Ballantine, 1973) that he "had somehow been born without feelings" (p. 141). This was my experience as well.

s   *The Patchwork Girl of Oz* was the second most favorite book of my respon-

Originally called Ojo the Unlucky, he is later renamed Ojo the Lucky by Princess Ozma. His hat has little bells hanging from it (fig. 5.6).

Two other citizens of Oz from the books are very concerned with their appearance. Perhaps not coincidentally, both are also learned. Introduced in *The Marvelous Land of Oz*, H.M. Wogglebug, T.E., was once a tiny bug in a Winkie schoolhouse. He listened to many lectures and became thoroughly educated (hence the "T.E."). When he escaped from under a microscope he became highly magnified ("H.M."). Now that he is

5.6 Ojo and Button-Bright, from *The Patchwork Girl of Oz*, 1913

thoroughly educated and highly magnified, he dresses like a dandy (fig. 5.7). While some questionnaire respondents disliked the Wogglebug for his authority and pedantry, one fan identified with the Wogglebug for being erudite and gentle. A human-sized frog called the Frogman, who first appears in Baum's *The Lost Princess of Oz* (1917), also dresses in fancy clothing (fig. 5.8). The Wogglebug and the Frogman were several fans' least favorite characters. The reasons given were not about dandiness specifically, but this negative gay stereotype may have played into the dislike.

After Dorothy, the Scarecrow is fans' most beloved Oz character; when two young fans realized they couldn't play Dorothy in a public

> dents, after *The Wonderful Wizard*. It introduces Ojo and other marvelous characters such as the Patchwork Girl, the Woozy, and the Glass Cat. The plot is compelling as well: Ojo goes on a quest to find the ingredients for a spell to bring his petrified uncle back to life, and in the process goes to prison for breaking the law. Ojo and Button-Bright become chums in the Baum series, and one gay fan, Paul Dana, features them in his two superb extensions of the canon, *The Law of Oz and Other Stories* (2013) and *The Magic Umbrella of Oz* (2014).

5.7 H.M. Wogglebug, T.E., from *The Magic of Oz*, 1919

5.8 The Frogman, from *The Lost Princess of Oz*, 1917

performance, the Scarecrow was the second choice of each. The Scarecrow is generally not mentioned with respect to gender issues explicitly.[t] The reasons that fans give for liking him often have to do with his relationship to Dorothy; she meets him first, and in the MGM film she tells him she will miss him the most when she gets back to Kansas. But the Scarecrow is certainly a nontraditional male. In the film he sings of conferring with the flowers; and slipping and sliding, he seems to have no backbone. This physical flexibility contrasts with the rigid, upright, John Wayne kind of straight male. Fans relate to the abuse the Scarecrow suffers and to his apparently low self-esteem. For teetering on the edge of gay, the Scarecrow as portrayed by Michael Jackson in the film version of *The Wiz* is one fan's favorite character.

The Wizard of Oz in the main story is the quintessential powerless male. With no real magic, he has no real power. This makes him laughable.[u] But creating illusions has its allure, and some fans admire the "All

---

t   A 1971 survey conducted by the *Baum Bugle* found that the Scarecrow was the favorite Baum character of Oz Club members, followed by Dorothy.

u   In the print and stage *Wicked*, however, the Wizard is more powerful and more actively evil.

Powerful Oz." In a transformation surprising to those who know only the movie, the Wizard is reformed by Baum in later Oz books. Now a good guy, he learns real magic from Glinda, and then he is more powerful and hence more appealing. To critics and to questionnaire respondents as well, the Wizard can stand for fathers.

Gay men who feel alienated from their (presumably heterosexual) fathers may enjoy the Wizard's loss of power. As the resident authority in Oz, the Wizard can be seen as the patriarchy or society as it is currently constituted. The unmasking of the Wizard is the overthrowing of patriarchal values, and the positive message gay men can take away from the story is that there is no reason to become a "real man." The Wizard's becoming good in later Oz books can perhaps model the possibility of our forgiving the fathers who distanced themselves from us.

Combining Masculine and Feminine

Rigid gender-role expectations are also softened in Oz when characters' identities or names change. When Oz is performed on the stage or screen, many male roles are played by females and vice versa. From the first 1902 musical, performances of stories set in Oz often used men in female roles, and females in men's. Notable examples include Bessie Wynn as Sir Dashemoff Daily and the chorus girls as Munchkin Boys in the 1902 play *The Wizard of Oz*; Violet MacMillan as Ojo and Pierre Courderc as Scraps, the Patchwork Girl, in the 1914 silent film *The Patchwork Girl of Oz*; Frederick Kovert as the Peacock Lady in the 1925 film *The Wizard of Oz*; the female terrier Terry as the male character Toto in the 1939 film; and Fred Barton as Miss Gulch in his 1994 cabaret act, *Miss Gulch Returns*. (See Appendix D, "Cross-Dressing in Oz Performances," for the complete list.)

Billina, the Yellow Hen, began life as Bill; she didn't have a sex change, just a name change. Dorothy meets the hen at the beginning of *Ozma of Oz*. Upon discovering that the hen can talk, Dorothy asks her what her name is. The hen says it is Bill, but Dorothy refuses to call her Bill, which she insists is a boy's name. She calls her Billina instead.

Perhaps the most startling gender-related incident in the Oz canon is the transformation of the boy Tip into the fairy princess Ozma at the climax of *The Marvelous Land of Oz*. Tip, a mischievous slave to the witch

Mombi, runs away from her. Near the end of the story, Mombi is forced by Glinda to explain what happened to the child Ozma, who was to inherit the throne of Oz. She looks at Tip.

> "Yes," said the old Witch, nodding her head; "that is the Princess Ozma—the child brought to me by the Wizard who stole her father's throne. That is the rightful ruler of the Emerald City!" and she pointed her long bony finger straight at the boy.
>
> "I!" cried Tip, in amazement. "Why, I'm no Princess Ozma—I'm not a girl!"
>
> Glinda smiled, and going to Tip she took his small brown hand within her dainty white one.
>
> "You are not a girl just now," said she, gently, "because Mombi transformed you into a boy. But you were born a girl, and also a Princess; so you must resume your proper form, that you may become Queen of the Emerald City."
>
> "Oh, let Jinjur be the Queen!" exclaimed Tip, ready to cry. "I want to stay a boy, and travel with the Scarecrow and the Tin Woodman, and the Woggle-Bug, and Jack—yes! and my friend the Saw-Horse—and the Gump! I don't want to be a girl!". . .
>
> . . . Then he added, hesitatingly, as he turned to Glinda: "I might try it for awhile, just to see how it seems, you know. But if I don't like being a girl you must promise to change me into a boy again."

Glinda replies that changing Ozma back to Tip would beyond her powers, and she goes ahead with the transformation. Ozma appears as a young girl, dressed in gauzy robes and dainty slippers made of satin. As children, gay Oz fans have varying reactions to this presto change-o. Some are put off, registering regret, bother, and shock at the strange plot device. Others react more positively. One fan identified with Tip for not wanting to change to Ozma. Presumably, like Tip, he enjoyed being a boy. The gay filmmaker Kenneth Anger was excited by the sexual terror and reversal of gender in this development. One transgender child so identified with the transformation of Tip to Ozma that he began to cry when his mother read him this scene. And just as they feel more positive about the MGM

Cowardly Lion and Glinda after coming out, adult fans are more likely to delight in the Tip-into-Ozma transformation.

Sadly, once Tip becomes Ozma, his/her previous existence is never mentioned. A gay writer, Jack Snow, who wrote two Oz books that are part of the official canon, actually brought Tip back. His story "A Murder in Oz" begins with the discovery that Ozma is dead. It turns out that Tip didn't like being disembodied and took his life back from Ozma. The Wizard solves this problem by promising with his magic and Glinda's to return Ozma to life and keep Tip alive as well. Tip thus becomes Ozma's twin brother![v]

The typical girls' story—*The Secret Garden* (1911) or *Heidi* (1881), for example—has a young girl as a main character and centers on character and feelings. The typical boys' story—*Treasure Island* (1881–82), to name one—has adventure, gadgets, and good guys versus bad guys, and often there is a lone male hero. While Oz stories are considered girls' stories, the plots often combine elements of each of these genres. Conflict and violence exist in Oz, but they are not enacted in the classic western or sci-fi or *Star Wars* mode. In Oz, disputes are resolved without fighting, by a collaboration of male and female characters, unique individuals who stick together. In fact, the plot of the original story can also be seen as a combining of masculine and feminine, thus modeling gender nonconformity. Gay Oz fans are able to take feminine aspects of the story to heart. They get the lesson that they don't have to be macho; they can be gentle males.

With the girlish boys and boyish girls in Oz stories, the males who appear in the clothing or names of females and vice versa, Baum—who himself had female alter egos, writing stories for children as Laura Bancroft, Edith Van Dyne, and Suzanne Metcalfe—has created a world in which gender-atypical boys feel at home. Not behaving like a boy or man is only one way to be different. In fact, Oz stories show an acceptance and celebration of difference in general, the topic of the next chapter.

---

v   David Maxine, who published the story posthumously, thinks Snow's resurrection of Tip may have been part of an attempt to integrate his own divided homosexuality; see the Afterword to *Spectral Snow: The Dark Fantasies of Jack Snow* (Bloomfield, NJ: Hungry Tiger Press, 1996), p. 81.

Difference in Oz

Writers of fantasy aren't bound to depict social reality; they can imagine and depict utopian alternatives. In fact, utopian novels are sometimes considered a subgenre of fantasy. It was in this tradition that Baum created Oz. He saw much lacking in the American landscape of 1900, and Oz was his vision for an alternative to the misery he had seen in his life. Owing in part to the way social relations are depicted in Oz stories, the land itself can be considered a utopia.[a]

Friendship and Community

Friendship is a strong theme in all versions of Oz stories. In most of the stories set in Oz, we see friends exploring together. This pattern is set with Dorothy's befriending the Scarecrow, the Tin Woodman, and the Cowardly Lion in the main story. In later Oz books, the Scarecrow and the Tin Woodman become especially close; at their reunion in the second Oz book, *The Marvelous Land of Oz*, the Woodman "caught the

---

[a] In the first Oz book and the movie, Oz isn't particularly utopian. But in later books, utopian social values are elaborated, and the two MGM songs heard when the four companions first see and then enter the Emerald City do set a utopian tone. The Emerald City is "the most glorious place, on the face of the earth or the sky," and citizens "laugh the day away in the merry old Land of Oz."

6.1 The Tin Woodman and the Scarecrow, from *The Marvelous Land of Oz*, 1904

Scarecrow in a close and loving embrace that creased him into many folds and wrinkles" (fig. 6.1). Fans young and old often view familiar Oz characters as friends. Dorothy's companions on the Yellow Brick Road can become companions of the young gay Oz fan.[b] Books in a series, in particular, allow this relationship to develop, and getting a new Oz book for a birthday or Christmas allows the young fan to see old friends in new settings.

Friendship and caretaking are important aspects of gay male sensibility and culture. Gay boys, adolescents, and grown men without gay peers may fantasize about meeting a "special friend" who understands them perfectly and shares their values and point of view.[c] Some research has shown that the role of friendship is different in the lives of gay men and heterosexual men. Gay men have more of a need for sympathetic peers and tend to have closer friends than heterosexual men, a "circle of loving companions."

Lonely children often turn to books, and gay Oz fans are no exception. A fan who was a "very introverted" child and an unhappy adolescent reports that some of his happiest childhood memories involved the thrill of reading new Oz books. Oz helped another fan, an only child, feel comfortable when he was alone. The themes of kindness, caring, friendship, and love resonate with fans who were actively scorned by their peers

---

b   Characters can become "fellow travelers" in the "familiar world of the text"; see Roger Aden, *Popular Stories and Promised Lands* (Tuscaloosa: University of Alabama Press, 1999), p. 160.

c   For those who haven't come to grips with their sexuality, "special friend" may be a euphemism for a lover or boyfriend.

as boys.[d] The more gay boys and men feel the pain of being different and isolated and of being teased, the more they need the balm of friendship. How characters feel about one another can therefore model relationships for gay fans. The native inhabitants of Oz are gentle, generous, and tolerant. What better way to characterize the kinds of friends a gay child might want to have?

Living in harmony is a related Ozzy value; the Oz stories show how communal feelings could thrive. Robert Sabuda, the pop-up children's book artist and paper engineer, learned from the MGM film that very different friends working together toward a common goal can solve any problem. Fans like the fact that the four companions in the MGM movie support one another in danger and hardship. The Scarecrow facilitates this common activity. Fans consider him an "unsung hero" because he is the de facto group leader, organizing and providing a plan of action. Cooperation is shown in the MGM Kansas, too.

While cooperation is valued in Oz, so is independence. Luckily for the citizens of Oz, Ozma is a hands-off ruler who believes that you can do what you want so long as it doesn't hurt someone else. People in Oz are allowed to live their lives free from coercion.[e] In fact, the efforts of individuals to impose their values on others cause conflict and thus drive many Oz plots. The lesson Baum teaches is that individuals must shed their prejudices and not impose their views on others.

Integration and Segregation

At a social level, there are two ways to deal with people who are different. Society can integrate them: allow them to become part of the fabric of life. Or society can segregate them: facilitate or encourage them to have a separate but equal subsociety of their own. The culture of Oz embodies both integration and segregation.

---

d   Fans in general pick up on the love permeating Oz; see Suzanne Rahn, *"The Wizard of Oz": Shaping an Imaginary World* (New York: Twayne, 1998), p. 107.

e   We see more direct freedom from oppression in the first story, when Dorothy helps free the Munchkins from domination by the Wicked Witch of the East, and the Winkies from subjugation by the Wicked Witch of the West.

Society in the Emerald City is integrated. Humans from the United States, including the Wizard, Dorothy, Trot, Betsy Bobbin, and Button-Bright, live in the City. Humans born in Oz, such as Ojo and the former General Jinjur, also live in Ozma's palace at the center of the City or its environs. Humanoid creatures, among them the Scarecrow, the Tin Woodman, and Scraps the Patchwork Girl, attend Ozma's councils and banquets. "Flesh" animals, such as Billina the hen and the Cowardly Lion, and "meatless" animals, such as the Glass Cat and the Sawhorse, are also valued members of the community. And of course Ozma herself is a fairy, a humanlike creature with magical powers.

But Oz itself is made up of wildly different independent communities. Each of Baum's Oz books contains at least one such country defined by its own customs and inhabitants. In *The Wonderful Wizard*, Dorothy and her companions venture into the China Country. Much of the plot of *The Emerald City of Oz* is an introduction to many autonomous communities within Oz and the other races that live outside the marvelous Land. The MGM movie contains subtler examples of separate cultures within Oz. The size, costumes, and behavior of the inhabitants of Munchkinland differentiate them from the taller citizens of the Emerald City. The Winkie soldiers of the Wicked Witch of the West are a third distinct community. These segregated communities within Oz keep their own culture and values; there is never an attempt to integrate or assimilate them.

Before meeting other gay people or seeing gay images in the media, children and adults with a same-sex orientation often feel they are the only ones in the world. At this point they could relate to the unique Oz characters. Most, but not all, of the famous unique creatures live in the Emerald City, where difference is integrated. After we come out and meet other people who share our sexual orientation, we feel less alone. Even if we don't live in a gay ghetto, we can become part of an active gay community. In Oz, creatures cut from the same cloth, such as the kitchen utensils of Utensia, tend to live in one community. Here we have difference being segregated. Thus Oz reflects difference in both of the ways that gay children and adults experience it.

Equality

Oz's government is a monarchy, since the Land is ruled by one person who inherited the throne. But the values of the Land are democratic. Princess Ozma often plays merrily with her less regal girlfriends (fig. 6.2). Humans, animals, and animated creatures are all of more or less equal importance in Oz, and animals talk and have positions of authority in Ozma's court.^f This equality as a social value exerts a strong pull for gay fans.

6.2 Trot, Ozma, Dorothy, and Betsy, from *The Magic of Oz*, 1919

f   The Cowardly Lion and the Hungry Tiger are in fact Ozma's bodyguards. In Oz, animals or humans might choose to be servants because of their love for the person they serve; see S. J. Sackett, "The Utopia of Oz," in *The Wizard of Oz: The Critical Heritage*, ed. Michael Patrick Hearn (New York: Schocken Books, 1983), reprinted from *The Georgia Review* 16 (1960): 275–90. While the various creatures are considered equal, they have different needs. The Scarecrow, the Tin Woodman, and others don't have bodily needs like sleep and hunger. At banquets there is a separate table for those who don't eat. This may be efficient for serving, but it always struck me as segregation. While class issues are nonexistent and different species are treated with respect in Oz, the race divide is more problematic. A content analysis of eleven of Baum's books by Ann Prentice revealed two instances of racial and ethnic groups being represented, neither in a good light ("Have You Been to See the Wizard?" *Top of the News* 27 [Nov. 1970]: 32–44, especially p. 39). In the first instance, in Baum's *Rinkitink in Oz* (Reilly & Britton, 1916), a Hottentot is described as a lower form of man, black with animal skin (p. 295). In the second, in Baum's *The Patchwork Girl of Oz* (Reilly & Britton, 1913), the song sung by the universally disliked phonograph is "Ah wants ma Lulu, mah coal black Lulu" (p. 137). Adult fans notice this stereotyping and are bothered by it as well. On the other hand, fans appreciate that the MGM *Wizard* makes a good point about stereotypes. When she first meets Glinda in Munchkinland, Dorothy is surprised that Glinda is a witch, because she had assumed all witches were "old and ugly." Of course the fact that "only bad witches are ugly" is problematic as well.

The traditional power differential between children and adults is reversed or at least leveled in Oz. Dorothy is a Princess of Oz. Two other young girls from the United States, Trot and Betsy Bobbin, also have special status as friends of Dorothy and Ozma. Fans like the fact that children in Oz are powerful and respected. And in the course of the books, children become more and more prominent.

Upon closer inspection, however, not everyone is equal. The unique individuals are considered superior to the common folk. The main characters in the books—"celebrities," as they are sometimes called—seem to be exempt from work entirely. Dorothy and other adventurers encounter farmers and laborers of all kinds in their travels. But transplanted humans such as Dorothy, Button-Bright, Trot, and the Shaggy Man or the fleshy Ozians such as Ojo never seem to do work of any kind. Neither do the created creatures such as the Scarecrow, the Tin Woodman, Tik-Tok, or the Patchwork Girl.[g] This elitist view would appeal to boys who think they are different: they're better than the commoners. While not acknowledging this elitism explicitly, questionnaire respondents appreciate the protagonists' freedom to play and have adventures.

Oddballs and Outsiders

The most important utopian value for gay fans of Oz is the celebration of difference, especially in the Oz books. Baum not only accepts diversity but encourages and celebrates it. Beings in Oz are judged by their behavior, not by what they look like.

In Oz, difference is usually manifested physically: your body shows what you are made of and where you come from. Living beings can be fairies like Ozma, humans like Dorothy, talking animals like the Cowardly Lion, or composites of formerly inanimate objects like the Scarecrow or the Tin Woodman. Gay boys and men are fond of the many fairies, humans, animals, and composites Baum created. Polychrome, the Rainbow's Daughter, is a sky fairy. The Shaggy Man's clothing and hair

---

g The larger celebrity beasts, such as the Cowardly Lion, the Hungry Tiger, and the animated Sawhorse, carry people on their backs or draw wagons behind them. Smaller animals, such as the dog Toto, the Glass Cat, and Eureka, the Pink Kitten, retain their status as pets.

are always shaggy; he doesn't want to settle down or get repaid by people who owe him money. The Hungry Tiger wants very much to eat babies, but his conscience won't let him. Bungle, the Glass Cat, has pink brains and a hard ruby heart that can be seen inside her glass body, and she's proud of her appearance. Jack Pumpkinhead's body is made of thin hickory sticks; his head is a carved pumpkin that has to be replaced when it spoils. Tik-Tok is a copper mechanical man who needs to be kept wound up; when he speaks, he enunciates each syl-la-ble e-qual-ly (fig. 6.3).

6.3 Endpapers of *The Royal Book of Oz*, 1921

The way Dorothy befriends the Scarecrow, the Tin Woodman, and the Cowardly Lion in *The Wonderful Wizard* and the MGM movie initiates a pattern that is repeated in many Oz stories. While on a journey, a human protagonist discovers an eccentric. They quickly become friends and travel together.[h] This models the idea of valuing diversity, because everyone is accepted into the larger community. As a society populated by eccentrics, Oz is an attractive place for readers and viewers who feel different.

---

h   A protagonist may also actually create an eccentric, as Tip builds and brings to life both Jack Pumpkinhead and the Sawhorse in the second Oz book. In later books the oddballs can be protagonists themselves.

There is nothing objectively wrong with being different, of course. But because conformity is valued in our society, nonconformity and difference are often considered morally or socially wrong. Oz is more than a repository for misfits; it's a place where oddball creatures are famous and celebrated precisely because they are different, out of the ordinary. In Oz, being different is actually being *better*.[i] The strange characters are Oz's celebrities. The characters use this philosophy to cheer up others who feel bad about themselves for being one of a kind. The Scarecrow points out to Tommy Kwikstep, a boy with twenty legs, "You have the pleasure of knowing you are unusual, and therefore remarkable among the people of Oz. To be just like other persons is small credit to one, while to be unlike others is a mark of distinction."

The human protagonists in Oz stories are put in unusual circumstances, often surrounded by nonhumans, and are therefore perceived as outsiders by gay fans. Dorothy, in particular, is an outsider in both Kansas and Oz, especially in the MGM version of the story.[j] For many gay Oz fans, the MGM movie is about feeling different and fitting in. Like Dorothy, fans consider themselves aliens. They identify with Judy Garland's Dorothy in the Kansas sequence, who felt that she was an adopted outsider and that people didn't understand her.

Outsiders in other versions of the first Oz story, and in succeeding stories, evoke similar responses. The African American gay activist Keith Boykin, who saw the movie version of *The Wiz* as a youngster, understood Dorothy's ambivalence about her family because he was going through things he knew his family couldn't comprehend. Elphaba, the heroine of the novel *Wicked* and the musical, is green-skinned, and her political beliefs put her

---

i   Oz is certainly not alone in children's literature in celebrating those who are different. Another favorite childhood story of gay men is Hans Christian Andersen's "The Ugly Duckling," as Will Roscoe notes in *Queer Spirits* (Boston: Beacon Press, 1995).

j   While fans talk about acceptance in both book and movie versions of Oz, alienation is a stronger theme in movie versions such as the 1939 *Wizard* and *The Wiz*. In Baum's *Wonderful Wizard*, there is no indication that Dorothy is alienated from her home life; the only contrast between Dorothy and her foster parents is that she laughs and they don't.

at odds with the government. Her difference and alienation evoke strong feelings of identification in gay fans. One other book character who is a fan favorite is Ojo. He is probably the most alienated person in all of the Oz stories, rebelling against the government of Oz because the law won't allow him to find ingredients for a potion to break the spell on his uncle.[k]

Responses to Celebration of Difference

Oz gives the young fan a vision of belonging and acceptance. People who are different can find a home there. As Joe Yranski put it in his questionnaire, the Land of Oz offers

> the sense of acceptance so that everybody is able to fit into the fabric of Oz regardless of their own peculiarities. . . . This concept gave me great solace, as a child, aware of how different I was from my classmates, due to my unnatural desire for boys and men, rather than girls. In the realm of fantasy, I might be able to belong, without being labeled as a "monster" or worse.

Many gay boys are treated badly because of their actual or perceived differences. Several young fans were frequently subjected to teasing, humiliation, and actual violence and—understandably—wanted to escape. School was "hell" for one "scrawny, pimple-faced and extremely unathletic" young fan, who wanted so much to live in a world where he would be accepted, understood, and not discriminated against.

Young fans identify with Dorothy because she ran away from bullies and searched for a better place. Oz symbolizes a place away from the oppression of being a gay child, a safe harbor from teasing, and a place of refuge where one can be oneself. The stories are about misfits with unusual identities who find imaginative and courageous ways to get away from persecution, and end up being respected and famous. Oz stories give a young gay boy a glimpse of another way his life could be. They offer happier endings to one's own story.

---

[k] Young fans feeling the pressure to conform may like Ojo for his willingness to break a law. Other reasons fans like Ojo have to do with gender roles, as we saw in Chapter 5.

Adult gay fans also respond to Oz's celebration of difference. Gay people are archetypal outsiders, the "other." As they grow up, many gay men more consciously feel isolated and alienated, seeing themselves as strangers in a heterosexual world. Unlike American society with its judgment and prejudice, Oz is a place where gay men can fit in. For grown-up fans, Oz is a better world where there is no homophobia or hatred of any kind of difference. You can be your own unique self there, and be friends with other oddballs. Fans feel they would not be surprised to find a gay man in the company of Oz's eccentrics. The whole original story thus becomes a metaphor for being gay. As the respondent Marvin Martin explained it:

> We feel like strangers in a strange land, searching for the place where we belong. To find happiness we must make our own "family" of friends who, like ourselves, have never quite fit in to the larger culture into which we were born.

Adult gay fans escape to Oz in their imaginations, and some imagine how they would be treated in Oz if they actually arrived there. They know they would be welcomed in Ozma's court, and perhaps even more comfortable there than in the Castro. Acceptance of difference in Oz can also become a lesson for the real world. Fans attest to Gore Vidal's claim that reading the Oz books can make you more tolerant and imaginative. Society would be improved, fans believe, if we all followed Baum's example of tolerance and respect.[1]

---

[1] Ozzy values might have helped engender the social rebellion of the 1960s; at the very least, they resonated with youthful rebels of that era. See Raylyn Moore, *Wonderful Wizard, Marvelous Land* (Bowling Green, OH: Bowling Green University Popular Press, 1974), p. 4.

7
Messages and Uses of Oz

Because heterosexuality is a societal norm, conformity is a particularly poignant issue for homosexuals. Reacting to the pressure to conform, gay males (and lesbians) often construct a "false self" in order to fit in. A few attempt to become straight by undergoing voluntary shock therapy or "reparative" pseudo-therapy. Others just pretend to be straight, dating the opposite sex, getting engaged, and even marrying to please parents and the larger culture. Even gay men who do not try to be straight often suppress their impulses toward the same sex and shy away from pursuing any interests that might seem unmanly. And many go through a period of hiding, secrecy, and shame before coming out.

Deceit and humbug are disparaged in all the Oz books, but in a gentle and sometimes subtle manner. Ironically, the title character of the beloved story is one of the most hated of all Oz characters, often because of his phoniness: he is a fraud and a liar. Fans do not generally identify with the Wizard, although a few relate to him as someone with secrets. The Wizard does take steps toward honesty and truth by "coming out from behind the screen." Perhaps fans subconsciously feel that the Wizard's dilemma absolves them of the dishonesty of their closet. One fan identified with the Wizard because of his own "secret identity" as a humbug. Similarly, at an early age, another fan identified with the scalawag Randy from Thompson's *The Purple Prince of Oz* because of his "secret other life" as the Prince of Regalia.

Given parental assumptions that you are straight, peer pressure to conform, and the overwhelming number of images of heterosexuality from Madison Avenue, being your own true self is no easy feat. How can gay boys and men manage to do this? Therapy can help; so can symbols, fantasy literature, and myths. Literature in general, and fantasy in particular, can help us see the reality behind everyday illusion. As works of fantasy, stories set in the Land of Oz can help us find "reality." Myths enable people to be themselves and follow their bliss, and as a contemporary American myth, *The Wizard of Oz* can help show us our bliss.

For many, the message of *The Wizard of Oz* is that "you have everything you need inside you." Gay boys and men get the subtle message from society that they aren't real men. The idea that you don't need to rely on others, you are your own powerful person, is thus a compelling one. The bisexual actor Alan Cumming, who played a Scarecrow character in the 2007 television miniseries *Tin Man*, made a similar point in an interview: "Certainly *The Wizard of Oz* resonates strongly with gays. . . . I believe the idea that everything you need to make you happy is right inside of you—you have to find out about yourself. It's all about self-empowerment." Many fans echo the sentiment that once you look within, you can find your talents.

But the message of Oz is deeper than self-reliance. By using the Ruby (or Silver) Slippers to get what she wants at the end of the story, Dorothy finally understands the power she possesses. Because many of the personages in Oz stories are so weird, and their weirdness is accepted as normal, they model authentic individuality for the reader or viewer. Being yourself entails figuring out what your true self, your identity, is. A final piece of the process is integration: assimilating the old and new aspects of your identity. Along with the message of self-reliance, then, *The Wizard of Oz* imparts messages of self-understanding, authenticity, identity, and integration, all of which are especially relevant to gay men and boys.[a]

---

a Oz helps fans grow in many ways, and of course some fans derive psychological benefits unrelated to these messages. One important type of benefit is the role models Oz provides. Readers and viewers may identify with characters that embody characteristics they don't have, in an attempt to acquire those admirable characteristics themselves. A second benefit concerns ex-

For some, going to Oz is not escaping to somewhere else, but going inside. When gay fans first encounter Oz in their early childhood, much of their psychic life is unconscious. Symbols in Oz stories can tap into the unconscious, and symbols in movies can evoke both projection and introjection.[b] Using Oz as a route to the unconscious, readers and viewers can bring previously inaccessible feelings into conscious functioning; they can access inner truths and grow. Things gay fans may be ashamed about, such as homosexuality, can also be accepted without gay fans' compromising themselves.

One type of self-discovery for a gay man is realizing for the first time that he is gay; another is getting back in touch with early feelings that he

    pertise: Oz fans can try out new physical and social skills in make-believe. In addition, collecting Oz books and objects or becoming an expert on Baum, Oz, or the MGM movie can give the child or adult fan a sense of accomplishment and mastery. Third, Oz can help gay fans deal with unpleasant parts of real life. Around the age of four or five, many children have heightened concerns about "danger, disaster, and physical mutilation" (Dorothy Singer and Jerome Singer, *House of Make-Believe* [Cambridge, MA: Harvard University Press, 1990], p. 74). Young children may not be able to separate fantasy and reality, and a monster may seem quite real to them. If parents and teachers "accept such emotions as a part of the child's reality [and] . . . allow the child to play the monster game again and again, such fearful feelings may eventually dissipate" (Singer and Singer, *House of Make-Believe*, p. 174). In a similar way, being repeatedly scared by the Wicked Witch can be a way to work through feelings of fear.

b   Projection involves expelling bad aspects of oneself onto a symbol or object; introjection entails absorbing good qualities from an external object and unconsciously regarding the qualities as part of one's own self (Elizabeth Wright, *Psychoanalytic Criticism* [New York: Routledge, 1998], p. 72). Identification is a more general process, where "the attitudes of another are taken over as if they were one's own" (Frances Wickes, *The Inner World of Childhood* [Englewood Cliffs, NJ: Prentice-Hall/Spectrum, 1978], p. 9). Introjection and projection together create back-and-forth movement between what ones sees in a film and the unconscious, giving everyday images new meanings and bringing up to consciousness symbols hidden in the unconscious (John Izod, "Active Imagination and the Analysis of Film," *Journal of Analytical Psychology* 45 [Apr. 2000]: 267–85; see especially p. 273).

may have repressed. When we come out, we no longer heed authorities on sex and gender and start to see with gay eyes. We can then get rid of the false self we may have constructed to get along in an overwhelmingly heterosexual society. In myths and legends, quests are metaphors for psychological journeys. Like the heroes of old, Dorothy is on a journey of self-understanding. Shamanism is a practice of healing via the imagination, and Dorothy's visit to Oz can be seen as a shamanic journey. She learns to trust her own truth; she finds out what she is capable of and where she fits in the universe. Dorothy's quest thus parallels that of gay men, finding out about their own homosexuality. The MGM movie in particular can be seen as a shamanic journey toward self-knowledge for gay men. For some fans, other versions of *The Wizard of Oz* may emphasize self-understanding more. The movie of *The Wiz* made an impression on one fan in his early teen years, especially the song "Home" with "its themes of growing up and self-discovery," which were more explicit in *The Wiz* than they were in Baum's original book or the MGM film.

Many gay boys and adolescents suffer from poor self-esteem and shame caused by external oppression and internalized homophobia. When gay men are closeted, they, like the Wizard, hide their true selves. Beings in Oz are self-reliant and autonomous, free of pressure to conform; they are free to be who they really are. The young gay fan finds in Oz a model society where outsiders and misfits are not just tolerated but celebrated. He sees that different does not equal bad. Oz stories encourage him to be his authentic self; he can feel better about himself, develop a positive self-image, and even feel pride in who he is.[c]

---

[c] Coming out is only the beginning of being an authentic person. (See the interesting discussions in Peter Sweasey, *From Queer to Eternity: Spirituality in the Lives of Lesbian, Gay and Bisexual People* [London: Cassell, 1997], and Deborah Blincoe and John Forrest, "The Dangers of Authenticity," *New York Folklore* 19, nos. 1–2 [1993]: 1–14.) You have to present an authentic image of yourself to the world, a persona, and heterosexist patriarchal society gives gay men two options: be straight or be a sissy. So the task for gay men is to create personas that are authentically their own, and the MGM film can help with that as well; see Robert Hopcke, *Jung, Jungians and Homosexuality* (Boston: Shambala, 1989).

Because we rarely encounter role models within our families, gay people perhaps struggle with the identity question more than most. One gift of being gay is that we have the opportunity to ask ourselves who we are. When we come out to ourselves and the world, we have a chance to forge a new authentic self. Myths help people establish their identities, and many fans in fact do cite Oz and Oz fandom as part of their identity. Young gay fans experience Oz as a journey of self-actualization. Like Dorothy exploring Oz, gay men can reinvent themselves in a new world.

The Scarecrow lacks brains, the Tin Woodman wants a heart, and the Lion is searching for courage. Once Dorothy has helped them become complete and the Wizard learns magic from Glinda, they are all self-actualized, with new identities. Many of the characters in Oz literally create and recreate themselves, as when the Scarecrow gets restuffed or Jack Pumpkinhead carves himself new heads. They become metaphors for creating your own identity. Characters from the Land of Oz as well as the Land itself may also play a role in strengthening a developing gay boy's identity and help him to individuate, as Jungian psychologists call it—that is, help him to become more truly himself. In Oz, all the characters are comfortable with their identities and can model this comfort for a young gay fan, thus illustrating a journey of individuation for gay men.

Becoming whole, putting together aspects of yourself, is a related theme in Oz and gay men's lives. Leaving your family, coming out, and creating a new identity in a new, more accepting or anonymous environment can alienate you from your past. Another challenge for gay men is to integrate aspects of our earlier lives into our current psychic situations. We also need to integrate our gay identities into the rest of our identities. Since the psyche is itself made up of subpersonalities, Dorothy's companions can also represent aspects of herself that need to be developed and integrated. Dorothy helping her companions become whole—getting their brains, heart, and courage—can be a metaphor for Dorothy becoming whole herself. In the first book and the MGM movie, despite her incredible adventures, Dorothy is back home and things are the way they were. These last scenes can symbolize the impulse toward wholeness and restoration.

The process of gay males understanding themselves, becoming authentic, claiming a new identity, and integrating their old and new selves has a name: coming out. It should not be a surprise that Dorothy's journey from Kansas to Oz is interpreted as an allegory for accepting oneself as gay and coming out. Fans offer many correspondences, mostly with respect to the movie. The drab black-and-white of the movie and the grayness of Kansas in *The Wonderful Wizard* symbolize life in the closet, the world of patriarchy and heterocentrism. Dorothy's yearning for a place over the rainbow stands for a gay boy's yearning for self-understanding, an identity, acceptance, and community. The turbulent cyclone in Kansas is like the crisis many gay men go through when they discover they are different from other boys.

Dorothy's adventure without supervising adults parallels coming out on your own terms. Going from a small town to a big city is the journey many gay men travel when coming out. Going to Oz is embracing the fabulous in gay life. The famous contrast of the black-and-white scenes in the MGM movie with the Technicolor of Oz is like the difference between life before and after coming out. True reality for Dorothy and gay men is shown via Technicolor magic. Gay men are drawn to cities for their anonymity and possibilities, and the Emerald City can symbolize the city-full-of-possibilities. When the Wizard grants the wishes of the Scarecrow, the Tin Woodman, and the Cowardly Lion, he understands their desires and is helping Dorothy's companions achieve their deepest wishes. This parallels the result of coming out: making peace with your previously hidden and shameful desires and putting yourself on the road to satisfying them. Dorothy's return to Kansas is even like coming home after being immersed in a gay community. When you come out to others, you are not always treated seriously and respectfully.

Oz as Myth

A myth tells a story for an individual, a group, a subculture, a society, or a country. Its characters are often archetypes, that is, they embody significant traits or characteristics. Myths are metaphors for cosmological, metaphysical, sociological, and psychological truths and help us be open to and experience the transcendent. Via their archetypal images, myths can also bring about communication between the unconscious and the conscious mind. The narratives of myths give individuals a sense of where they fit into the larger scheme of things, answering such questions as

Where am I from? Who am I? Where am I going? In short, myths are stories to live by.

The Wonderful Wizard and its MGM movie incarnation are often described as peculiarly American myths, and Oz stories in general can be understood as, and experienced as, myths. In mythological adventures from cultures around the world, a hero sets off on a quest, going through the stages of separation, initiation, and return. During the quest the hero (or heroine) overcomes obstacles aided by companions met along the way. The core story of *The Wizard of Oz*, with Dorothy as questing hero, fits this structure pretty closely. The story of *The Wizard of Oz* is true in the sense of conveying universal truths in the way that a myth does.

Stories set in Oz are also replete with specific mythic imagery and archetypal symbolism. In many quests the hero encounters an authority or father figure who is overthrown or whose authority is undermined or supplanted by the hero. Dorothy's encounter with the Wizard, showing him to be a humbug, can be read as an example of this mythic theme. The Wicked Witch of the West can represent the "bad mother," and Glinda, the Good Witch, can embody aspects of the "good mother." The Friend is an archetype that reminds us of our connection to others, and Dorothy's companions on the Yellow Brick Road can symbolize archetypal friendship. The Scarecrow, Tin Woodman, and Cowardly Lion, who in the course of the story gain their missing parts, also individually embody the archetypal qualities of intelligence, compassion, and courage. Witches, magic, monsters, half-human beings, and androgynous beings are mythogems, or mythic ingredients, and they occur in stories set in Oz in spades. Animal helpers in particular are mythic and fairy-tale characters. In addition to Toto and the Cowardly Lion, a flying birdlike creature called the Ork and Billina the hen play important helping roles in the Oz books. Billina the hen is also an archetypal trickster.

Mythology offers many transcendental messages. Some of these are nicely embodied by stories set in Oz:

EXPERIENCE THE RAPTURE OF BEING ALIVE. The wonder that Oz evokes as a fantasy can be rapturous. And animating objects such as a scarecrow or a sawhorse helps readers and viewers think about what it means to be alive.

FOLLOW YOUR BLISS (BE IN TOUCH WITH YOUR OWN BEING). In Oz, oddballs are celebrated; all are recognized for their special gifts and allowed to follow their own path to happiness.

AWAKEN YOUR HEART TO COMPASSION AND BE CONNECTED WITH OTHER HUMANS, ALL BEINGS. The Tin Woodman symbolizes compassion and even cries when he steps on a flower. Communities within Oz such as Utensia and the China Country are populated with creatures that would be mute animals or inanimate objects in our world. By animating them all, Baum could be saying that we are all connected: bears and flowers and even china plates have feelings.

LIFE AND DEATH ARE TWO ASPECTS OF THE SAME THING: BECOMING. Another cosmic question that myths deal with is whether death is an end or a beginning. When the Scarecrow finds his stuffing scattered all around or becomes waterlogged, he picks himself up, dries himself off, and starts all over again. When his old head begins to rot, Jack Pumpkinhead carves himself a new one. The magical Powder of Life animates such inanimate creatures as the Sawhorse and the Patchwork Girl. Death and physical destruction are not absent from Oz, but they are made gentle, part of life's continuum.

Oz as Personal Mythology

Like Dorothy's trip to Oz, coming out has the form of a hero's journey, and in fact gay people lead "mythical lives" every day. That is, our lives have mythic structure that would easily lend itself to mythic narratives. Collectively, however, gay people don't have myths, and mainstream writers rarely acknowledge the heroic aspect of gay lives. A gay myth, if there were such a thing, would help give meaning to our lives. And knowing such gay myths would allow us to find out who we are.

When a culture lacks significant myths, either sociological or religious, that everyone buys into, individuals often develop their own personal myths and mythologies.[d] A personal myth, with its unique tone,

---

d   It is also possible to internalize the myths in your culture and then develop new "counter-myths" to better meet your needs. The myths limited you; the counter-myths expand you. See David Feinstein and Stanley Krippner,

ideology, and characters, can speak to one's individual needs. In particular, a personal myth can provide a sense of who one is, becoming the basis for one's identity. A personal mythology is the set of myths that filters one's perceptions, guides one's behavior, gives meaning to one's life, and locates one's place in the wider scheme of things.

There are clues that stories based on Oz are actually used as personal myths by gay men and boys. Mark Thompson, a therapist, uses the Oz story as a myth in his work with gay men. In his questionnaire responses one fan calls the film "our myth, our metaphor, our parable." Another fan's connection to the MGM movie is "deep, mystical and nourishing." Of course, how Oz operates as a personal myth will vary with each individual fan and with the same individual over time. And while Oz can contribute to a few themes or myths, Oz-inflected myths won't necessarily make up the complete set of stories a given fan lives by.

The process of developing a personal myth based on Oz would begin early. All children have complex and active inner lives that include "myth-making material." Before the self-conscious myth-making of adolescence, young gay boys can collect material to be used in the eventual full-blown personal myth via the unconscious processes of identification, resonance, and appropriation. The young gay fan may initially be drawn to the visual aspects of the film or the illustrations shared with him by the person reading the book aloud. The preschool child will also absorb images from the family via bedtime stories and from the culture at large, especially popular culture and advertising. When a gay boy is three or four or five, the archetypal images in an Oz narrative are reaching down into places of his unconscious. Dorothy in her checked dress, the tornado, the change from black-and-white to color, the Ruby Slippers, the Wicked Witch, the Lion with a bow in his hair, the Emerald City, the Wizard's throne room, the Witch's Castle, the hourglass timer, and the poppy field are all arresting images from the MGM movie

---

Personal Mythology: The Psychology of Your Evolving Self (Los Angeles: Jeremy Tarcher, 1988), pp. 208–9. Many of the messages that Oz stories offer can be taken as counter-myths to unquestioned assumptions of the culture of heterosexuality, heterocentrism, and heteronormativity (the idea that heterosexuality is the normal or preferable state).

that might find their way into gay fans' personal myths. The Wicked Witch is a particularly potent image for preschoolers. Seeing pictures of the Scarecrow, the Tin Woodman, the Lion, Glinda, the Patchwork Girl, and other colorful characters in illustrated Oz books, or hearing them described, might lead to their becoming important mythic images as well. The map of Oz with its four countries (red, yellow, blue, and purple), with a green Emerald City in the center, can also make a strong impression.[e]

The tone and general form of a personal myth will be based on experiences of the preschool child. Feelings of hope and trust that are present or absent during infancy and early childhood will contribute to the narrative tone. When a very young gay boy first sees the MGM movie or hears an Oz story read to him, he might be scared or overwhelmed or delighted. The jolly and companionable feelings generated by the Oz books would give rise to a very different story to live by from that inspired by scary aspects of the movie.

Characters who began as simple images in the preschooler's mind will be seen to have motives by the child in his elementary school years and will get more differentiated as he reaches adolescence and young adulthood. Conflicts in a fan's life can be played out by different characters in his personal myth. The characters might stand for the fan himself, for significant people in his life, or for different aspects of his personality. Dorothy's three companions can also express important parts of the gay fan and become characters in his personal mythology. Fans identify with many other Ozzy characters—male and female, good and bad, old and young—and have favorites of all kinds. Outsiders and misfits such as Dorothy, Ojo the Unlucky, the boy Tip who becomes the Princess Ozma, the Patchwork Girl, and the Wicked Witch of the West might represent traits of the gay fan and be absorbed as characters in his personal myth.

At subsequent tellings and viewings, the gay fan's understanding of

---

[e] The Shaggy Man's Love Magnet from a Golden Book version of an Oz story was the hook for one six-year-old. Another's was the first viewing of the movie at age two: "I recall being told at a little over age 2 that I was too young for the film. . . . The moment (after a commercial break) when Dorothy opens the door to Technicolor is one that I vividly recall."

the story will become more sophisticated and different issues will resonate depending on his emotional state and current circumstances. These viewings and readings might also be supplemented by other recreations of the story, such as fantasy play, retellings within his imagination, creative writing, and drawing. These recreations can be tailored individually, focusing on the aspects of Oz that matter most. Eventually the separate bits and pieces will coalesce into the gay fan's own personal mythology.

Different life stages will present new problems, and one's myths, including the Oz myths, will change and adapt or be replaced. The core Oz story of Dorothy's quest to return home could become a myth for one very young fan. A potent image might be of one door closing and another opening. A feeling or belief associated with this story at this stage might be "It's wonderful to go away for a while, but home is where you want to be." At a later time in life, a fan might focus on utopian aspects of the more complex social arrangements in Oz, or on Ozzy gender politics. Or the Oz myth might become a nostalgic return to the Eden of an innocent childhood. Another fan could extract several mythic themes or messages to live by, such as "You can be a lovable and valuable member of society if you are a nonaggressive male like the Scarecrow, the Tin Woodman, or the Lion." Or "It's OK to be different. Equality, nonviolence, and cooperation are worthwhile values that can make your life happier." Or "You need to escape from your home and family and become independent of them, but you can still hold them dear in your heart." Or "Become your own true self. Characters in Oz are authentic, and you can be, too." Drawing from all these themes, the gay fan can extract larger messages, such as "It's OK to be gay. You need to define yourself differently from what your family and society expects. This will entail moving away and perhaps becoming part of a gay urban culture."

A personal mythology based on aspects of Oz can be used by the gay fan in many arenas from concrete to cosmic. Some fans use Oz in specific domestic ways, such as having a screen saver that says, "Pass me the Ruby Slippers, Dorothy, it's time to go home!" Many fans quote lines from the movie, or hear bits of dialog in their heads. Others have used it to guide their career choices, how they view the world, and what qualities they look for in their friends. For older fans, Oz can be a source of support in times of great sadness. Within a period of three years, the respondent

Jim Whitcomb experienced the deaths of his mother, a dear friend, and his father, the suicide of his roommate's sister, and the need to put one of his dogs to sleep:

> It was at this point in my life that I drew strength from my love for *The Wizard of Oz*. In my own way, I went looking for "something" just like Dorothy did. I know now that what I was looking for were all of the virtues for which Dorothy and her friends were "Off to See the Wizard." During this horrible period in my life, I truly felt like I was going mad, thus I had no brains. My heart was breaking due to all of the loss I experienced. I didn't have the nerve or the courage to deal with my problems at that time in a positive or constructive manner. And, I so much wanted to go back home, to the place I remembered as a child; where all of the people I loved were still alive and well. So, I may no longer have in my life "my Auntie Em, Uncle Henry, or my little dog, too," but in my heart I know there is "NO PLACE LIKE HOME."

Arnie Kantrowitz structures an entire memoir of life before and after gay liberation, *Under the Rainbow: Growing Up Gay*, around metaphors taken from the movie. Kansas stands for a true home; freedom and excitement are seen in Technicolor; a better place to escape to is called both Oz and over the rainbow; and looking for a solution to life's problems is going off to see the Wizard. Any place or state of mind that has the answers Arnie is searching for is the Emerald City. Truth revealed is found behind the curtain. Since Arnie sees the Wizard as a granter of wishes, the Wizard becomes a metaphor for a perfect man. And when Arnie's two best friends die of AIDS, he feels he has lost his Scarecrow and Tin Man.

Oz gives meaning to fans' lives, and it becomes a guide for living. As the respondent Mark Griffin put it:

> I have adopted the message of the 1939 film as a way of life. The lesson that Dorothy learns about finding everything she needs right in her own backyard is a vitally important one. I've experienced the truth of that so often in my own journey. The Ruby

Slippers symbolize this so beautifully. You can go anywhere you want. The trip is up to you. We are all wizards. We give ourselves the greatest gifts. . . . I've tried to make that the theme of my life. . . . The long and the short of it is that it means EVERYTHING to me. I can't stress that enough. *The Wizard of Oz* has provided a beautiful framework for my life experience. In my daily dealings with co-workers, friends and relatives, I strive to live up to the beauty and grace of the story.

▪ ▪ ▪

To be sure, gay fans might not use the term "personal mythology" to describe their relationship to Oz, but their use of Oz stories is similar to the use of myth in earlier times and in other cultures. Individual gay fans are also part of a larger mainstream culture and, to a varying extent, of gay subculture as well. Their fandom thus has social and cultural contexts, which I explore in Part Three.

PART THREE SOCIAL AND CULTURAL CONTEXTS

8

The Subcultural Phenomenon

The chapters in Part Two described individual responses to Oz stories and the reasons gay boys become and stay fans of Oz stories as adults. What is the relationship between these individual fans' love of Oz and the status of the MGM film in gay culture in general? As we have seen, it is stories set in Oz in any format, not just the 1939 film, that appeal to gay men, but images from the film are what appear in gay contexts. It may be that there is a self-fulfilling prophecy at work here: the assumption that the movie is better known is part of the reason that the movie is better known. Imagine a fan who likes the books and the movie equally deciding to dress up as a character from the books, such as Ojo or Ozma, for Halloween or gay pride. When he realizes that most people won't know who he is supposed to be, he will probably go as the MGM version of the Scarecrow or Dorothy instead.

How do individual childhood responses turn into a collective subcultural phenomenon? The short answer is that Oz fans often want to share their fandom. Young fans are surrounded to a greater or lesser extent by a network of family members, friends, and schoolmates. As they grow up and come out, they also develop some kind of relationship with the larger gay community or subculture. They will likely have some gay friends and romantic partners. They might belong to gay organizations, subscribe to gay periodicals, visit gay websites and blogs, and attend events within the gay community.

Of course, some young Oz fans enjoy their fandom in isolation; their love of Oz was and still is an intensely personal experience. That is the case for Mark Thompson, who as a ten-year-old retreated to his local public library to read the Oz books and get away from his family. For another Oz fan, it wasn't until high school that he felt secure enough to tell his friends that he knew the MGM film by heart and that it mattered deeply to him. Adults may also prefer to appreciate Oz by themselves because they see their relationship to Oz as a personal and private matter. Enjoying the MGM version of Oz in solitude is especially striking, since movie viewing is often a social experience. Paul Dana, who has written Oz stories he wants others to read, likes to watch the movie by himself, or with friends who stay quiet. Since he's never known any other serious Oz fans, his pleasure essentially comes from inside. Mark Griffin, who talked about Oz all the time as a child, is hesitant to talk to male peers now about his fandom.

But other young fans sleep, breathe, and eat the story, and everyone in their households knows of their obsessions. Young fans often find siblings, friends, neighbors, or schoolmates who are at least somewhat interested in Oz. In addition to playacting, boys will enjoy Oz in a social way by reciting lines from the movie, borrowing each other's books, pooling allowances to buy books, and reading aloud to younger kids. Many adult fans want to share their love of Oz as well. Some want to meet other Oz fans who are gay, to share their enthusiasm with kindred spirits. One respondent wondered if others had tried to write their own Oz books, either as children or adults. Another proposed an Oz reading group for gay men.

Many fans are lucky enough to have gay friends who are also into Oz. One pattern is to have met a handful of friends via conventions, book collecting, the Internet, or piano bars. Or a given fan might know only one other Oz fan, such as a partner, a former lover, a best friend, or a work assistant. Those who do count Oz fans among their gay friends tend to appreciate the connection, although some say Oz isn't the basis for their friendship.

Adult gay fans who are in relationships have the opportunity or challenge of explaining their fandom to their partners. This can occasionally result in a conversion to interest, if not full-fledged fandom, on the part of the significant other. Some partners attend Oz conventions as active participants, but a more common situation is for partners of fans to be somewhat supportive or to simply tolerate the quirks of the devotee. Some gay Oz aficionados, however, are fortunate enough to find a partner whose level of interest is similar to their own. David Maxine and Eric Shanower met at an Oz Club convention in 1983, when David was twenty and Eric nineteen. Oz was such a strong bond between Joe Yranski and his partner, Joe Cantlin, that Yranski temporarily lost interest in Oz when Cantlin died in 1988.

Social fans may attempt to share their fandom with members of a younger generation, but it does not seem that love of Oz itself can be passed along. Godchildren, nieces, and nephews are often the recipients of Oz books or other presents. The younger person may react with appreciation or enthusiasm, but these attempts at cross-generational Oz bonding are not always successful. Brian Finnegan reports that his son liked *The Wizard of Oz* when he was younger, but by age eleven, "being a very straight boy (!), couldn't care less."

I had expected to find at least a few fans who became enamored of the movie after finding out it was a big deal within the gay male community. Keeping up with the Joneses or the Bruces wouldn't explain all of Oz fandom, but it is conceivable that at least some appreciation of an aspect of gay culture could be explained by learning that it's a gay thing and then cultivating an appreciation for it.[a] But Oz fandom rarely works this way, it seems. Learning about Judy Garland or Bette Davis, or seeing a movie one hadn't heard of before, could be useful for holding up one's end of the conversation. But fans don't develop a love for something because someone tells them it's popular. Almost without exception, fandom based on either the movie or the books begins very early in life. Oz is not a cultivated taste, like opera, fine wine, or Limburger cheese.

The adult fan's impulse to reenact and control a trip to Oz via performance and creation is often played out in specifically gay contexts,

---

[a] One stage of becoming part of gay culture is serving as a model for others entering the culture. See Joseph Goodwin, *More Man Than You'll Ever Be: Gay Folklore and Acculturation in Middle America* (Bloomington: Indiana University Press, 1989).

which have been noted in gay culture for at least a few decades. Also common are stories with Oz allusions in which the protagonists are gay men or boys. William Mann and Geoff Ryman have depicted gay boys' early obsessions with the MGM movie in their novels. Jameson Currier's collection of stories about gay men and AIDS, *Dancing on the Moon* (1993), includes the short story "What They Carried," in which the characters gather at a sick man's home during a television broadcast of the MGM film. Howard Cruse ends his 1984 satirical comic strip "Cabbage Patch Clone" with Dorothy and her companions appearing to a lonely gay doll. A few adult fans have even written Oz stories with gay characters for adult readers. *Son of a Witch*, Gregory Maguire's 2005 sequel to *Wicked*, includes a love affair between two men.[b]

Fans occasionally get to perform Oz in a gay context. James Heintz was on a camping trip in 1993 or so, with a dozen gay friends. When someone played the CD soundtrack of the MGM movie, a spontaneous reenactment of the movie took place. Dorothy had a wicker basket and a stuffed dog, and everyone joined in with most of the lyrics. Ted Genova starred in a production of *The Wizard of Oz* in a gay bar in 1985, the same week Margaret Hamilton died. And John Kenrick sings along in piano bars whenever he can.

The gay Oz fan's urge to become his favorite Oz character is given an outlet at both gay pride and Halloween. Some people make their own costumes; others buy theirs in stores. Attending parties, demonstrations, and concerts with gay friends also allows adult fans to dress

---

b   Although I am talking about fiction here, gay fans have used Oz in their nonfiction creations as well. Around 1990 Larry Hermsen wrote "Over the Rainbow, Into Our Hearts: *The Wizard of Oz* and the Gay Experience." Ryan Bunch's master's thesis in musicology was "'Over the Rainbow': Difference, Utopia, and *The Wizard of Oz* in Queer Musical Experience." Alexander Doty, Patrick Horrigan, and Reid Davis have all written about their own responses as gay men or boys to the MGM *Wizard*. "OZ—The 'Other' Side of the Rainbow" is Brian Bogdan's website. "It allows me the freedom to speak my mind, politically and humorously," he writes. "I am a friend of Dorothy's after all."

up in Oz drag. Friends from the Chicago area regularly go together to the Oz festival in Chesterton, Indiana, in MGM Oz costumes. Dorothy in blue gingham and pigtails is a common sight in gay venues in particular. Scott Robinson dressed up as Dorothy to be in the audience for *Miss Gulch Returns* (fig. 8.1). When Brian Finnegan programmed the Dublin Lesbian and Gay Film Festival in 1999 and 2000, he included a Cine-oke sing-along of the MGM movie. A drag Dorothy sang "Over the Rainbow" along with the Dorothy on the screen. The MGM Glinda is another popular image in gay contexts. During the March on Washington for LGBT Rights in 1993, Camo Bortman dressed up as Glinda. Halloween has seen Glindas, Wicked Witches, and Scarecrows.

8.1 Scott Robinson as Dorothy on the set of *Miss Gulch Returns*, 2000

While the MGM characters are more recognizable to the public at large, at Oz conventions one might see one of W. W. Denslow's or John R. Neill's illustrations from the Oz books come to life. Joe Yranski and his partner went to an Oz Club convention in 1984 dressed as Munchkins from the books. They also wore these costumes to the Halloween parade in Greenwich Village later that year, flanking a gay male friend dressed as Dorothy.[c]

There are also established ways to share your appreciation of Oz in a communal gay context. Some groups of gay friends get together to watch

---

c Not all gay Oz fans are enamored of the idea of dressing up as Oz characters, however. One fan hates to "see hairy drag queens dressing as Dorothy," and another thinks those who spend all their energy getting dressed up are "in sore need of a life."

8.2 Friends watching the movie before the pride march, Madison, WI, 2001

the movie, and many regularly give or attend Oz-themed parties (fig. 8.2). Public showings of the movie in gay neighborhoods are scenes of mutually reinforcing hilarity and recognition. Several fans, some of whom don't even live in San Francisco, revel in the sense of community created by seeing the movie at the Castro Theatre in the heart of gay San Francisco. Reid Davis first saw the movie as an adult at the Castro. He noted "liberation-cheers" and "howls of laughter" at all the moments with special meaning for the gay audience: "We're not in Kansas anymore," "Only bad witches are ugly," "It's very tedious being stuck up here with a pole up your... back." Davis's experience inspired him to write an article about the group dynamics of viewing the movie with hundreds of other gay men.

Adult sharing is a natural extension of childhood sharing, and gay adults will want to share their love of Oz in a gay context. The adults will have more resources than children and can make their love more visible. Thus gay fans contribute to the visibility of the MGM movie in gay culture, boosting Oz in various ways, and people start to notice. They give their travel agencies, hair salons, websites, bars, events, and organizations such names as Land of Oz, Yellow Brick Road, Emerald City, Toto Tours, This Ain't Kansas, and Dorothy's Surrender. They suggest *The Wizard of Oz* as a theme for floats and events. Oz characters are regularly seen in pride parades, the film is put on the program at gay film festivals and on lists of gayest movies, and allusions to Oz show up in gay writing of all sorts. All these individual decisions enable individual love of Oz to become a cultural fact.

Feelings About the Oz–Gay Connection

As gay fans share and boost Oz, the knowledge that gay men love the MGM *Wizard* becomes established at the subcultural level. And as part of the gay subculture, this knowledge gets passed along from one generation to the next.[d] How fans themselves learn this offers a window into how gay men become part of the larger gay community.

It is when they are in high school, in college, or just after college—long after they have become fans themselves—that most gay fans find out that the MGM *Wizard* is considered a gay favorite. Many encounter the gay connection at more or less the time they come out. In some cases, though, it happens later. Gregory Maguire didn't find out about gay love of the MGM film until he did book tours for his novel *Wicked*. Despite being out for many years, he was a recluse with respect to gay culture.

The discovery can happen in many ways. One out gay individual can pass the knowledge of the gay connection to another. Other fans see or hear a reference to the MGM film within an aspect of the larger gay culture. Oz images appear in gay publications. Gay choruses sing "Over the Rainbow." Entering a gay bar and having everyone say "You're not in Kansas anymore" to you can be a clue. So is seeing the movie at the Castro Theatre in San Francisco with hundreds of other cheering gay fans. Just as you see Oz in a gay context, you might see gay in an Oz context, perhaps noticing other gay fans at an Oz convention.[e]

Finding out that Judy Garland is a gay icon is often related to the discovery of the Oz–gay connection. Amazingly, three questionnaire

---

[d] Two recent novels use Oz imagery to show that gay culture—appreciation for certain movies and movie stars, for example—is passed along from older men to younger. William Mann's *The Men from the Boys* (1997) includes a scene in which members of the older generation lament the youngsters' lack of knowledge about gay icons and talk about teaching them how to "be gay." In Jameson Currier's *Where the Rainbow Ends* (1998), the protagonist's first lover is an older professor who explains about Oz.

[e] Seeing other gay men in an Oz context can help individuals overcome internalized homophobia. One fan says that meeting other gay men at gatherings of the International Wizard of Oz Club helped him to realize that gay people "weren't evil."

8.3 Rockshots card: "Toto, I don't think we're in Kansas anymore!"
(© 1982 Warren Fricke and Rockshots Greeting Cards)

respondents mentioned the same Rockshots greeting card of Judy as Dorothy in a gay bar, surrounded by men looking very much like the Village People, with the message "Toto, I don't think we're in Kansas anymore!" inside (fig. 8.3). One fan came across the card in his mid-teens, before he was out, and added it to his Oz collection. Another avenue of discovery of the Oz–gay connection is hearing the expression "friend of Dorothy." Someone may explain to the fan that the Dorothy in question is Dorothy Gale, as portrayed by Judy Garland; in other cases the fan simply makes that assumption himself.[f]

Fans themselves have both positive and negative reactions to the Oz–gay connection, related to the degree to which they accept their own homosexuality. Seeing other gay Oz fans in public—at Oz Club conventions, as fellow volunteers for a stage version of *The Wizard*—often comes

---

f In fact, Judy Garland's role in the MGM film may or may not be the origin of the expression. See Chapter 9, "Oz and Judy in Gay Folklore."

as a surprise. The revelation that one's own fandom is shared by other gay men can be deeply gratifying and powerful. The nineteen-year-old Brent Terrien writes in his questionnaire:

> I really felt a sense of weird Oz/Gay pride considering I found this out after I realized I was gay. It was really cool to find out that something I had loved since I was born to be a "gay favorite" *laughs a bit*

Being part of the gay stereotype is fine with many fans. One found it funny that he was so "typically gay" in being an Oz fan. Another fan thought that finding out about the Oz–gay connection was great and fitting, since he was also a big fan of Judy Garland, Liza Minnelli, Barbra Streisand, and the history of Hollywood. He realized he was "a dyed-in-the-wool gay guy in progress."

Knowing about the Oz–gay connection rarely *creates* fandom, but it can reinforce it; being gay and loving Oz can feel like a wonderful double dose—or, as one fan said, "a miracle" and "a double whammy of epic proportions." Many fans, especially baby boomers, feel a strong connection to other gay adults of the same age. They now see *The Wizard of Oz* as part of their new cultural heritage and are thrilled to talk about their childhood love of the film or the books. The connection with other gay fans when seeing the movie at a gay venue such as San Francisco's Castro Theatre can be overwhelming. The respondent Mike Duffy described the scene:

> Had I never heard of the film before I saw it with 2,000 other queens at the Castro Theatre, I would have been immediately drawn in . . . just by being swept up in all the love that so freely flowed through that theatre. It was an incredible bonding experience.

Gay love of Oz becomes a delightful secret that straight society does not know about, with many gay fans using the metaphor of belonging to a special club. The knowledge that other gay men are into Oz can also make you see your earlier life differently; your humdrum childhood—or what you saw as a humdrum childhood—now has secret meaning.

Having a gay identity—that is, being a self-aware and self-acknowledged gay man—can affect your relationship to Oz in many ways. As we saw above, out gay fans can appropriate Oz through their personal use of it in a gay context; they can make it their own through creation and performance with a gay spin. Oz itself looks different through gay eyes. Camp, performance, artificiality, and irony may feature in gay perceptions of Oz.[g] The heightened or artificial aspects of the movie are seen by some fans as reflecting their gay ways of perceiving the world. One fan points out the irony of the text in the original ads for the movie: "The Gaiety! The Glory! The Glamour!" The MGM characters of the Cowardly Lion, Glinda, and the Wicked Witch are now seen as delightfully camp, or, as one fan says, "deliciously over-the-top." Another fan notes that coming out allowed him to cross-dress as Glinda on Halloween; others note that the Lion, who was boring to them when they were children, is obviously queer now. Watching the movie with friends after coming out allows fans to appreciate the Lion's humor and gay undertones, especially the dandy-lion reference in his song. But the Lion isn't the only companion seen with new gay eyes; one out and ironic respondent comments that all three of the companions are "intensely queeny." For some fans, the idea of performing an identity is highlighted in Oz, in both the books and the movie.

The MGM visuals also speak to some fans' gay sensibilities. Oz can offer gay men fantasy and fabulousness. For some fans, gayness is everywhere in the movie's Technicolor images, costumes, and sets. Oz's esthetics are linked to a gay way of being, and this connection can begin in boyhood. The respondent Michael Griffo put it this way:

> As a gay man it obviously offers a lot more. It showed me a world of color, glitter, costumes, music, etc. as a young boy that even though I didn't categorize as "gay" or of the "gay world," I grew up to understand it was part of my culture.

---

g   Two of the top three favorite movies of respondents, *All About Eve* and *Auntie Mame*, are camp classics. Some of the favorite books that were mentioned by more than one respondent were camp or gay classics as well, such as Patrick Dennis's *Little Me* (1961) and Armistead Maupin's *Tales of the City* (1978–2014).

Looking at Oz through gay eyes can involve speculation. Fans who appreciate Oz's respect for diversity like to imagine how a gay person might fit into the Land of Oz. In Eric Shanower's short story "Abby," published in *Oz-story* magazine in 1996, a character who went to Oz as a child in a canonical Oz book returns to that magical land as an adult gay man. One Oz lover dates his fandom from when he thought Baum might be gay. He had seen the movie on television as a teenager, but he didn't think any more about Oz until he was in college and had to do a term paper on an author of children's books. He chose Baum because he had a vague memory of Baum as the author of Oz books. He felt drawn to the picture of Baum on the cover of a book, and hoped to discover that Baum was really gay. (See Appendix C, "Was Baum Gay?")

In contrast to the many fans who rejoice in knowing that other gay men are into Oz, there are some fans who claim that when they learned of the Oz–gay connection they felt nothing, they never thought about it, or they just didn't care. When they say the connection is not particularly relevant to them, their reactions seem to me to border on the defensive. I suspect they don't want to be associated with stereotypical gay frivolity, in much the same way that some fans want to distance themselves from the MGM Cowardly Lion's sissyness.

Fans can go further than dismissing the connection as irrelevant; some actually object to the idea that being gay might have anything to do with their own love of Oz. They would like to think that their preferences are a matter of choice, not determined by influences beyond their control. But the idea that solitary readers (or viewers) make their judgments in a vacuum is a myth. Responses to books and films are influenced by factors outside our control in many ways. If many gay men have similar readings of and appreciation for Oz, the most logical explanation is that they share some characteristics that enable them to have the same reaction. This is scary and threatening to many gay men who want to preserve their individuality, their free will. Once you admit the influence of genetics or culture and context, where do you draw the line?[h]

---

[h] If your choices in books and movies are conditioned by social or genetic factors, it's hard not to wonder whether the qualities you are attracted to in certain men are determined by forces outside your control as well. Thinking

The social context of gay fandom also includes reactions of others to the gay fans of the MGM *Wizard*. Some people think being gay and loving Oz fulfills a stereotype. Rufus Wainwright cites wanting to be Dorothy as a reason people knew he was gay at a young age. In the case of another fan, his family and friends, knowing he was gay, simply assumed that he loved Oz. Buying Oz-related presents is one way for family members to acknowledge and support a fan; these folks really "get it." Thoughtful family members can even let young closeted fans know of the gay connection. The parents of one had gay friends and regularly gave an "Oz gay Xmas party."

Families sometimes react negatively to a young boy's fascination with a story whose protagonist is a girl, and a small negative comment from a parent can loom large in the mind of the young fan. Steve Sando remembers feeling hurt when his father said to his grandmother that Dorothy was stupid. Michael Griffo's earliest memory of the MGM movie is tied in to his mother's displeasure when he was eight or nine:

> I remember kneeling on a chair in my kitchen staring at the clock. I was mentally willing it to move faster because *The Wizard of Oz* was starting at 7:00 and I couldn't wait for it to begin. I remember my mother telling me, "The clock's not going to move any faster if you stare at it." I'm not sure if she was annoyed by my behavior or my obvious passion to watch a "gay" classic, but the moment had a profound effect on me and has stayed with me all these years.

Learning about the gay connection from family members can be part of a negative message. One young fan was teased by his brother in a way that led him to believe his love of Oz was a gay thing. Another fan's parents forbade him to watch the movie when he was twelve; it was then, he suspects, that he got the message that there was something gay in Oz.

Some parents go one step further than saying bad things or tolerating

---

politically, you might wonder whether society's values have something to do with why you are only attracted to muscular men, for example.

8.4 Patrick Quigley with *The Wizard of Oz*, 1973

teasing by siblings; a handful attempt behavior modification. This might take the form of withholding the expected Oz present and giving the young boy something more manly. Patrick Quigley's father told him he wasn't allowed to take out any library book with a title containing the word "Oz" or beginning with a girl's name (fig. 8.4).[i] When John Nickolaus was a young teenager, his father ridiculed him, he was sent to a psychiatrist (in part because of his love of Oz), and his Oz collection was taken away. Joe Yranski had a similar experience: when he was ten, his parents, too, gave his Ozzy objects away and prohibited him from watching the film.[j]

Parents' negative reactions can also turn one friend against another. Paul Dana had a childhood friend who shared in his imaginative Oz play. But when the acquaintance's father taunted his son for it, the friend turned against Paul. Paul stood firm, knowing the problem was with his friend, not himself. But some young fans internalize the negative messages they get about their love of Oz and then keep their interest to themselves.

Oz fans can also be mocked by siblings or schoolmates for their

---

i   Oddly, perhaps, Patrick's father didn't have the same reaction to Barbra Streisand. When Patrick talked about her, his father would ask him to play Streisand records.

j   According to Rik Isensee in *Growing Up Gay in a Dysfunctional Family* (New York: Simon & Schuster, 1991), parents' removal of favorite toys is a form of emotional abuse and "psychological terror" (p. 39).

enthusiasm. Barry Kriebel Jr. was teased in kindergarten for bringing in his Mego Dorothy doll to show-and-tell, and Mark Thompson's family members always made fun of him when he cried at the end of the movie. Atticus Gannaway's older brother would deride him mercilessly about his love of Oz, questioning his masculinity; his peers would snicker as well. Jeff Miller's whole family disparaged his obsession. His brother tortured him about an Oz play Jeff wrote, hiding it and pretending to have destroyed it.

What is wrong with Oz? Why is it considered inappropriate for young boys? Conrad Jarrett's brothers thought Oz was only for little kids. A more common objection is that Oz is for girls. Seeing their young boy engrossed in a tale about young girls, adults would hope for or offer more manly alternatives, such as *Johnny Tremain* (1943) or He-Man or BraveStarr action figures. Within the Oz universe, a parent can also try to channel interest away from the female characters and into the male Scarecrow, Tin Woodman, or Lion. The most extreme reaction is gay panic: fearing that their sons will turn gay if they spend too much time in the fantasyland of Oz, parents forbid them to have any contact with Oz at all.

Young boys may be bothered by negative reactions, but this doesn't stop them from loving Oz. Many respondents held on to Oz in trying circumstances. Barry Kriebel Jr. didn't give up when he was taunted for bringing his Oz dolls to kindergarten, since they were his friends; he would brush and braid his Dorothy doll's hair despite the teasing. Young Oz lovers can come up with clever ways to get around adult bans, often finding collaborators who support their interest. Aaron Almanza was teased by his older brother but had cousins who gave him their book collection. When Patrick Quigley wasn't allowed to get an Oz book out of the library to read, he asked his aunt to give him Baum's *Wonderful Wizard* for his First Communion present. The wily Patrick also bought Oz books through the Scholastic Books program at school, which his father didn't know about. In John Nickolaus's case, the psychiatrist his parents sent him to couldn't cure him of his love of Oz. He eventually got his Oz collection back, and later his family embraced and even encouraged his fandom. Taking away Oz objects or denying access to Oz changes a young fan's love as successfully as reparative therapy "cures" homosexuality—which is to say not at all. In both cases, you may be able to change behavior but not deep-seated orientation or feelings.

Of course, what is considered cute in a young child is sometimes less appreciated as the fan grows older, and many parents and friends expect, perhaps not unreasonably, that a fan will outgrow a childhood interest. Parents, friends, and relatives of other fans may offer gentle teasing or accept the weirdness with eye rolling, condescension, or quiet resignation. Attitudes can sometimes change if the fan explains the seriousness of Oz scholarship, but some people may never really understand how important Oz is to the devotee.

When heterosexuals find out about the Oz–gay connection, their reactions run the gamut from acceptance to downright hostility, depending on how they feel about homosexuality in general. People who accept gay people tend to accept gay love of Oz. At the annual Oz festival in Chesterton, Indiana, the gay friends from the Chicago area who participate in the Oz Fantasy Parade have won the costume contest more than once. In 1999 a reporter singled them out as embodying the surreality of the parade:

> And then came the tallest and most bizarre Dorothy of them all—a man wearing 6-inch red glitter platform shoes, a braided wig and a short, short Dorothy dress. Only in this surreal world of Oz—Chesterton style. "Oh look, it's my favorite—Wizard of Oz in drag," said Laura Sullivan of Beverly Shores. "They're the best act in the whole parade." The group of men Sullivan referred to first made their appearance six years ago . . . and have become a whimsical part of the parade ever since. . . . "Exactly what I would expect," said Marc Lehnerer of Lansing, Ill., laughing as the pack marched by.

At least one mother appreciates that gay men are into Oz. Rebecca Rivers and her children dressed up as Oz characters for a 1999 Halloween party in New York's Central Park. "I was Glinda the Good Witch. Only gay guys knew who I was. Everybody else noticed my breasts."

On the flip side, homophobia can manifest itself in response to Oz being found in gay contexts. One member of the board of directors of the Oz Club opposed my speaking on gay men and Oz at the club's centennial celebration in 2000, and actually tried to steer people away from the room in which I was speaking. I have also received some very hostile comments about my research. For the most part, though, non-gay Oz fans have been curious about and receptive to my research. Some already know about the gay love of Oz, usually because they have gay friends who are into Oz, but most are surprised. On November 28, 2000, after my research was posted on the Oz Club's website, I got one online flame from someone calling himself or herself or themselves PurpleFlamingo12:

> hello you are a dork!!! the wizard of oz has nothing to do with dorothys mestral cycle!!! if you were a true oz fan you would knowthat her slippers were origialy silver!!! peoplelike youmakethe wizard of oz seem so unlike what frank baum wated it to be like when he wrote it!!! he wrote this as a childre's book the only reason gay men like the wizard of oz is because of the movie not because of any thing the story is about!

In 2005, my exhibit of Oz items at the DuBois Library at the University of Massachusetts, Amherst, included one case devoted to the gay connection. In the midst of the positive reactions in the exhibit's comment book was one upsetting one: "I could see how the display would appeal to a bunch of Sodomite perverts." After reading about my exhibit at UMass, the director of the public library in nearby Southbridge asked me to set up an Oz exhibit that would include items relating to the Oz–gay connection. He envisioned this as part of the town's first Gay and Lesbian Awareness Month, in June 2006. After the exhibit opened, one member of the town council expressed his homophobia:

> I think it's wrong. . . . I don't think young kids should be subject [sic] to see these things. . . . If it's not cancelled, I hope the people of Southbridge boycott the library for the month of June. What these people do in their homes is their business, but they shouldn't be promoting it in a public building.

And not everyone thinks the Chicago dragsters mentioned above are whimsical. A few days after the 1999 parade, the *Chesterton Tribune* printed a letter to the editor objecting to the drag Dorothy. The writer said she was upset by the short skirt—"this guy is prancing around, in my opinion, making a mockery of the whole event in a dress that barely covers his rear-end"—and wasn't happy with the drag either. She didn't refer to homosexuality explicitly, but it is hard not to see her outrage as having something to do with homophobia.

Homophobic straight individuals also made the connection between Oz and gay men in Draper, Utah, in October 2002. The gay director Jesse Dolce gave four actors colored flags to carry during the curtain call of a production of *The Wizard of Oz* at a local community theater. Dolce's idea was to add color to the mostly black Kansas set where the curtain call took place. Apparently members of the cast or their parents decided to make a stand against the director trying to make Oz gay. Seven members of the cast threatened to quit the show because they thought he was promoting the gay agenda through a "veiled reference" to the gay pride rainbow flag. On opening night, the president of the board of the theater told Dolce to take the flags out. He quit to protest what he perceived as homophobia.

Other fans have not encountered such dramatic homophobia, but they worry about the possibility nonetheless. Joe Yranski was apprehensive when he and his partner went to the Oz Club's Munchkin convention dressed as Munchkins from the books. He was relieved when nobody blinked at seeing men in their thirties wearing blue satin hats with bells on them.

· · ·

Reactions of both gay and straight people to the Oz–gay connection seem to reflect how they feel about gay people and homosexuality in general. The more positive fans themselves feel about being gay and the more aware they are about gay issues in a political sense, the more likely it is that they will embrace the Oz–gay connection. Oz fans who are not gay will also accept the gay love of Oz to the extent that they accept gay people in general. If gay people are OK, then the fact that they love Oz is OK too. If gay people are seen as bad or icky, then their love of Oz is threatening; their association with Oz will sully the homophobic person's treasured childhood memory.

The knowledge that gay men love the MGM film has thus become part of gay subculture. More specific beliefs about the film and about Judy Garland have become part of gay culture as well. It is to those beliefs that I turn in the next chapter.

9

Oz and Judy in Gay Folklore

As gay fans of the 1939 MGM *Wizard of Oz* have shared their love of the film with one another, the movie has assumed a special place in gay culture. The movie is part of gay culture in a broader sense as well, in that beliefs about the movie are held by many gay men, whether they are Oz fans or not.[a] Among the commonly held beliefs about Judy Garland and *The Wizard of Oz* are these:

1. The Oz–gay connection began when the MGM film came out in 1939.
2. Love of Judy Garland is the main reason gay men love the film.
3. The Dorothy in "friend of Dorothy" refers to the character Dorothy Gale as performed by Judy Garland in the MGM version of *The Wizard of Oz*, and has been in use since the 1940s or 50s.
4. Grief in the gay community over Judy Garland's death and

---

a   Gay culture, which is really predominantly white urban gay male culture in the English-speaking countries, is more properly thought of as a subculture, sometimes in opposition to and sometimes not that different from mainstream culture.

funeral contributed to the frustration that erupted as the riots at the Stonewall Inn in 1969, which gave birth to the modern gay liberation movement.

5. The rainbow was chosen as a symbol of gay pride in part because of the song "Over the Rainbow."

Examining the evidence for these beliefs—which may or may not be true—yields insights into the relationship between Judy Garland, the MGM *Wizard*, and gay culture. It is important to keep in mind, though, that while it is the 1939 Technicolor masterpiece that is visible in gay culture, some gay men feel more drawn to other versions of the Oz story.[b]

BELIEF #1—THE TIMING

When did the Oz–gay connection begin? Some writers assert that it arose when the movie appeared, in 1939. But if it is aspects of Oz itself and not the MGM movie per se that gay men are responding to, gay men should have had deep and lasting connections to the Oz books and other versions of the story before that time.

There is some anecdotal evidence that the Oz books did appeal to gay boys before the movie was made. My father, Martin Michel, was born in 1919. He and his siblings had many Oz books as children, but Martin, the gay one, was the custodian of them all and became the lifelong Oz fan. Among my respondents, a handful of older gay men became fans upon first viewing the movie in 1939 and 1940. One saw the movie in 1939, when he was seven, but his fandom began when he read the books

---

b As I mentioned in Chapter 1, the role Oz has played in the gay community has probably changed over time; see Ryan Bruce Bunch, "'Over the Rainbow': Difference, Utopia, and *The Wizard of Oz* in Queer Musical Experience" (master's thesis, University of Maryland at College Park, 2001), p. 3. There are also many problems with generalizing across time about Judy Garland fandom. See, for example, Richard Dyer, "Judy Garland and Gay Men," chap. 3 in *Heavenly Bodies: Film Stars and Society* (New York: St. Martin's Press, 1986), and Frank Browning, *A Queer Geography* (New York: Crown, 1996), p. 18.

in 1941. Other pre-boomer fans became enamored of the movie or the books when they were young boys in the late 1940s or early 1950s. Older respondents estimate, variously, that they learned about the gay–MGM movie connection in 1954, 1961, 1965, 1967, and 1970.

Documented references to and uses of Oz in a gay context would demonstrate a shared knowledge that *The Wizard of Oz* was important to gay men. This kind of evidence for a cultural connection seems to appear in the early 1970s, when gay media began to flourish in the wake of the 1969 Stonewall Riots. In 1972, for example, the first play of the Hot Peaches, a New York gay drag theater company, was *The Wonderful Wizard of U.S.*, "a hallucinatory musical send up of the Baum/Fleming classic." In 1978, the Houston company Ozzo Unlimited marketed "Oz" poppers to gay men (see fig. 1.8).[c] By the 1980s, there were explicit mentions of the Oz–gay connection. Comparing Oz to Middle Earth, Ethan Mordden wrote in 1984 that "Oz[,] as a cult, counts an unusually high gay component, while Tolkien seems to have no appeal to the gay readership. The only gays I know who have read Tolkien did so because they ran out of Oz." Michael Bronski wrote about the film in 1986, noting that Holly Near considered "Over the Rainbow" the "gay national anthem." Judy Grahn noted the following year what a "gay story" the film was. And as I mentioned in Chapter 1, a gay character in the 1988 film *Love Bites* says he's seen *The Wizard of Oz* sixty-two times.

It could be that many gay adults who saw the MGM movie in 1939 loved it and cherished it, but we have no evidence that this love was shared in a cultural sense. In contrast, the generation of boys who saw the movie on TV in the 1950s became adults in the post-Stonewall era. Gay culture was no longer underground in the 1970s, and these Oz fans had access to an open gay press. By the 1980s and 1990s we see allusions to Oz in their writing and guides to gay movies listing *The Wizard of Oz*. Men of this post-Stonewall generation were also creating hundreds of gay-identified organizations and businesses, some of which gave a nod to Oz in their names.

---

c   See Appendix E, "Early Allusions to Oz in Gay Contexts," for a longer list.

BELIEF #2—JUDY

After hearing about my research into Oz's appeal for gay men, many people, both gay and straight, have replied dismissively, "It's the cult of Judy." The logic is that Judy Garland starred in the movie and gay men love Judy, and thus the movie is a gay favorite because of her performance. Judy Garland's role as Dorothy Gale is certainly an unforgettable aspect of the MGM movie, and her performance is a perfectly good reason for liking the movie. But as I showed in Chapter 2, Judy Garland is not the *cause* of gay love of Oz.

BELIEF #3—"FRIEND OF DOROTHY"

What about the expression "friend of Dorothy," gay slang for a gay man? Most people think the Dorothy in question is the character Dorothy Gale in the MGM movie, and reference works for slang expressions either cite the movie exclusively or mention it as the most likely source.[d] Note that the phrase does not refer to Judy Garland herself ("friend of Judy") but rather—or so the theory goes—to the character she played in the MGM movie. Since the three companions who were her friends in the movie were all non-macho males, they could collectively stand for gay men. Further, "friend of Dorothy" is a coded expression, the meaning of which is known only by those familiar with the gay subculture. Thus the Garland explanation of "friend of Dorothy" represents the nexus of gay male culture, the cult of Judy, and the fact that the MGM movie is a gay favorite.

Garland probably became a gay icon during the 1950s, more than a decade after she starred in the MGM film. After being fired by MGM, Garland tried to kill herself in 1950. And because she couldn't work in

---

d   Even in their "Gay and Lesbian Music" article in the *New Grove Dictionary of Music and Musicians* (London: Macmillan, 2001), Philip Brett and Elizabeth Wood say, "In the cult of the queer, Judy Garland is a saint, heaven is 'Somewhere over the rainbow' (from *The Wizard of Oz*) and 'friend of Dorothy' the secret mantra of its votaries." See Appendix F, "The Origin of 'Friend of Dorothy,'" for a more complete list of sources that include, and sources that do not include, the expression.

movies, she began to give "dazzling" concerts. This comeback was part of her appeal. Gay men were among the most ardent and vociferous members of the audiences at Judy's concerts. Seeing one another in these public spaces helped them feel part of a community.

The second most often mentioned candidate for the Dorothy in question is Dorothy Parker. She certainly has her gay bona fides. Many gay men admired her bitchy and clever remarks and writing. She married the bisexual Alan Campbell twice and lived with him a third time, and she had warm relationships with gay men such as Alexander Woollcott, George Oppenheimer, and Clement Brace. She also liked Truman Capote much more than the macho Norman Mailer, appreciated Capote's writing as well as that of E. M. Forster, and visited Christopher Isherwood and Don Bachardy.

There are two eras when Parker spent a lot of time with gay men: circa 1933 in New York City and circa 1961 in Los Angeles. Gay men would have been aware of Parker's genius in 1933 New York, when she was publishing poems and short stories and was a member of the Algonquin Round Table. While she might have been less famous in 1961, she still had plenty of gay admirers in West Hollywood. Parker had a love/hate relationship with gay men: she sometimes put them down in her writing and behind their backs. Given the times, however, her mixed feelings are not entirely surprising. And if gay men idolized Parker in spite of her ambivalence toward them, it wouldn't be the first time that gay men fed the hand that bit them.

Another minority candidate for the original Dorothy is Dorothy King, a socialite in early twentieth-century London. According to one source, the gay men who congregated at her soirees eventually used the expression "friend of Dorothy" as a way to identify each other. Dorothy Dean—another possibility—was a well-connected woman who preferred the company of gay men when she was a student in Cambridge, Massachusetts, in the 1950s and in the New York City literary and art world from 1962 to 1980. She was profiled in a *New Yorker* article, "Downtown Chronicles: Friends of Dorothy," and the title of the article alone seems to have given rise to the theory that Dean is the Dorothy in question. Of course it may be that the expression does not refer to any of these

Dorothys—Gale, Parker, King, or Dean—or, in fact, to anyone in particular.[e]

Pinning down when the expression first appeared might help settle the question. Some people claim that it was used by soldiers in World War II. The writers Ben Brantley, Michael Bronski, and Randy Shilts all assert without evidence that "friend of Dorothy" was used in the 1940s, 50s, or 60s. After having looked at scores of reference sources and been in touch with gay historians, linguists, and folklorists in an attempt to track down the origin of the expression and the dates when it was used, I doubt that it is so old. Here's why.

"Friend of Dorothy" does not appear in the many sources in which one would expect to find it.[f] None of the eleven lists of gay slang that were published between 1941 and 1988 list the term. Neither does it appear in the seven empirical research studies published between 1965 and 1986 that have documented gay slang. It is not until 2002 that a serious, empirically based collection of gay slang includes the expression. The phrase also does not appear in the six academic discussions of gay codes and coded language published from 1976 to 2006. Later sources do cite the phrase, however. Several general dictionaries, slang dictionaries, gay slang dictionaries, and gay guides from the 1990s onward list the expression,[g] usually citing the MGM *Wizard* as the origin. The

---

e   Expressions can be invented and then stick if the name "sounds right." The proverbial expression "drunk as Cooter Brown," for instance, might not have a referent (Arnold Zwicky, personal communication).

f   There is documentation from 1972 of another gay slang expression related to Oz. An entry in Bruce Rodgers, *The Queens' Vernacular: A Gay Lexicon* (New York: Straight Arrow Books, 1972), reads: "DOROTHY AND TOTO. 1. gay boy and his dog. 2. dominating effeminate homosexual man with his paid-for escort. 3. extended to any male couple whose effeminate partner is in command. 'When's Dorothy and Toto getting here with the chest of drawers?'" (p. 66). Although the expression seems not to have been widely used—it doesn't appear in any other slang dictionary—it might have given rise to "friend of Dorothy."

g   The earliest date given by the *Oxford English Dictionary*, 1984, is problematic. The *OED Online* cites p. 82 of a 1985 edition of *The Slanguage of Sex* by Brigid McConville and John Shearlaw, saying that this source cites an actual

expression also appears often in the gay press and popular culture beginning in the 1990s.[h]

There does not seem to be any evidence that "friend of Dorothy" was used in the 1950s and 1960s. One would think that if use of the expression was part of the subculture generally, it would be noted in at least one of the many published lists of gay slang, research studies on gay slang, or discussions of gay codes and language. Of course, the fact that something is not listed doesn't prove that the term was not in use at the time. And slang is, by nature, spoken rather than written. But the lack of evidence is certainly startling.

But could this particular piece of gay slang be receding into the distance because it is a *secret* code? For the half-dozen dictionaries and reference works that list the expression, dozens and dozens do not. It is conceivable that as a secret expression it was withheld from researchers when thousands of other terms were offered or put into print. But given the embarrassing and explicit nature of other terms collected by researchers in their fieldwork, deliberate withholding seems unlikely. It could be that "friend of Dorothy" was used as early as the 1950s and 60s, but only by a few people, and that it spread into more general gay usage in the 70s. Or it might not have been coined until the mid- or late 70s.

The fact that printed evidence goes only as far back as 1984 might help in deciding between the origins. Dorothy King flourished around the turn of the century. Dorothy Parker was in her heyday in the 1930s

---

usage from 1984. None of the bibliographic databases I searched contained any trace of a 1985 edition of *The Slanguage of Sex*. There is a 1984 edition by McConville and Shearlaw, with "FRIEND" appearing on p. 83, but it does not list "friend of Dorothy." The *OED* also cites "Dorothy and Toto" from the 1972 *Queens' Vernacular*, and a Feb. 12, 1988, issue of *Capital Gay*.

h   For example, two recent gay films are titled *A Friend of Dorothy* and offer the Judy theory of origin. One of them, a short film written and directed by Raoul O'Connell (1994), tells the story of Winston, an NYU student, who loves Barbra Streisand but doesn't care for Judy Garland. Winston meets a Judy fan in a record store who says to him, "You are a friend of Dorothy, aren't you? You know? Judy Garland? *The Wizard of Oz*?" And in the mainstream 1995 film *Clueless*, one character explains another is gay by calling him, among other things, "a friend of Dorothy."

and 40s. Judy played Dorothy Gale in 1939; she probably became a gay icon in the 50s, and her iconic status was strong in the 60s, 70s, and 80s. Dorothy Dean had her salons in the 70s. If references are found to the phrase before 1939, that would eliminate the Judy-as-Dorothy explanation. In fact, for the phrase to be used by GIs during the time of American involvement in World War II (1941–45) and refer to Judy as Dorothy, the movie would have had to appeal not just to individual gay males but to those who had enough of a connection to gay culture to know that the movie was something special to gay men *collectively*. It seems unlikely that a shared knowledge of the movie's appeal could have existed just a few years after the movie's release in 1939. If the phrase wasn't used until the 50s, the Judy derivation would make more sense, because Judy Garland had become an adored entertainer for many gay men by that time.

Most of the people I've talked to, and the editors of the slang dictionaries that list it, assume that the expression refers to Dorothy Gale as played by Judy Garland in the MGM *Wizard of Oz*. It's amazing that so many people have converged on that explanation without hard evidence. But the Oz resonance is a strong one; we *want* the Judy explanation to fit.

BELIEF #4—JUDY'S FUNERAL AND STONEWALL

Judy Garland's funeral took place in Manhattan on June 27, 1969. That night saw the beginning of the Stonewall Riots, violent confrontations between police and patrons of the Stonewall Inn, a gay bar in New York's Greenwich Village. Many associate Garland's funeral with the riots. At anniversaries of Stonewall—which set in motion the modern era of gay liberation—Judy and even Oz are often evoked. In 1994, on the twenty-fifth anniversary of the riots, two plays about Judy and Stonewall were produced in New York City.[i] At the thirtieth anniversary, a radio interviewer made the connection to both Judy and Oz:

---

i   The two plays were *Stonewall: Night Variations*, by Tina Landau, and *Judy at the Stonewall Inn*, by Thomas O'Neil. See Ben Brantley, "Why Oz Is a State of Mind in Gay Life and Drag Shows," *New York Times*, June 28, 1994, pp. B1, B5; reprinted in *The Gay Rights Movement: The New York Times 20th Century in Review*, ed. Vincent J. Samar (Chicago: Fitzroy Dearborn, 2001).

The woman and the movie are loved by millions, but they have special resonance in the gay community. This being Gay Pride week and the 30th anniversary of Judy Garland's death, we thought we'd take a little trip down the yellow brick road to find out why *The Wizard of Oz* and Garland are so important to gay culture.

Others go beyond simply associating the funeral with the riots: they believe that gay men's distress over Judy's death contributed to their reaching a breaking point on that particular night. A co-founder of the Stonewall Veterans' Association said on camera in 1999, "I was at the Riots. Judy had a part of it. She was in our minds, she was in our hearts, she was in our souls." But historians of the riots discount the idea that Garland's funeral played a causative role, for two reasons.[j] First, the main fighters were street youths who listened to rock and soul, not Garland. Second, contemporary accounts do not mention Garland's death or funeral as a cause.[k]

Garland's death can be also seen as symbolic of the change between the old order and the new. The gay film expert Vito Russo, who was a big Garland fan, had been to the funeral that day and the bar that night. He later wrote that Garland's death didn't cause the riots, but he made the argument for a symbolic connection. The coincidence of the death of Judy Garland with the Stonewall Riots has developed into a myth of the gay subculture. The story that Judy's funeral contributed to the riots is concrete and colorful and somehow empowering. It is such a nice story, it has to be true.

---

[j] Many activists think citing Judy as a cause of the riots trivializes gay oppression. See, for example, Martin Duberman as quoted in Christopher Guly, "The Judy Connection," *The Advocate*, June 28, 1994, p. 49.

[k] But even those who don't think Judy Garland's funeral caused the patrons of the Stonewall Inn to fight back on that particular night often feel the need to say so. Mentioning Judy just adds to the legend. See Stephen Maddison, "Fags, Female Icons and Stonewall," in *Fags, Hags and Queer Sisters: Gender Dissent and Heterosocial Bends in Gay Culture* (New York: St. Martin's/ Scholarly Press, 2000).

9.1 Rainbow flag in Twin Cities Gay Pride Parade, 2013 (photo by Tony Webster)

BELIEF #5—THE RAINBOW FLAG

Judy Garland's performance of "Over the Rainbow" in the MGM *Wizard of Oz* was so powerful that fans demanded she sing it in concerts, and it became her signature piece. The song, by Harold Arlen and E. Y. Harburg, is considered a gay anthem or theme song. It is sung often by gay choruses, and has inspired at least one master's thesis in musicology, "'Over the Rainbow': Difference, Utopia, and *The Wizard Of Oz* in Queer Musical Experience."

"Over the Rainbow" is perhaps the best-known expression of longing to leave a hostile environment. The idea of leaving home is especially poignant for gay boys and men, and this song is preeminent among "hometown" songs that appeal to gay men. In fact, its unaffected longing for a utopian haven may have contributed to Garland's devoted gay male following.

In 1978 Gilbert Baker designed the rainbow flag to make the San Francisco gay pride parade more colorful. The set of vibrant stripes (fig. 9.1) has since become a symbol of the gay community, gay pride, and, to some, gay consumerism, and many people associate the flag with

"Over the Rainbow." In an ice-skating competition in 1998 Rudy Galindo draped himself with a rainbow-colored scarf and skated to Melissa Manchester's rendition of the song. When the competition was televised, the announcer explained the gay meaning of the rainbow flag. When asked how they feel about the rainbow flag as a symbol of gay pride, gay people sometimes mention the Oz connection, and many assume that Baker was thinking of "Over the Rainbow" when he created the flag.[1] In fact, Baker did not have the song in mind; he was much more into "psychedelic music" than he was into Judy Garland. But in just the way that the Stonewall Riots bring to mind Judy Garland's funeral, the gay rainbow flag conjures up Oz.[m]

The Need for Gay Myths, Legends, and Folklore

What is going on with these widespread beliefs about Judy Garland and the MGM *Wizard of Oz*? What needs could they fulfill? Gay culture has evolved in part because gay people are oppressed and marginalized, and have developed their own subculture in opposition to mainstream culture. Culture provides individuals with a sense of history and identity, answering questions such as "Who am I?" and "Where do I come from?"—the same questions that myths answer, as we saw in Chapter 7. In traditional societies, culture is passed along from adult to child, within the family and in other group settings. In modern society, print and other communication media transmit cultural knowledge as well. Since gay children are rarely brought up by gay parents, gay culture operates

---

[1] In 2008 the textile artist and teacher Liz Collins created an art installation project, *Knitting Nation*, in which teams of knitters produced a huge rainbow flag for Rhode Island Pride. Collins also posted a poll on various websites from around the world asking people what the rainbow flag meant to them. Some of her respondents cited the entire lyrics to the song. Others mentioned Dorothy or "you're little dog, too [sic]." (Personal correspondence.) See also Brian Jewell, "She Breaks [sic] for Rainbows: Unfurling the Pride Flag at R.I. Pride," *Bay Windows*, June 19, 2008, pp. 1 + 28IbF, http://www.lizcollins.com/kn.html, http://www.youtube.com/watch?v=v5V3ee7FTNs.

[m] One respondent points out that the rainbow has become the gay emblem when discussing Oz's meaning for gay males.

outside the family, with groups of friends operating as surrogate families, passing along gay cultural practices, traditions, and beliefs. Gay media have also been available to post-Stonewall generations. Such media are especially useful for gay men not living in urban centers. Individual fandom, love of Oz by gay boys and men, is not itself passed along. But beliefs about *The Wizard of Oz* are handed down by both individuals and gay media.

Folklore, which may or may not be "true," was traditionally passed along without being written down, through stories and songs and performances. Modern urban folklore is often passed along and given credence by appearing in print as well. Folklore and the folk process develop, express, and maintain bonds that help forge a group's identity. Because we have been systematically oppressed, folklore and oral communication have played a particularly central role in gay communities.

Why do so many people think the Dorothy in "friend of Dorothy" is Dorothy Gale, as portrayed by Judy? Or that the rainbow flag was created at least in part because of the song "Over the Rainbow"? Or that the MGM movie was a gay favorite back in the 1940s or 50s? Or that Judy Garland's funeral caused the Stonewall Riots? These notions are not legends or myths in the technical sense, because they aren't full-fledged stories with narrative content and details. They might more accurately be called folkloric beliefs. That there is this cluster of folkloric beliefs about Judy Garland and the MGM *Wizard* is not entirely surprising; the movie has generated a good deal of folklore—consider the urban legend that there is a hanging Munchkin in an early scene in the movie. But within gay culture, the *Wizard*-related folklore focuses on Judy Garland (chart 9.1).

The belief that the Stonewall Riots were caused by gay grief over Judy Garland's death is not an Oz issue per se, of course. But I include it here because Judy is linked with gay history, and her status in gay mythology is related to her role in the MGM film. It is important to remember that other movies Judy was in have not risen to the status of gay favorites. So it is her role in the MGM movie that matters: Judy becomes Judy-as-Dorothy in the minds of gay men. While Judy isn't explicitly part of the idea that "Over the Rainbow" inspired the rainbow flag, she is involved indirectly. Judy sang the song in the movie, it became her signature tune,

FACT	FOLKLORIC BELIEF
Judy starred in the MGM film.	The MGM film has been a gay favorite since 1939.
Judy played Dorothy in the MGM film.	Judy is the Dorothy in "friend of Dorothy."
The Stonewall Riots began hours after Judy's funeral was held.	Judy's funeral was the cause of the Stonewall Riots.
Judy sang "Over the Rainbow" in the MGM film.	"Over the Rainbow" inspired the rainbow flag in 1978.

Chart 9.1 Folkloric beliefs about Judy Garland and the MGM *Wizard of Oz*

and she became a gay icon. Similarly, the idea that the movie was a gay favorite right from the beginning could be tied to Judy in that she was the star of the movie and gave it its emotional power, and people often cite Judy as the reason that the movie is a gay favorite in the first place. It seems likely that Judy is related to these two folkloric beliefs in a subconscious way, in terms of their connotations and associations.

How do folkloric beliefs develop? As with other cultural practices, it's hard to pinpoint the exact route. The general picture is that an individual comes up with a story, an idea, or a new way of doing something, and then either it takes or it doesn't. Like new words in the language, most potential bits of culture are not successfully adopted by a large percentage of the population; many never go beyond a small group. But other bits of oral communication are taken up by more and more people and make it to the "tipping point." A new belief of that kind survives and spreads because it strikes a chord in those who tell it and those who hear it; it fills some cultural need. Once a piece of folklore is institutionalized within the culture at large, it takes on a different status. It becomes part of what gets passed along by mentors in a self-conscious way. It might also become visible in print and other media in a way that is outside traditional folk processes. When these aspects of gay culture are passed down from generation to generation and also travel geographically, they become part of the gay cultural heritage.[n]

As we saw in Chapter 7, Oz can function as a myth in the lives of individual fans. The five folkloric beliefs have a similar function at the subcultural level. The five beliefs are about gay culture and history and are held by Oz fans and non-fans alike. They help to provide gay people with a sense of identity and history. In its depiction of two gay men kissing, Michael Breyette's 2010 painting *Once in a Lullaby* speaks to our nostalgic longing for a shared history. The painting is a fantasy—it is unlikely that two men would have engaged in such an open display of affection in 1939—but the emotions it conveys are very real (fig. 9.2).[o]

Gay men feel the need to be connected with something larger than themselves. Gay boys who grow up isolated, thinking they are the only ones, want to feel that they belong. Because we feel different from family members or are even rejected by them, our families often don't provide this sense of belonging. Folklore can give us a feeling of belonging and being part of something bigger than ourselves. One function of the gay subculture is to offer knowledge of the world in general and the group in particular; another function is to shape identity. Having these shared folkloric beliefs about Oz and gay history thus helps us feel we are part of something larger than ourselves and reinforces our gay identities.

n   Screenings and sing-alongs of *The Wizard of Oz* by gay groups are not only evidence of the Oz–gay connection but also a nice example of how the special status of the movie is maintained and transmitted (passed along). This transmission occurs in a physical and public way that could never have happened in the pre-Stonewall era. See Monica Lawton and Leonard Norman Primiano, "Gender and Folklore," in *American Folklore: An Encyclopedia*, ed. Jan Brunvand (New York: Garland, 1996).

o   On the webpage for this painting (https://www.breyette.com/prints/once-in-a-lullaby), the artist elaborates on its meaning: "As they left the theater they felt moved not only by the spectacle and songs, but also by the underlying theme of the film. Throwing caution to the wind they kissed on the street in public. Something very taboo for 1939. They closed their eyes and wished, perhaps one day they would not have to hide their lives in the shadows, but simply live and love freely in a land that they heard of once in a lullaby."

9.2 *Once in a Lullaby* by Michael Breyette, 2010 (www.breyette.com; used with permission)

Beliefs about Judy Garland and *The Wizard of Oz* appeal to members of the gay subculture as myths or legends of gay history. Because we don't have evidence of early gay fandom of the movie, the point where myth becomes history is unclear. It could be that the idea of early fandom was created as a myth about our past to give us a shared history.[p] The actual historical roots of these associations may be beside the point. For many gay folks, Oz is connected to these aspects of gay culture and history. The three other beliefs—the beliefs about "friend of Dorothy," Judy Garland's funeral and Stonewall, and the rainbow flag—reinforce each other and probably arise from a similar need for a known and explainable history.

---

p   Individuals experiencing a historical event such as the Stonewall Riots don't think of it as mythic at the time. It is only after, when interpreted by a community or culture, that it gains mythic dimensions. See Robert Brockway, *Myth from the Ice Age to Mickey Mouse* (Albany: State University of New York Press, 1993), p. 81.

Many traditional myths are origin stories—tales of how something came to be. Three of the five folkloric beliefs are, in effect, origin stories: Garland's funeral caused the Stonewall Riots;^q Garland's role as Dorothy Gale is the origin of the expression "friend of Dorothy"; the song "Over the Rainbow" is the inspiration for the gay pride rainbow flag. While they are not full narratives, these beliefs are very short stories about the origins of important aspects of gay culture. In addition to giving us a sense of history in general and identity and belonging, these beliefs ground us by explaining aspects of our culture.

History, origins and identity: mythic Oz is the perfect peg to hang all these needs on. According to these folkloric claims, *The Wizard of Oz* explains a lot in gay history. The origins of "friend of Dorothy," the rainbow flag, and the Stonewall Riots are all related to the gay appeal of Oz. It is pleasing to have one explanation for diverse phenomena, and even those gay men who are not fans of Oz find comfort in gay love of Oz.

. . .

q The idea that the Stonewall Riots were the beginning of the gay movement is itself a folkloric belief. As Robert Hopcke points out, it can be one of our creation stories ("Gay Relationship as a Vehicle for Individuation," in *Mirrors of the Self: Archetypal Images That Shape Your Life*, ed. Christine Downing [Los Angeles: Tarcher, 1991]). Of course, there were important public gay activities on the West Coast before 1969. What was different—the reason one might see Stonewall as the beginning of something new—was the sudden rise of more radical groups in New York and elsewhere soon after the riots; see John D'Emilio, *Sexual Politics, Sexual Communities: The Making of a Homosexual Minority in the United States, 1940–1970* (Chicago: University of Chicago Press, 1983). Furthermore, as more than one writer has noted, pre-Stonewall gay life wasn't uniformly closeted and repressed; see George Chauncey, *Gay New York* (New York: Basic Books, 1994) and John Loughery, *The Other Side of Silence: Men's Lives and Gay Identities* (New York: Holt, 1998). Nevertheless, the myth persists that the riots in Greenwich Village opened gay windows to light and openness and happiness. The idea that "friend of Dorothy" was a common code word in the 1940s and 50s fits into this picture of the closet before Stonewall.

Gay love of Oz is more than the MGM movie, but it is folkloric beliefs about Judy Garland and the MGM movie that persist despite any evidence of their objective truth. They feel right because they give gay people a more satisfying sense of their own history. The MGM film has thus become part of gay folklore and gay history. What status will Oz have in the minds and hearts of individual gay men and boys, and in gay culture in general, in the future? Will stories set in Oz be replaced in the hearts of gay boys and men by another work or set of works? The next chapter explores these questions.

10

The Oz–Gay Connection Now and in the Future

There is abundant evidence that the Oz–gay connection is alive and well, both with individual gay adults and at the level of the gay subculture. There are nods to gay Oz fans in Andrew Lloyd Webber's 2011 stage version of the MGM film; the Lion, who is more obviously gay this time around, actually says, "I'm proud to be a friend of Dorothy!" One of the teams of gay men in the 2013 Bay to Breakers race in San Francisco wore Oz costumes, and many of the team members were young. The 2013 convention of the International Association of Gay and Lesbian Country Western Dance Clubs, held in Seattle, was called the Emerald City Hoedown.[a] The organizers made the connection between Seattle's nickname and Oz by using yellow bricks as the path to a Seattle looking a lot like the Emerald City (fig. 10.1). When the U.S. Supreme Court overturned the anti-gay Defense of Marriage Act (DOMA) in 2014, the online business Queer Getting Married created a graphic of the Wicked Witch as DOMA, saying "Ding-Dong Da DOMA's Dead" (fig. 10.2).

The travel section of the Sunday *New York Times* of June 1, 2014, featured four articles on LGBT travel with two Oz references; one was a cartoon with the caption "I have a feeling we're not in San Francisco

---

a   The association included a "Friend of Dorothy" sponsorship option when registering.

10.1 Poster for Emerald City Hoedown, 2013 (designed by Jim Drew; used by permission of the Rain Country Dance Association)
10.2 Defense of Marriage Act graphic, 2013 (illustration by Mike Curato)

anymore . . ." The theme of a 2014 gay Academy Awards event to raise funds for an AIDS organization in San Francisco was "Return to the Emerald City." In Melbourne, Australia, a sculpture was installed in 2014 to recognize the gay and lesbian community; it consisted of a man on a yellow brick road shedding a Cowardly Lion skin. Frameline39, the 2015 San Francisco International LGBTQ Film Festival, was called "There's No Place Like Here," and its trailer was an Oz parody. "Wizards of Drag," the sixth episode of the eighth season of *RuPaul's Drag Race*, which aired on April 11, 2016, saw the contestants give members of the TV show *Little Women: LA* "makeovers in the style of *The Wizard of Oz*."

Gregory Maguire's novel *Wicked: The Life and Times of the Wicked Witch of the West* has had an enduring connection to the gay community since its publication in 1995.[b] *Wicked* the novel, which appeared on

---

b   Although Maguire is openly gay, he didn't set out to write a story that would appeal especially to gay men. In fact, he didn't even know that *The Wizard of Oz* was a gay favorite until his book tour for *Wicked*. See Peter Galvin, "A Wizard with Words," *The Advocate* (Oct. 17, 1995), pp. 56–59.

bestseller lists after the musical version opened in 2003, is venerated by gay bookstores.[c] The heroine, Elphaba, born with green skin, is ostracized for her very recognizable difference. She stands up for the rights of a downtrodden minority, animals who can talk, and is vilified for being against the established order of the Wizard. In the best-selling sequel that appeared in 2005, *Son of a Witch*, Elphaba's son, Liir, has an affair with another man;[d] the gay press, gay bookstores, and gay book clubs had a field day with that. *Wicked* the musical, a blockbuster, opened on Broadway in 2003.[e] While the book includes a heterosexual romance between Elphaba and her male lover, Fiyero, the musical is much more about the relationship between Glinda and Elphaba, and as such it can be considered a queer love story.

Wicked the musical has been taken up with fervor by some gay men. Both its Broadway opening and its subsequent tours have been featured prominently in the gay press.[f] It may be Elphaba's outsider status, stemming from her green skin, that makes her a new gay icon. "Green is so the new gay," says one gay audience member. "Defying Gravity" was the second most popular song to sing along with videos at the gay bar Splash in New York City in 2008. At a retreat for gay men in September 2005,

---

c In 2007 a gay gift shop in Manhattan, Rainbows and Triangles, featured *Wicked* in its Halloween window display, and the following year it also carried *Son of a Witch*, a coffee-table book about the musical entitled *Wicked: The Grimmerie* (2005), and Robert Sabuda's pop-up *Wonderful Wizard of Oz* (2000). Boston's LGBT bookstore, Calamus, carried all four of Gregory Maguire's Wicked Years books.

d The Wicked Years series continued with *A Lion Among Men* in 2008 and *Out of Oz* in 2011.

e Many touring companies set box-office records around the country with *Wicked* in 2009, and the musical is still making money on Broadway in 2017.

f One could argue that this press coverage may be just a matter of "Gay men love musicals" and "Gay men love dueling divas"—think of Jerry Herman's "Bosom Buddies," sung by Angela Lansbury and Bea Arthur in the original *Mame* (1966), or the uber-bitchy cast of *The Women* (1939). But when it comes to gay interest in *Wicked*, there is more going on.

two men wore *Wicked* souvenir apparel, a hat and a T-shirt.[g] In 2007 the gay brother on the television show *Brothers and Sisters* was depicted as a big fan of the musical *Wicked*. Idina Menzel, who created the role of Elphaba on Broadway, has also been embraced by gay fans,[h] and the original Glinda, Kristin Chenoweth, appeared in 2005 at the New York City LGBT Community Center to talk in a series called "Broadway Divas as Gay Icons."

One of the best arguments that Oz will endure in gay hearts is that it is not just aging baby boomers who revere it; Oz resonates with a much younger generation as well.[i] The theme of the 2005 True Colors LGBT youth conference was "Over the Rainbow and Out of the Box: Deconstructing Labels." The youth pride celebration in Boston chose *The Wizard of Oz* as its theme in 2006. In 2007 the gay student group at the University of Connecticut, the Rainbow Center, created an award-winning Oz-themed banner as its entry in a homecoming competition (fig. 10.3). The Boston Alliance of Gay, Lesbian, Bisexual, and Transgender Youth advertised its 27th Anniversary Celebration and Alumni/ae Reunion in 2007 with two pairs of footwear: black stomping lace-up boots and ruby slippers. The LGBTQ group for students and allies at Northwestern Connecticut Community College picked Oz as the theme for their exhibit for National Gay and Lesbian History Month, October 2009. In 2016, the thirty-one-year-old gay performance artist Todrick Hall toured with a live show, *Straight Outta Oz*, based on his YouTube album of the same name.

---

g   The hat said, "*Wicked*, defy gravity," a reference to the Witch's big song, and the T-shirt was from the athletic department of Shiz University, the (fictional) school that is the setting for much of *Wicked*'s first act.

h   Menzel, a white woman whose first marriage was to an African American man, also played a lesbian in *Rent* (1996).

i   It should be mentioned, though, that Oz fandom in general may be falling off with the younger generation: the International Wizard of Oz Club has fewer young members than it used to. This trend might be due to a general falling-off in clubs and social organizations in the online age, as people become more involved in virtual communities, or to a lessening of Oz fandom specifically.

10.3 UConn's homecoming float banner, 2007 (designed by Jesse Kohut and Braden Jockmyhn and used with permission)
10.4 Cover of Brian Andersen's *Friend of Dorothy*, issue no. 1, 2010 (art by Neftali Centeno; used by permission of Brian Andersen)

Oz allusions continue to appear in gay literature for teens and in works by young writers. *The Tragedy of Miss Geneva Flowers* (2005), by the young author Joe Babcock, contains a handful of allusions to Oz. A gay teen narrates Paul Ruditis's *The Four Dorothys* (2007), about a high school production of *The Wizard of Oz*. In 2010 Brian Andersen created a comic called *Friend of Dorothy*, about a gay boy who is visited by Gorlinda, a hunky male good witch, who dubs him "Oz's Friend of Dorothy" (fig. 10.4). YouTube contains dozens of homemade films mentioning or exploiting the Oz–gay connection. In 2009 the thirty-one-year-old editors of the "Breeder's Digest" blog created a code to explain colored handkerchiefs worn in your back pocket. It includes the entry, "BLUE GINGHAM: left: likes Judy Garland; right: is Judy Garland."

Pop singers from a younger generation have also referred to Oz in their performances and songs. Rufus Wainwright, as I mentioned earlier, has talked about dressing up as both Dorothy and the Wicked Witch when he was little. Three of the five members of the pop band Scissor Sisters are young gay men. Their 2004 song "Return to Oz" refers to different characters and creatures from the Oz books. The gay duo What Time Is It, Mr. Fox? released an EP in 2005 titled *Songs for the Tin Man*. The title tune is about a gay man going to the bars and not finding love. And several young gay bloggers are fans of the MGM movie, the original Oz book, *Wicked*, or some combination of these.

There are, however, some signs that gay attitudes toward Oz are changing a bit. Some gay men poke fun at aspects of Oz, replacing reverence with ridicule.[j] Oz sing-alongs are a good example of reverence and ridicule rolled into one. At both official "mainstream" Oz events and those in gay venues, gay men show up in costume, along with the kids, and irreverently throw things at the screen while still being moved by the story. Several commercial products poke fun at Oz. There are blatantly sexual greeting cards, a rug and a postcard featuring Betty Boop on the Yellow Brick Road, and "Hate you, hate Kansas" T-shirts. While these items have nothing explicitly gay on them, they are often found in gay gift shops. The campy and disrespectful nature of these items may suggest we're in a new era; we can make fun of Oz and the Oz–gay connection.

The Wicked Witch may be replacing Dorothy in the hearts of many gay men. Celebrating the villain could be a camp response to the film, as opposed to the more serious identification with the heroine that earlier fans felt. Gay fans' embrace of Elphaba, the Wicked Witch in *Wicked*, can likewise be both campy and serious. These days, in another piece of evidence that the subculture values the movie less than it used to, the MGM *Wizard* doesn't appear in every list of the top gay movies.[k]

---

j   The phrase "from reverence to ridicule" is Daniel Harris's from *The Rise and Fall of Gay Culture* (New York: Hyperion, 1997), p. 22; it is probably a play on Molly Haskell's *From Reverence to Rape* (1974). This irreverence can be seen as pre-Stonewall camp or postmodern irony.

k   One example of a list that doesn't include *The Wizard of Oz* is "The Fifty Greatest Gay Movies!," compiled in 2008 from an online poll. The titles that made the grade all have gay characters, although this wasn't an explicit criterion (see http://www.afterelton.com/movies/2008/9/50greatestgay-movies). The MGM film isn't on the 2007 list called "The Ten Gayest Movies," either. The entries on this list are all pretty recent, with *Some Like It Hot* (1959) and *The Sound of Music* (1965) being the oldest; see Scott Boardman, "The Ten Gayest Movies," *Cybersocket* magazine, April 2007, pp. 36, 38.

The Oz books are not automatically on every gay reading list, either. And Judy Garland herself may not be an icon for younger generations of gay males. Writers on Judy's lack of relevance to today's gay men consider her a pre-Stonewall icon, but I have yet to see any lengthy parallel arguments being made about Oz. Perhaps it is more fun to dethrone divas than films, or perhaps Oz is going to outlast Judy as a gay icon. In any event, some gay men do think public, subcultural gay love of Oz is old-fashioned, from an earlier era. In a rant about gay conformity and consumerism, one journalist wrote in 2000, "Gays and lesbians have come to realize that *The Wizard of Oz* is increasingly useless as both theology and security blanket. When you get over the rainbow, you get over the rainbow." Comments like these make one wonder whether Oz stories in general, and the MGM *Wizard* in particular, will continue to hold a special place in gay male culture.

▪ ▪ ▪

If Oz does become less beloved by gay fans in the future, what might the reasons be? First, the sensibilities and outlooks of the fans themselves could change. Second, the environment—the context in which we learn by taking in information and live our lives as social beings—might change in a way that makes it less likely for the Oz stories to resonate with gay fans. And even if gay sensibilities and the environment remain the same, another story or set of stories could become more popular.

Similar patterns of behaviors, propensities, and talents have been observed in many gay men. While not all gay males have the same sensibility, they seem to have a propensity for certain ways of being in the world. Recent research shows differences at earlier and earlier ages; these may very well be inborn. Qualities such as gentleness, imagination, creativity, cherishing things of the past, gender atypicality, love of home and domesticity, romanticism, estheticism, theatricality, connection- and continuity-mindedness, peacefulness, care taking, and friendship form a gay sensibility or way of being in the world. These qualities do not come in response to a homophobic culture. Some claim that as gay oppression lessens and we are more accepted into society, not just gay culture but also the gay sensibility itself will change or disappear. But just as gay boys manifest differences soon after birth, they become Oz fans before they encounter homophobia, see gay images or become aware of the lack of gay images, and so forth.[1] Thus, changes in societal attitudes about being gay wouldn't necessarily affect the early fandom of gay boys.

Other aspects of being gay come from the culture around us, such as feeling like an outsider or sharing the experience of being oppressed with other gay men, and thus different generations of gay males do have different issues to a certain extent. The closet and closed-mindedness of the 1940s and 50s have given way to the in-your-face queer culture of the 90s and beyond. And while still influential in gay culture, the pre-Stonewallers and the Boomers who came out soon after 1969 are getting old. As the political and social environments change in ways that improve life for gay men and boys, might their enthusiasm for Oz wane or become indistinguishable from that of their straight peers?

With teen support groups, gay–straight alliances, and Internet social networking sites, gay youth are not as isolated as they used to be. A new generation will have new experiences growing up, and their culture will have new values and issues. But homophobia—in schools, among peers, and from parents—is still very much with us and will probably continue for some time. Even if institutional homophobia and heterocentrism were to disappear, gay people would remain a numerical minority. Schoolyard bullies will always look for scapegoats and pick on those who

---

[1] Some anecdotal evidence that Oz fandom in gay boys is related to inborn characteristics is the fact that homosexual siblings seem to be more likely to be into Oz than heterosexual ones. One fan has a lesbian sister who is "wild about" the MGM film, in contrast to the rest of his family, which is only "OK" with it. Gay brothers seem particularly likely to share a passion for Oz. Nikita Simmons and his brother, both gay, were ardent about Oz as kids and are equally interested as adults. Roger Sutton's whole family loved the movie, but only his gay younger brother and he went on to read the books. While anecdotal evidence suggests that gay brothers are the most likely to share an enthusiasm for Oz, sisters seem to be more likely to do so than straight brothers. Fans also talk of finding out that the friends they shared Oz with as children ended up being gay as well. Erick Neher found a kindred spirit, John, at the age of six. He and John read all fourteen of the Baum books, exploring Oz together and talking about it constantly. They came out to each other when they were fourteen, and are still friends.

are different—minorities of any sort. Redheads, for example, are picked on just because they are different from the majority. And it is unlikely that there will ever be a perfect utopia of total gay acceptance.

The environment with respect to gay-positive information and representation has changed greatly since the middle of the twentieth century, when the bulk of my Boomer respondents were growing up. There is now a huge variety of potential sources for the kinds of information and images that gay boys and men need, and many gay teens grow up seeing images of people like themselves in the mass media.[m] They see gay couples getting married, and they no longer feel like second-class citizens. Publishing and filmmaking have changed as well; there are now more pieces of nonfiction writing and documentary films that provide information and images to gay boys and men. Fiction can also be sources of positive gay images. Scores of books with gay characters are created each year, and films, musicals, and television shows now include gay characters as well. It is not just the small, alternative publishers and producers who are creating these works; mainstream or "straight" publishers and producers do so as well.[n]

What about a replacement for Oz regardless of the changing environment? One possibility, in my view, is a subterranean gay work—a work of fiction that has no explicitly gay characters but includes themes

---

m Gay man and youth can also get their needs met from gay-related folk knowledge. See, for example, William Leap, *Word's Out: Gay Men's English* (Minneapolis: University of Minnesota Press, 1996).

n While some activists have decried mainstreaming, it has undeniably brought gay images and words to isolated gay people who had no access to them before. The works can be from the domains of both "high art" and popular culture, and are aimed at children, young adults, and adults; in some cases, adults read gay young adult fiction (Kate Pavao, "Joining the Club," *Publishers Weekly*, Dec. 1, 2003, p. 25). As more and more gay authors of children's books come out, they are role models, and also enable more gay content (Michael Giltz, "Not Just Kid Stuff: Robert Sabuda and James Howe, Two Successful Creators of Children's Books, Talk About Coming Out in Their Corner of the Publishing World," *The Advocate*, Dec. 25, 2001, pp. 66–67).

important to gay people.º Explicitly gay books, with gay characters, are available to a small fraction of those who might benefit from them. Subterranean gay works, in contrast, have a wider audience; they are more widely distributed and are more likely to avoid censorship.ᵖ Parents are more likely to present a subterranean gay work to their child; a child reading such a book is more likely to avoid disapproval of peers and adults; and gay boys are more likely to choose such a book for themselves.

There are also several textual reasons—that is, reasons having to do with the nature of the text—why a replacement to Oz is likely to be a subterranean gay work. Because of the symbolism involved, the subterranean approach often reaches deeper into the subconscious. And since they are not written to prove a point, subterranean works are more likely to be "artistic" and lasting.ᑫ They also lend themselves easily to appropriation.ʳ

o   The term "subterranean approach" comes from personal communication with Deborah Hautzig, author of *Hey, Dollface* (1978). Subterranean gay works cannot, by definition, include issues that apply to gay people uniquely, such as homophobia, anti-gay violence, or coming out as gay.

p   Avoiding censorship by using the subterranean approach might be considered letting homophobes define the terms of the debate or blaming the victim. I'm not saying we shouldn't have any explicitly gay books for kids. While one can take a subterranean approach to the issues that gay kids deal with, direct mention of gay people and homosexuality is crucial for validating gay kids' very existence. LGBT parents may look for books with images of households headed by a same-sex couple or those that challenge gender stereotypes, and non-LGBT parents who think diversity is important may expose their children to a wide range of images, including those in LGBT picture books. See Michael Ford, "Gay Books for Young Readers," *Publishers Weekly*, Feb. 21, 1994, pp. 24–27.

q   The authors of didactic books are trying to make a point rather than create literature, so those stories tend to be realistic, preachy, and lacking in imagination, as Melynda Huskey points out in "Queering the Picture Book" (*The Lion and the Unicorn* 26, no. 1 [Jan. 2002]: 66–77). *Heather Has Two Mommies* and *Daddy's Roommate* established this tradition in 1989 and 1990. (Even *Heather*'s author, Leslea Newman, admits it was "didactic"—see Dana Rudolph, "Heather Author Discusses Her Two New Books About LGBT Families," *Bay Windows*, June 25–July 1, 2009, p. 4.) The problem is not with LGBT lit alone; books whose agenda is "psychological self-help" often

Any work that replaces the collection of stories set in the Land of Oz would have to satisfy several criteria:

- It would probably have been created with children in mind but also appeal to adults.ˢ
- It would most likely be a work of recent vintage. If older works such as *Alice in Wonderland* (1865) and *Peter Pan* (1904) haven't replaced Oz by now, there is no reason to think they would in the future.
- It would be available to a large segment of the population, in many formats. Books that appear in series have the advantage of quantity—more titles available—as do books that are made into movies. Series, sequels, and versions in other media foster great anticipation, as fans look forward to the next one in a series or the film version of their favorite book.

have this flaw. See Ellen Handler Spitz, *Inside Picture Books* (New Haven, CT: Yale University Press, 1999).

r Unlike appropriation by a dominant culture (which is a no-no), when a gay reader appropriates a text for his own use, it can be seen as revolutionary or countercultural act. Two examples are *A Separate Peace* and the Harry Potter books. For more on the uses to which *A Separate Peace* has been put, see Rob DeKoven, "Banning GLBT Literature," Beyond the Briefs, *Gay and Lesbian Times*, Mar. 21, 2002, p. 38. For Harry Potter, see Michael Bronski, "There's Something About Harry," *The Phoenix.com*, June 27–July 3, 2003; Joel Brown, "When Harry Met Draco: Halloween Confab in Salem to Explore the 'Metaphorical Queerness' of Harry Potter," *Bay Windows*, July 21–27, 2005, p. 4; Catherine Tosenberger, "Homosexuality at the Online Hogwarts: Harry Potter Slash Fanfiction," *Children's Literature* 36 (2008): 185–207; and Annette Wannamaker, "Men in Cloaks and High-Heeled Boots, Men Wielding Pink Umbrellas: Witchy Masculinities in the *Harry Potter* Novels," *Alice's Academy* 10, no. 1 (Jan. 2006), http://tlg.ninthwonder.com/rabbit/v10i1/alice4.html.

s Many children's TV shows work on two levels—consider the obscure puns and references in *Rocky and His Friends* (1959–64), or the adult fans of *SpongeBob SquarePants* (1999–). Margaret Wise Brown's *Goodnight Moon* (1947) is a very simple classic that adults enjoy, but my guess is that the replacement for Oz, if there is one, will be longer and more complex than a picture book.

- It would probably be a fantasy, or at least have some fantastic elements. Fantasy has the advantage of allowing unrealistic characters and events to be taken in stride. Fantasy can also more easily tap into the imagination and creativity and unconscious of gay boys.
- It would present themes that resonate with gay boys and men. The society depicted could be a utopia with inhabitants who value diversity. Characters should reflect nonstandard gender roles. Aspects of friendship, family, and home might be highlighted, as might the idea of becoming your own true self. A replacement might also have other gay-relevant themes that aren't found in Oz stories.
- It would most likely present these themes in a subterranean way (see above).
- Finally, it would meet the many needs—social, psychological, and spiritual—of gay boys and men. Social needs include friendship, community, history, belonging, and lessening the sting of being different. Psychological needs are such things as helping to form an identity, building confidence and self-esteem, helping one to stay true to oneself, and offering gender-atypical role models. Spiritual needs might be creating a safe space to travel to, offering the possibility of living a different kind of life, and showing the transcendence of another world.

The protagonists of Disney films are often outsiders and misfits, and Disney's 2013 animated *Frozen* has been lambasted by right-wing Christians as being pro-gay. *Frozen* certainly has many positive themes, including a brief glimpse of a gay family, but it is too early to say whether it will be taken to heart by lesbian and/or gay kids. Of course, it's impossible to predict the next big thing, either in the culture at large or in the gay subculture. Who could have said Harry Potter would become the phenomenon it has? New works are created all the time, in old media. And new works will undoubtedly appear in new media and new forms of distribution. There may never be exactly the same mixture of gay-relevant themes in another work, but perhaps something new will have other themes that will speak more directly to gay boys and men inhabiting a different environment in the future.

Once and Future Oz

Even very young children know Oz. How that happened has its roots in the history of the book and the MGM movie. The original story, L. Frank Baum's *Wonderful Wizard of Oz*, was a huge success as a children's book in 1900; it became a major stage hit in 1902. Baum and others kept Oz new and in the public awareness for decades by creating a whole series of Oz books. In 1939 *The Wonderful Wizard* was made into a magical movie, one that may even have been an improvement on the original book because it tightened up the plot. Although the movie didn't make money, it was hugely successful in terms of the number of tickets sold. After a few decades, baby boomers got to see the movie annually on television, and watching the movie became a ritual. Between the TV viewing and the repeated theatrical releases, the MGM film became one of the most widely seen movies ever made. Meanwhile, both before and after 1939, Oz merchandise of all sorts was created. New stories and editions proliferated when the books began to enter the public domain in 1950. Dolls, games, and peanut butter containers with Oz images abounded, and still do. All of this has facilitated access to Oz for very young kids.

Oz is an open-ended phenomenon, with new stories in new formats being created all the time. While the movie still appears on television, many fans can watch it whenever they want; they own a copy or can rent or borrow a video or DVD from a library. Scenes are currently available on the Internet, and the whole movie is available via commercial streaming. Made-for-television movies and miniseries, such as 2007's *Tin Man* or 2017's *Emerald City*, are another venue for experiencing Oz. Theatrical versions also provide access to Oz for thousands of fans, from community theater and school productions of *The Wiz*, to stage versions of the movie, to Broadway and professional touring productions of *Wicked*, to live sing-alongs of the MGM film. Fan fiction is available over the Internet, as are self-published unofficial continuations.ᵗ

As I have argued, Oz's appeal for gay boys and men stems from both inborn characteristics and social conditions. For many decades, from at

---

t   Transmedia storytelling uses different digital media to bring out different aspects of a story; see Henry Jenkins, "Transmedia Storytelling: Moving Characters from Books to Films to Video Games Can Make Them Stronger

least the 1930s to the 1990s, themes from Oz stories have resonated with gay boys. Young gay boys see their gender atypicality, difference, and gentleness reflected in aspects of the stories. Their imaginations and creativity are fueled by Oz. Their feelings of being alone and not understood disappear when they travel to Oz in their imaginations. Their yearning to escape is fulfilled as well. Gay adults, too, have found Oz a nurturing place. In addition to reflecting their values and providing an escape, there is a sense of nostalgia in revisiting the storybook land of one's youth. Both gay boys and men have also used Oz for therapeutic purposes, and to fulfill social and spiritual needs. Oz has nourished the souls of gay boys and men as a gay space, a personal myth, and even a Jungian other life. And for some, the fact that the MGM movie is a gay favorite at the cultural level has increased their individual appreciation of both the movie and Oz in general.

Oz's appeal to the population at large is timeless. Perhaps Oz's appeal to the gay population is, too. We don't really know, of course, if Oz affected gay boys or men in the beginning of the twentieth century when the books first appeared. In 1921, an adult male fan wrote to Baum to say that he had read the Oz books all his life and that the characters were more real than any others he had encountered. He cherished them with "a love that would seem ridiculous to one who did not understand." The mother of one young boy wrote to Baum in 1920 about her sick son who begged for Oz stories. On his last morning, "he muttered 'Princess of Oz, Princess of Oz' and died as he had lived, in fairyland." These two early book fans may not have been gay, but their sentiments certainly are consonant with the intense feelings of gay boys and men now.

Maybe love of Oz can be passed along after all. When parents read a story they love out loud to their children, they pass on their values to the next generation. Fantasy and science fiction fans can get their

---

and More Compelling," *MIT Technology Review*, Jan 15, 2003. The best examples use rich fictional worlds, of which the Land of Oz is a perfect example. There is the potential to tailor fan fiction in different media to different fan bases, and we might even see more Oz stories created specifically for gay fans, along the lines of Bob Kanefsky's slash story or Brian Andersen's comic book *Friend of Dorothy*.

appreciation of *Star Wars* or *Star Trek* (1966–) from their parents. Some gay Oz fans—I'm one of them—got their first taste of Oz from their parents, who were fans when they were kids themselves. Now that we have a generation of out gay adults choosing to have kids, some will expose their kids to Oz. My youngest respondent says that it makes him happy to hope that he can bring Oz's values and magic into his own children's lives someday.

When we are little, our parents are in charge. They read us stories, take us to the movies, and give us films to watch. Later we ourselves choose which works to continue to interact with. These stories take us out of everyday sensory reality and shape who we are. In particular, within a given text, we latch on to those aspects that speak to us. We construe, appropriate, interpret, appreciate, respond to, and create meaning from the parts that resonate with our needs, wants, desires, and situations. Whether the process is active, consciously sought out, or part of a serendipitous encounter, the result is the same: we get what we need from the work. When we return to the work because it meets our needs, we become fans. As we get older we can reflect on our encounters, be self-conscious about it. We can joke about our fandom and be ironic and campy.

The gay subculture will undoubtedly change. New divas have already replaced old ones. New favorite movies will appear on lists and be shared at the subcultural level. The MGM film will probably fade in importance in gay culture. But it is impossible to predict if any one work will replace it as a touchstone in gay culture. Will any other work have enough rich imagery to regularly inspire themes for pride parades and other gay events? Will any other work lend its terminology to gay businesses, books, and folklore? I doubt it.

And there will always be gay boys—different in many ways from other boys—making their way in a society that does not always respect their natures. Whether or not social conditions change enough to affect gay needs for and uses of Oz, there will still be a need for some special story for gay males to relate to. The fact that *The Wizard of Oz* is a mainstream classic guarantees its ubiquity. It is unlikely that another work will come along that is as famous and as widespread. While the numbers of fans may change and perhaps the intensity of the fan feelings, Oz in all its versions will always speak to many gay individuals, young and old.

Not having explicitly gay content works in Oz's favor. Stories set in this fabulous land can speak to the unconscious in a way that today's didactic and explicitly gay works for children do not. Because of their subterranean themes and wide availability, many gay boys are nurtured by stories set in Oz before they themselves realize they are gay. In Oz, authority figures get their comeuppance; diversity and being true to oneself are celebrated. Oz also gives a budding gay boy another way of conceptualizing himself. The stories are full of depictions of other ways of being: non-macho males, incomplete men, and strong women. A gay boy can see himself in Dorothy or Ojo, Glinda or the Wicked Witch, the Scarecrow or the Patchwork Girl.

Oz is full of magic, fantasy, escape, and happy endings. Devoted Oz fans as young as three or four or five aren't escaping to Oz because of gay oppression. The appeal of *The Wizard of Oz* for individual gay men and boys is about more than escape from a negative environment, a fantasy of acceptance in a utopia. It is also about play, imagination, creativity, awe, joy, and transcendence. Oz's themes will continue to resonate for those gay boys who are exposed to Oz. New Oz stories, such as *Wicked* and its spinoffs, will help keep the flame alive. Despite improving social conditions, we will never reach gay utopia, and individual gay fans will always want to escape to the utopian Land of Oz.

APPENDIXES, NOTES, INDEX

Appendix A The Questionnaire

I am a gay man writing a book on the appeal of *The Wizard of Oz* for gay males. My project includes any manifestation of the Oz story, from L. Frank Baum's original book, to others in the series, the MGM movie, other versions such as *The Wiz* on stage and screen, Disney's *Return to Oz* and so on. As part of my research, I am asking people what the story means to them. I would very much appreciate your answering the following questions; this might take you an hour or so, depending on how much you get into it.

- For yes/no questions, put an X in the appropriate slot.
- Begin written responses on a new line after the question, and leave a blank line between your response and the next question.
- Have fun.

1 LOGISTICS

1.1 How much of an Oz fan are you? Put an arrow along the scale to represent your enthusiasm:

5 = Extremely enthusiastic fan (e.g., book or memorabilia collecting; member of an Oz club)
4 = Enthusiastic fan (e.g., have a refrigerator magnet or two; make friends watch the movie)
3 = Moderate fan (e.g., multiple viewings of the MGM movie in recent years)

2 = Mild fan (e.g., enjoy the movie or book, but no big deal)
1 = No particular enthusiasm for Oz

If you responded with a 3 or higher, please continue. If not, please stop here and let me know. Thanks for your time.

1.2 Your name: _____
Unless given permission below, I will not identify you by name.

1.3 Is it ok to use your name in writing up the results of this questionnaire?
YES _____
NO _____
If you like, provide a pseudonym: _____

1.4 Date filling out questionnaire: _____

1.5 Year of birth: 19_____

1.6 Sex: _____

1.7 Sexual orientation: _____

1.8 So that I may contact you with follow-up questions, please provide your preferred mode(s) of communication:

Telephone number: _____

Email address: _____

Mailing address: _____

1.9 Occupation, employment, job background: _____
_____

2 BEGINNINGS

2.1 What is your earliest memory of Oz? Please specify which version of the story this was (book, MGM movie, *The Wiz, Oz on Ice*, etc.), how old you were, and if there was a particular person (family member, friend, etc.) who introduced you to Oz.

2.2 When and how did you become an Oz fan, that is, when did you feel that a book or movie spoke to you in a special way? If this wasn't upon first exposure, how old were you and what were the circumstances? What about the book or movie particularly appealed to you, do you think? (If this is hard to say, don't worry.)

2.3 When you became an Oz fan, were other friends or members of your family exposed to the Oz story as you were?
NO _____
YES _____ Who were they and what were their reactions to the Oz story? Were their reactions the same as yours or different?

2.4 When you first became an Oz fan, did you share the fact that you were an Oz fan with any friends or family members?
NO _____
YES _____ If you can, please describe any reaction they had.

3 CURRENT INTEREST

3.1 Who or what is your favorite character in the Oz book(s) or movie(s), and why?

3.2 Who or what is your least favorite character in the Oz book(s) or movie(s), and why?

3.3 Is there a particular character in either the book(s) or movie(s) that you identify with?
NO _____
YES _____ Who or what? If you can, please explain why you identify with this character. If this is different from your favorite character discussed in 3.1, please explain.

3.4 Are there particular aspects of the Land of Oz (the place, not the book) that appeal to you?
NO _____
YES _____ Please describe them and, if you can, explain why they appeal to you.

3.5 Are there particular aspects of the Land of Oz that you do not like?
NO _____
YES _____ Please describe them and, if you can, explain why you don't like them.

3.6 Are there particular aspects of Kansas as depicted in the book(s) or movie(s) that appeal to you?
NO _____
YES _____ Please describe them and, if you can, explain why they appeal to you.

3.7 Are there particular aspects of Kansas as depicted in the book(s) or movie(s) that you do not like?
NO _____
YES _____ Please describe them and, if you can, explain why you don't like them.

3.8 Of the many different versions of the Oz story you have experienced (e.g., a particular book within the series, the MGM movie, *The Wiz* on film or stage), is there one you like the most?
NO _____
YES _____ Why is it your favorite?

3.9 Do you have any other opinions on the different versions or updatings of the Oz story (the book vs. the MGM movie, *The Wiz*, Geoff Ryman's *Was*, Gregory Maguire's *Wicked*, etc.)?
NO _____
YES _____ Please elaborate.

3.10 If you own any Oz books or Oz-related objects, do you have a favorite?
NO _____
YES _____ What is it and what about it makes it your favorite?

4 FANDOM

4.1 How does being an Oz fan express itself now (collecting, membership in a club, giving theme parties, etc.)?

4.2 Please describe any reactions your friends or family currently have to your being an Oz fan.

4.3 In addition to what you get from the story itself (see 5.1), please describe what you get out of being an Oz fan (e.g., pride in expertise, satisfaction with collecting, validation or friendship via fan groups).

4.4 Has your interest in Oz changed in any way over the years (e.g., you used to have a different favorite character, or your general interest has increased or lessened)?
NO _____ Please go to 4.6.
YES _____ Please describe.

4.5 What do you think might have caused this change?

4.6 Has *The Wizard of Oz* affected you in any way personally or professionally? Have you made use of Oz in any way?
NO _____ Please go to 5.1.
YES _____ Please describe.

5 MEANINGS

5.1 What is *The Wizard of Oz* about for you? What about the book or movie particularly appeals to you? Does it contain any themes or issues that speak to you?

5.2 If you were an Oz fan as a child, what do you think Oz offered you as a child?

5.3 What does Oz offer you as an adult?

5.4 Do you think the generation of which you are a part has anything to do with your interest in Oz?
NO _____
YES _____ In what way?

5.5 Do you think Oz offers you anything as a man?
NO _____
YES _____ Please describe.

5.6 Do you think Oz offers you anything as a gay man?
NO _____
YES _____ Please describe.

6 A GAY CONNECTION?

6.1 How old were you when realized that you were gay?

6.2 How old were you when you starting coming out to others?

6.3 Do you know that the MGM film of *The Wizard of Oz* is considered a gay favorite?
NO _____ Please go to 6.7.
YES _____ When did you realize this?

6.4 Did you find out that the MGM *Wizard* is a gay favorite before or after you yourself became an Oz fan?
BEFORE _____
AFTER _____

6.5 How did you feel when you found out about this Oz/gay connection?

6.6 Do you think this embracing of the film of *The Wizard of Oz* by parts of the gay community has anything to do with your being an Oz fan?
NO _____
YES _____ In what way?

6.7 Do you yourself think that the story of *The Wizard of Oz* has any special meaning for gay males?
NO _____
YES _____ Please describe.

6.8 Do you know any other gay Oz fans?
NO _____
YES _____ What kind of contact or socializing do you have with them?

6.9 Would you like to be put in touch with other gay Oz fans?
NO _____
YES _____

7 FINAL THOUGHTS

7.1 Do you have any other favorite books?
NO _____
YES _____ Please list them, saying what is special about each.

7.2 Do you have any other favorite movies?
NO _____
YES _____ Please list them, saying what is special about each.

7.3 Please add any other thoughts that didn't get addressed by the above questions.

7.4 Do you have any photos or other images that relate to your Oz interest that you might be willing to share for reproduction in my book? Pictures of you as a youth would be especially useful. I happily accept GIFs and JPGs.
NO _____
YES _____ Please describe.

Appendix B Methodology

Subjects

I found gay male Oz fans willing to answer my questions in a few different ways—by word of mouth, listing my research online, and making personal contact after my presentations. I also contacted gay writers who mentioned or wrote about Oz and owners and managers of gay businesses and organizations with Ozzy names, such as Toto Tours or the Land of Awes Information Service.

Once someone agreed to be a subject, I sent him a questionnaire via email. The first question in the questionnaire asked respondents to rate their degree of fandom on a scale of 1 to 5. Anyone who considered himself a 3, 4, or 5 was, for the purposes of my investigation, an Oz fan. I occasionally asked follow-up questions for clarification and to pursue ideas put forth in their answers in more detail. Two subjects preferred to be asked the questionnaire questions over the phone. I taped the conversations with them and later transcribed the answers.

In order to decide when I had enough data, I paid attention to the phenomenon known as "saturation" in qualitative research. The idea is that when additional data doesn't yield any new information, the data gathering can stop. After receiving 73 questionnaires, I analyzed them. Then, after another 31 came in, I tallied them as a separate pool. Both the specifics and the trends were very much the same, so I felt I could stop. After that point, for the sake of geographic diversity, I accepted as respondents a few fans who lived outside the United States.

I received a total of 109 completed questionnaires between 2001 and 2007. About half of the respondents were baby boomers; the oldest was born in 1930, the youngest in 1985. All but eight were from the United States, with three from Canada, three from the United Kingdom, and one each from Ireland and Australia. Among respondents there was a preponderance of professional occupations, helping professions, academia, and the like.

Almost half of those who answered my questionnaire considered themselves "extremely enthusiastic" fans; the other half was split between "enthusiastic" and "moderate." On the question of whether they preferred the movie or the books, there were twice as many respondents who chose the movie. Almost all respondents identified themselves as "gay"; a handful preferred "gay/bi," "bisexual," or "queer." Most respondents said it was OK to use their name, but I sometimes refer to them simply as "a respondent" or "a fan." A sizable number of respondents have always known they were gay (although they didn't have the word or even the concept for it), or have known since a very early age, such as five or six. The age at which respondents began coming out to others ranged from twelve to sixty-one.

Unfortunately, I did not ask questions about race and class. At the time, I had not considered how different the experiences of people unlike me in race and class (I am white and middle-class) might be. While not all my respondents were urban, white, middle-class, American baby boomers, my sense is that a great preponderance of them were. This reflects the makeup of the generic "gay community," which would more correctly be called "one of the more visible of the gay communities"—the urban, white, middle-class gay community that most people think of when they use the term "gay men."

While there were some yes/no questions and others that asked for numbers such as age of coming out, the questionnaire as a whole was designed to yield qualitative data. Answers given by my gay Oz fans varied greatly in degree of detail, explicitness, and content. This variety demonstrates that there isn't any typical gay male Oz fan. In fact, there were many opposing opinions about aspects of both the MGM movie and the

Oz books. Some fans loved the Cowardly Lion or the Wicked Witch of the West; others hated one or both. Respondents also had strong positive and negative opinions about the MGM dream ending and its "no place like home" sentiment, Baum's Shaggy Man character, and the lack of aging and death in Baum's Oz. They also disagreed about whether being gay affects their fandom, and differed greatly in the degree to which they shared their fandom with others.

The Appeal of a Work

Asking people why they like something is problematic. How many people can say why they like mint chocolate chip ice cream, or why their favorite color is blue? Explaining why they like a book or a movie may yield more information, but people cannot always analyze and articulate the reasons for their preferences. If we believe with Freud that much of our behavior is affected by unconscious factors, it makes sense that people cannot offer complete explanations of why they prefer what they prefer, or what they get out of a particular behavior they engage in. Some kinds of behavior have multiple causes, and people who engage in those behaviors may well be aware of only some of the causes. Furthermore, some people are more articulate and analytical than others. Even if their reasons are theoretically available to their conscious minds, they may not have the vocabulary or the inclination to talk about their reasons.

My investigation of the gay appeal of Oz by asking people about their fandom is in the spirit of qualitative anthropology or sociology. The advantage of such an approach was that my conclusions would be based on actual responses from gay fans—reality-based data—rather than on my own reading and theorizing. The disadvantage was that the data would be only part of the picture, because people can't always explain their behavior. Before I developed my questionnaire I looked at the published literature for themes in Oz stories that were also themes in the lives of gay men, such as home or gender roles.[a] It turned out that many of

---

[a] For the results of comparing themes in Oz with themes in gay lives before I interviewed anyone, see Dee Michel, "Not in Kansas Anymore: The Appeal of *The Wizard of Oz* for Gay Males," *Baum Bugle* 46, no. 1 (Spring 2002): 31–38.

the themes that emerged from the questionnaires were the sorts of issues I had identified by my literary method. This gave me confidence in both types of investigation.

In addition to keeping an open mind about different methodologies, I felt it was important to be open to different theoretical frameworks or points of view. For the same reason that different methods might yield different results, so would different intellectual approaches. A Freudian will see sublimated sexuality as the reason for behavior, a Marxist will see economic forces as crucial determinants, and a feminist will pay special attention to gender roles. I decided to take from different frameworks whatever seemed useful. I had no hypothesis or preconceptions about the answers I would find, except perhaps that there wasn't likely to be one answer to the question of what Oz meant to gay men.

At some point I had to grapple with the question of what it means to say that a book or movie has a particular meaning to readers and viewers. Reader-response theory sounded like a helpful approach, but I soon discovered that hardly any writing in this area was based on hard data about readers forming meaning. Combining aspects of reader-response theory and Jungian literary criticism, I came up with a model of interactive meaning, resonance, and fandom, described in the Introduction.

Frequently Asked Questions

When I've presented my project to friends and public audiences, certain questions have come up repeatedly.

1. *"The appeal of Oz is universal. Why talk about Oz's appeal to a particular group?"*

What does it mean to say the appeal of Oz is universal? That Oz appeals to everyone? That is clearly false, because some people are not Oz fans. Perhaps Oz's appeal being universal means that Oz appeals to all its fans for all the same reasons. That doesn't make sense either. If you speak to any two fans, you may get similar reasons, but they won't be exactly the same. If the first two fans happen to give you identical reasons (assuming they can articulate all the reasons for their fandom), keep going: by the third or fourth person, you will most certainly get additional, or fewer, or differently flavored reasons.

A third conceivable interpretation of "The appeal of Oz is universal" is that reasons for its appeal are completely random, that no patterns or generalizations could be made about why anyone likes any aspect of Oz. This seems a funny interpretation of the word "universal" indeed. Besides, this claim of random reasons would mean that there are no patterns of fandom whatsoever. (By "patterns of fandom," I mean that similar groups of people would have similar reasons for loving Oz.) This interpretation of "Oz is universal" forecloses any real discussion of the appeal of Oz. If any and all reasons are possible and equally likely in the same strength for every reader of every Oz book and every manifestation of Oz in movie form, what more is there to say? The most likely and most logical distribution of reasons for fandom among fans is neither identical for everyone nor totally different for everyone. In other words, patterns of fandom exist.

I think saying "The appeal of Oz is universal" is really a somewhat grandiose shorthand for saying that there are no a priori limits: Oz fans can be found in all shapes and sizes, and—in theory, at least—anyone can become one. While this is probably true as far as it goes, it doesn't really tell us much about what makes anyone like Oz. I think the question of why one likes Oz (or any literary work) is an interesting and important one.

One way to get at what seems like a universal phenomenon is to investigate a particular case in detail. By looking at what well-defined groups of people see in Oz, we can paint a more complete picture of Oz fandom in general. Once we identify a pattern, it is possible to ask how widespread the pattern is.

Now, the idea that tastes and behaviors of different groups might systematically vary is a controversial one. We like to think that human beings are all the same and that we enter the world with a clean slate where every choice is equally possible. But love and appreciation of cultural artifacts such as movies and books do not happen in a vacuum; they are determined *in part* by our culture. In the United States, women tend to read romances more than men do, and men like war movies more than women do. This is not to say that no men read romances or that no women like war movies; the point is simply that men as a group tend to differ from women as a group in their preferences. Or take the example of our romantic attractions. Most people would say that liking blonds or thin people is a choice made randomly, out of complete free will, like the choice of a favorite ice cream flavor; there are no politics involved. But consider all the online dating listings that specify a preference for a particular body type. The choice of a partner is conditioned by social reality. To say that we love Oz in a vacuum, aside from our other values, politics, and so on, is, I think, equally unrealistic.

2. *"Couldn't members of any minority relate to Oz's message in the way that you say gay males do?"*

Being gay in our society at this moment and in the recent past brings with it certain attitudes, feelings, and experiences. Not seeing yourself reflected in much literature, feeling different, wanting to be accepted at home, and needing to create your own identity are feelings gay males have *because they are gay*. Thus there are good reasons why the themes of gender roles, acceptance, home, and identity appeal to gay males.

This is not to say that members of other groups are not touched by some of these themes as well. Non-macho boys who are heterosexual probably also appreciate images of sissies. Members of other minorities, such as the disabled or African Americans, may feel that the acceptance aspect of Oz speaks to them. Salman Rushdie has said that the theme of home in the MGM movie is especially poignant for immigrants. The question of identity may be an important part of Oz's appeal to adolescents of all sexual orientations. And other aspects of Oz, such as the presence of strong female rulers, may be important to female readers. My argument in this book is simply that this particular *constellation* of aspects—the themes of feeling different, searching for home, and so on, taken together—holds special appeal for gay males. Furthermore, while individual non-macho heterosexual boys, disabled people, African Americans, immigrants, and adolescents may embrace Oz, their subcultures have not, as far as I know. It is only gay males who have institutionalized *The Wizard of Oz* at a cultural level, with the MGM film.

One might argue that everyone can feel the pull of these themes; why is it so different or special for gay males? Yes, adolescents or African Americans or people with a disability or redheads may also feel different. But gay people can also be adolescent or African American or disabled.

Being gay is not something that happens to you *instead of* being male or human or disabled or African American or an adolescent; it is there *in addition to* other aspects of your makeup. Those aspects of Oz that appeal to your gay side do so in addition to any others. Some people are more oppressed and more likely to be teased and feel different than others. A gay disabled African American man may feel the pull of Oz more strongly. Being gay is an extra reason—on top of all the reasons that most people, gay or straight, have—to feel different.

The themes I discuss are not meant to exclude other reasons a given gay male fan might have for loving Oz. They are why being gay makes it more likely you will be an Oz fan, or why being gay deepens fandom that would be there anyway. Being a gay male facilitates being an Oz fan, but it doesn't guarantee it. This is illustrated in chart 1.1 (in Chapter 1).

3. *"Shouldn't you have control groups and interview heterosexual men and women and lesbians? How do you know that what gay males feel about Oz is really different from what the rest of the population feels?"*

If I am going to try to characterize the gay responses as something unique, perhaps I need control or comparison groups. Is it possible to talk about gay male appreciation of Oz without comparing it with what lesbians and straight men and women feel? And what about bisexuals and transgender folks? The short answer is that I am not claiming that what gay males feel is different from what everyone else feels. I am just trying to figure out what the reasons are for gay boys and men.

Some people want to know about a control group because they assume I am doing quantitative research. But the question one asks in one's research will to some extent determine which methodology can best answer it. A question such as "Does A affect (or cause, or correlate with) B?" will necessitate measuring something, or more generally using a quantitative methodology.[b] Other questions, such as "why" questions, are more open-ended. Rather than measuring, one is exploring a territory

---

b Once I decided to talk to actual Oz fans myself, my research seemed "scientific," especially since some of my questions could be answered with numbers, such as age of coming out. That led people to think I was doing quantitative research, which was not the case.

and describing what one finds. A different method would be needed to answer a question such as "Do gay men respond to Oz differently from the rest of the population?" or "Do gay men respond in the same way but more deeply than other people?" The terms "differently," "same way," and "more deeply" refer to quantitative concepts; answering a question containing one of those terms would entail defining the concept "respond to" in a way that would allow for measurement. Using questions to be answered on a scale of 1 to 10 would yield numbers that could be compared across groups. The research would become quantitative.

But my methodology is like that of an anthropologist, looking at one culture or community and seeing what the motivations are behind a given phenomenon, in this case, the gay love of Oz. If an anthropologist looked at the coming-of-age rituals of adolescent girls in a particular culture, that would be a study in and of itself; nobody would say, "What about girls in other cultures?" or "What about those girls when they get older?" or "How about adolescent boys?" If a reviewer did ask these questions, it would not be to fault the study but rather to extend it or expand upon it. In academic parlance, these would be "questions for future research." Or consider a study that consisted of interviewing bus drivers to see what they like about their jobs. Upon reading the results, one might wonder whether bus drivers like their jobs for the same reasons as subway operators. The original study would not have addressed this issue, but a larger investigation of transportation job satisfaction might entail a comparison. One's research question always determines where one draws the boundaries of the investigation.

People who consider a comparison with straight people or lesbians to be a necessary part of this research may be assuming that there's only one reason for gay men's Oz fandom. If there were only one reason, I might be able to pinpoint it by asking gay men yes/no or multiple-choice questions, and then I could compare their responses with heterosexuals' and lesbians' answers to the same questions. But there is no single answer. Gay men find a rich tapestry of meanings in stories set in the Land of Oz, and a given fan may be touched by Oz in different ways at different points in his life. Some respondents give very specific reasons—the relationship between a character named Speedy and his uncle, or the Lion's calling himself a "dandy-lion," or discovering, after seeing the flowers in the set of the MGM movie, that flowers can be a source of beauty and pleasure. Other respondents have more abstract or general reasons. All these themes and feelings can't and shouldn't be reduced to numbers.

But might there be a hidden question that would need a quantitative answer? This would be the case if I were making claims about causality or correlation. Am I claiming that being gay causes you to be an Oz fan? No. Am I claiming that being gay correlates with being an Oz fan? Yes, in the sense that being gay makes you more likely to be a fan, or a bigger fan, I'm making a claim that there is a correlation. But I am not trying to *prove* the correlation. My research takes it as a given that gay men have a special affinity for Oz. What I'm looking into is *why* this is so. My study is therefore qualitative: I'm looking for themes and feelings and other ideas that are best described in words rather than measured in numbers. I agree that having comparison groups and numbers and statistics would seem like stronger evidence, more "scientific," but it might not get at the real truth of the phenomenon. Qualitative and quantitative methods both have their strengths, and ultimately researchers should use many different approaches to arrive at the most complete picture of this or any other social phenomenon.

Another way to look at the question of including heterosexuals in this study is to think about a baseline. Because researchers mirror the heterocentrism of the culture we live in, heterosexuality is usually assumed to be the default condition. There is a hidden assumption that research should begin with heterosexual behavior as some kind of baseline or control. A research study would then attempt to describe how homosexuals differ from this "norm," or perhaps find out that they don't. These assumptions in research and public discussion have parallels in sexism and racism. Research on health, for example, has been on men's health, with women's issues—or women's often quite different symptoms and prognoses for the same health problems—being considered only recently. But there is no prior research establishing a heterosexual baseline of appeal in the case of Oz; that is, I have not been able to find anything of substance looking explicitly at why the story appeals to anyone. So I am turning the paradigm around. The appeal of Oz to gay males can be the baseline in this case, and someone else can ask whether straight people turn to Oz for the same reasons as gay males. If other qualitative work about Oz is done with other groups in the future, it may turn out that the reasons straight people and lesbians are attracted to Oz are exactly the same as for gay men, or the reasons may be different. My guess is that it will be a combination.

Another possibility for future research is for someone to look at my conclusions and then formulate hypotheses that could be tested with quantitative research, such as "Fewer lesbians are into Oz than gay men," or "Lesbian Oz fans have many of the same reasons as gay males, but their responses to gender issues are different," or "Straight men are drawn to Oz for many of the same reasons, but not as intensely." My results are ideally part of a much wider series of investigations that would include not just comparison groups but also investigations of other works that gay males are drawn to. What about gay men's responses to modern retellings of fairy tales, erotic fairy tales for men, or other fantasies, such as *The Lord of the Rings*? How do gay males respond to other famous movies, such as *Gone with the Wind* (1939), or to Barbra Streisand movies and recordings? Clearly my investigation into gay love of Oz is just one piece of a much bigger puzzle.[c]

4. *"Is Oz really a big deal for gay men of all ages, or just baby boomers?"*

Almost one-third of my respondents were Gen Xers, born in 1965 or later, with one Gen Y born in 1985, who was nineteen when he filled out the questionnaire. There is also a good deal of evidence that Oz resonates with gay youth, as detailed in Chapter 10.

5. *"Perhaps gay men say they are into Oz, or become Oz fans, to conform to a perception that Oz is a gay thing. Isn't it just a matter of 'keeping up with the Bruces'?"*

No. See Chapter 2.

---

c   Richard Dyer is one of the few people who have communicated with gay fans in order to learn their reasons for fandom—in his case, why they loved Judy Garland. See Dyer's "Judy Garland and Gay Men," chap. 3 in *Heavenly Bodies: Film Stars and Society* (New York: St. Martin's Press, 1986); reprinted in *Rainbow: A Star-Studded Tribute to Judy Garland*, ed. Ethlie Ann Vare (New York: Boulevard Books, 1998).

6. *"Many gay Oz fans insist their fandom has nothing to do with their being gay. Doesn't this invalidate your claim that there is a special Oz–gay connection?"*

The widespread evidence in the subculture (see Chapter 1) suggests that the film appeals to gay people *as* gay people. Support for this interpretation also comes from people who have written about their own fandom. But it is true that some gay Oz fans, when asked, adamantly deny a connection between their love of Oz and their homosexuality. Their denial doesn't negate my thesis. I'm not claiming that being gay is the only reason for liking Oz. If this were so, there would be no straight fans. Since there are other reasons not related to being gay, it makes sense that some gay people will have other motives. What I *am* claiming is that being gay facilitates being an Oz fan. It gives you additional reasons or perhaps strengthens the reasons you have.

There is also the possibility that the fans who deny any connection between their gayness and their fandom are not fully aware of the reasons for their behavior. And those who believe that social forces do not influence individual choices and behavior in general will be resistant to the idea that their sexual orientation affects their Oz fandom. Internalized homophobia may also lead some to discount the idea that their being gay affects their choices in any way.

7. *"Why Oz? Since it's popular with non-gays as well, wouldn't it make more sense to study a movie that is really only beloved of gay men, such as* Whatever Happened to Baby Jane?*"*

The movie critic Mark Griffin has said to me, "Yes [I know *The Wizard of Oz* is a gay favorite], but it's a general fave for millions of people. *Whatever Happened to Baby Jane?* appeals almost exclusively to gay men. Important difference there." I agree that there is an important difference between a movie that is only or primarily loved by gay men and one that has mainstream recognition as well as gay adoration. Griffin was assuming that the point of my research was to illuminate gay film fandom in general. If that were my goal, looking at *Baby Jane* (1962) would certainly make sense. But my interest is in Oz in all its forms, not gay film fandom. And the fact that the MGM movie is a "general fave" means that the reasons I discover for gay fandom may be of interest to those looking at the Oz fandom of other groups in the future.

8. *"Isn't all this focus on Oz and gay men taking Oz away from the rest of us?"*

Some people think that talking about gay love of a mainstream work of literature or film makes the work gay by association. And once something is branded as gay, it will no longer be available for others. This is silly for many reasons. First of all, I am not claiming that Oz is exclusively a gay thing. Nor I am making Oz "bad" by talking about the Oz–gay connection, since there is nothing wrong with being gay. But the important point is that I'm not taking away anything from straight society. I'm giving everyone—gay, straight, and in between—a new way of looking at one aspect of the phenomenon of Oz fandom.[d]

---

d   Alexander Doty gives two examples of this fear in his article on a lesbian reading of the MGM movie: "I was discussing stardom with a graduate student, when she asked me to name some gay cult stars besides Judy Garland. As I began to rattle off a list, she stopped me at one name. 'Wait!' she said, 'Don't take Bette Davis away from us, too!' Before this, I hadn't thought of gay culture—or gay cultural studies—as taking anything away from anyone. Nor had I wanted to believe that anyone apart from white, straight patriarchal types would think that stars and texts were commodities to be owned by one group of cultural readers or another. Was I ever naïve: I guess most people out there really are lifting up their leg or squatting to mark their popular culture territory. Regarding the subject of this paper, there was one student at a college in Louisiana who let me know through her friends that she would not be attending my talk because she didn't want to have *The Wizard of Oz* 'ruined' for her by all my dyke talk about the film. Something similar happened in class during a discussion of *Thelma and Louise*." See Doty's "'My Beautiful Wickedness': *The Wizard of Oz* as Lesbian Fantasy," in his *Flaming Classics: Queering the Film Canon* (New York: Routledge, 2000), pp. 52–53.

Appendix C Was Baum Gay?

When I tell people about my project, many ask me if Lyman Frank Baum, the creator of Oz, was gay. Questionnaire respondents have wondered as well. The assumption is that material of such strong appeal to gay males is likely to have been created by a gay man.

There is no question that Baum was unusual in the arena of gender roles. One reactionary critic, Osmond Beckwith, paints an awful portrait of Baum as psychologically damaged, especially broken in the masculinity department. He claims that Baum has some unnamed strange fears that he dealt with in the original story; felt like an incomplete, unmasculine man; identified with little girls and wished he were one;[a] and thought two men can and should be able to create creatures without women or sex. Beckwith also claims that there is a lot of gender confusion in the Oz books. He clearly sees these qualities in Baum and the Oz books as negative, but these are only a problem for those who want all stories to reinforce strict gender roles.[b] Whether these issues of incomplete

---

a   Beckwith spills a lot of ink comparing Baum with Lewis Carroll, and Dorothy with Alice, but doesn't suggest that Carroll needs psychoanalysis. Apparently, in Beckwith's view, wanting to photograph little girls isn't as bad as wanting to have girls in charge, or having boys change into girls.

b   It is also a problem if you insist on interpreting the orphans, beheadings, gender bending, and the like psychoanalytically. Another critic makes

masculinity and the like are considered a problem or not, many of them could be issues for gay men.

But it doesn't take much imagination to realize that non-gay writers can write convincing portraits of gay men and create works that speak to gay men. Michael Chabon writes novels that are so gay positive and so full of convincing gay characters that he was included in a *Newsweek* article about gay writers, but he is heterosexual and happily married to a woman. In talking about the writer Selma Lagerlof, one critic says, "Although Lagerlof's work avoids explicit lesbian themes, it generally features confident, commanding female characters . . . and the author's sympathies are clearly with those who follow their true natures despite social convention." One could say the same thing about Baum. Does this make him an honorary lesbian? Or feminist? Or gay man?

Here's what we know about Baum himself. He was anything but your typical macho man. In fact, he shared a lot of characteristics with gay men. As a child, he was delicate and nonathletic and had nightmares; he didn't like sports or authority or giving or getting physical punishment. He was dreamy and a reader, often acting out fantasy stories, playing with imaginary friends, and inventing voices for his toys. He related well to children, animals, and flowers. He hated military school for its strictness, corporal punishment, lack of reason, and hierarchy; after some kind of incident, perhaps health-related, his parents brought him home. The adult Baum liked the theater and the theatrical; he acted in plays and also produced and wrote them. He put his theatrical imagination to work when he began to design window displays. He wrote the first articles about window dressing, even creating a book, magazine, and professional organization devoted to the subject. Later in life he grew prize-winning flowers and was extremely proud of his garden, which included goldfish pools and water lilies and chrysanthemums that spelled out the word "OZ" in contrasting colors. Throughout his marriage, his wife dealt with the household finances, and he liked it that she took charge of things.

many of the same observations about character and plot and simply says that Baum thinks that families and home aren't necessarily good. See Joel Chaston, "If I Ever Go Looking for My Heart's Desire: 'Home' in Baum's 'Oz' Books," *The Lion and the Unicorn* 18, no. 2 (Dec. 1994): 209–19.

He was always very tenderhearted. Once after spanking his son Kenneth, he felt so bad about it that he woke Kenneth up to apologize. Baum was also left-handed, which correlates somewhat with being gay. While all these qualities are consonant with a gay sensibility, we also know Baum was very much in love with his wife, and—for what it's worth—he loved watching baseball.

Baum certainly seems to have had many characteristics in common with gay men. Can there be such a thing as a gay sensibility in a straight man? Of course. No group has exclusive rights to any traits. Perhaps we can consider Baum an honorary gay man. Whatever we call him, Baum's having these qualities demonstrates that gay men are not the only ones to act and feel in ways not considered traditionally masculine. As a feminist and a nontraditional male, I like to think Baum would be honored and pleased that his books inspired gay boys to grow up into fully integrated gay men.

Appendix D
Crossing-Dressing in Oz Performances

Males Playing Female Characters

EARLY
- Ed Stone and later Joseph Schode as Imogene the cow, in *The Wizard of Oz* (1902 play)
- Pierre Courderc as Scraps the Patchwork Girl, in *Patchwork Girl of Oz* (1914 silent film)
- Frederick Ko Vert as the "Phantom of the Basket" illusion, in *The Wizard of Oz* (1925 silent film)
- Frederick Kovert as the Peacock Lady, in *The Wizard of Oz* (1925 silent film)

MODERN ERA
- Bille Brown[a] as the Wicked Witch of the West, in *The Wizard of Oz* (1988 original stage version of the movie by the Royal Shakespeare Company)
- Kurt Raymond as the Witch, in *The Wizard of Oz* (stage version of the MGM movie in Southern California)
- Christopher Passi as Ozma, in *Land of Oz* (1981 Minneapolis Children's Theatre Company)

---

a Born William Gerard Brown.

- Fred Barton as Miss Gulch, in *Miss Gulch Returns* (1994 cabaret)
- Alex O'Connell as Mombi, in *The Land of Oz* (2000 Puddlejump Players[b] original stage musical)
- Kurt Raymond as the Witch, in the sing-along *Wizard of Oz* (2003 Hollywood Bowl)

Females Playing Male Characters

EARLY

- Bessie Wynn as Sir Dashemoff Daily, in *The Wizard of Oz* (1902 play)
- Chorus girl as the Captain of the Patrol, in *The Wizard of Oz* (1902 play)
- Woman as Leo, Captain of the Guards,[c] in *The Wizard of Oz* (1902 play)
- Chorus girls as Munchkin Boys, in *The Wizard of Oz* (1902 play)
- Chorus girls as Snow Boys, in *The Wizard of Oz* (1902 play)
- Chorus girls as Cooks, in *The Wizard of Oz* (1902 play)
- Blanche Dey as Tip, in *The Land of Oz* (1905 play)
- Violet MacMillan as King Bud, in *The Magic Cloak of Oz* (1914 silent film)
- Vivian Reed as Quavo the minstrel, in *The Magic Cloak of Oz* (1914 silent film)
- Violet MacMillan as Ojo, in *The Patchwork Girl of Oz* (1914 silent film)
- Vivian Reed as the Leader, in *The Patchwork Girl of Oz* (1914 silent film)
- Mildred Harris[d] as Button-Bright, in *His Majesty, the Scarecrow of Oz* (1914 silent film)

---

b   A Boston-area children's theater company.
c   Originally played by a male actor, but by 1908 it was played by a woman.
d   The first Mrs. Charlie Chaplin.

MODERN ERA
- Terry as Toto, in *The Wizard of Oz* (1939 film)
- Shirley Temple as Tip, in *The Land of Oz* (1960 television show)
- Cheryl Letourneau as Uncle Henry, in *The Wizard of Oz* (1979 movie by Mark Griffin)[e]
- Cheryl Letourneau as the Guardian of the Gates, in *The Wizard of Oz* (1979 movie by Mark Griffin)
- Debbie Donohoe as the Scarecrow, in *The Wizard of Oz* (1979 movie by Mark Griffin)

---

e A homemade movie by Mark Griffin, age eleven.

Appendix E
Early Allusions to Oz in Gay Contexts

- In 1973, on his first visit to San Francisco, the gay historian Allan Bérubé went home with a man who lived on a hill above Castro Street. The next morning his host showed Allan his view of the city. "The lights were glittering all over the City and the Bay. And the host said, 'Welcome to Oz.'"

- *Sparkles: The Ultimate Fairy Tale* by Michael Lewis and Jim Murdock is a 1981 gay musical patterned on *The Wizard of Oz*. It tells the story of a gay hairdresser, Larry, who goes to "LALA Land" during an electrical storm.

- While at NYU drama school in 1981, the gay producer Dan Jinks (*American Beauty*, *Milk*, and *Big Fish*) created a show in which the lead dressed like Dorothy from *The Wizard of Oz*.

- In 1982 Klaus Nomi, a gay German performance artist, recorded "Ding Dong (The Witch is dead)."

- In 1985 Ethan Mordden published a collection of short stories, *I've a Feeling We're Not in Kansas Anymore: Tales from Gay Manhattan* (New York: St. Martin's Press). An ad for the book in the gay magazine *Christopher Street* that year (issue 99) says in bold letters, "Manhattan is even stranger than the Land of Oz!"

Appendix F
The Origin of "Friend of Dorothy"

Sources That List the Expression
JUDY GARLAND IS GIVEN AS ORIGIN
- 1992. John Ayto and John Simpson, *Oxford Dictionary of Modern Slang* (New York: Oxford University Press).
- 1993. OED Online, second edition additions.
- 1994. Kevin Dilallo and Jack Krumholtz, *The Unofficial Gay Manual: Living the Lifestyle, or At Least Appearing To* (New York: Main Street/Doubleday).
- 1995. Jonathan Green, *Macmillan Dictionary of Contemporary Slang*, 3rd ed. (London: Macmillan).
- 1997. Jeff Fessler and Karen Rauch, *When Drag Is Not a Car Race: An Irreverent Dictionary of Over 400 Gay and Lesbian Words and Phrases* (New York: Simon and Schuster).
- 1997. Rebecca Scott, *A Brief Dictionary of Queer Slang and Culture*, http://www.geocities.com/WestHollywood/Stonewall/4219/.
- 1998. Robert Scott, *Wizard's Gay Slang Dictionary*, a.k.a. Robert Scott's *Gay Slang Dictionary*, http://www.hurricane.net/~wizard/19f.html.
- 2000. Orland Outland, *Coming Out: A Handbook for Men* (Los Angeles: Alyson).
- 2002. Paul Baker, *Fantabulosa: A Dictionary of Gay Slang* (London: Continuum).

- 2002. Simon Gage, Lisa Richards, and Howard Wilmot, *Queer* (New York: Thunder's Mouth Press).
- 2002. Donald Reuter, *Gaydar: The Ultimate Insider Guide to the Gay Sixth Sense* (New York: Crown).
- [As of 2017.] *A Dictionary of Slang: English Slang and Colloquialisms Used in the United Kingdom*, http://www.peevish.co.uk/slang/f.htm.
- [As of 2017.] *Queer Slang in the Gay 90's*, started with information gathered in part from the *Alyson Almanac*, http://atleb.tripod.com/ordbok/queer_slang_in_the_gay_90s.htm#f.

JUDY GARLAND AND DOROTHY PARKER
ARE GIVEN AS POSSIBLE ORIGINS

- 1995. William Stewart, *Cassell's Queer Companion* (London: Cassell).
- 1999. David Bianco, *Gay Essentials* (Los Angeles: Alyson).
- 2006. Donald Reuter, *Gay-2-Zee: A Dictionary of Sex, Subtext, and the Sublime* (New York: St. Martin's Press).
- 2014. Wikipedia. http://en.wikipedia.org/wiki/Friend_of_Dorothy.

Sources That Do *Not* List the Expression

SLANG LISTS

- 1941. Gershon Legman, "The Language of Homosexuality: An American Glossary," in *Sex Variants: A Study of Homosexual Patterns*, by George W. Henry (New York: Paul Hoeber).
- 1957. Swassarnt Nerf et al., "Gayese-English Glossary," in *Gay Girl's Guide to the U.S. and the Western World*, 3rd ed. (Privately printed mimeograph.)
- 1960. Gordon Westwood (pseudonym for Michael George Scholfield), "The Homosexual Vernacular," Appendix C in *A Minority: A Report on the Life of the Male Homosexual in Great Britain* (London: Longmans).
- 1962. Richard Hauser, "The Private Language of a Minority," in *The Homosexual Society* (London: Bodley Head).
- 1963. Donald Webster Cory and John LeRoy, "A Lexicon of Homosexual Slang," in their *The Homosexual and His Society: A View from Within* (New York: Citadel).

- 1964. Strait and Associates, *The Lavender Lexicon: Dictionary of Gay Words and Phrases* (San Francisco: Strait and Associates).
- 1965. *Guild Dictionary of Homosexual Terms* (Washington, DC: Guild Press).
- 1965. A. F. Niemoeller, "A Glossary of Homosexual Slang," *Fact* 2, no. 1 (Jan./Feb. 1965): 25–27.
- 1972. Bruce Rodgers, *The Queens' Vernacular: A Gay Lexicon* (New York: Straight Arrow Books), a.k.a. *Gay Talk* (New York: Putnam).
- 1980. Panos Bardis, "A Glossary of Homosexuality," *Maledicta* 4, no. 1 (Summer 1980): 59–63.
- 1984. Judy Grahn, *Another Mother Tongue: Gay Words, Gay Worlds* (Boston: Beacon Press).
- 1985. Wayne Dynes, *Homolexis: A Historical and Cultural Lexicon of Homosexuality* (New York: Gay Academic Union).
- 1988. H. Max, *Gay(s) Language: A Dic(k)tionary of Gay Slang* (Austin, TX: Banned Books).

EMPIRICAL RESEARCH STUDIES ON GAY SLANG
- 1965. Donald Webster Cory, "The Language of the Homosexual." *Sexology* 32 (Oct. 1965): 163–65.
- 1969. David Sonenschein, "The Homosexual's Language," *Journal of Sex Research* 5, no. 4 (Nov. 1969): 281–91.
- 1970. Julia Penelope Stanley, "Homosexual Slang," *American Speech* 45, nos. 1–2 (Spring–Summer 1970): 45–59.
- 1972. Ronald Farrell, "The Argot of the Homosexual Subculture," *Anthropological Linguistics* 14, no. 3 (Mar. 1972): 97–109.
- 1973. Julia Penelope Stanley, Unpublished manuscript of research asking for terms matching definitions such as "any homosexual, male or female," "any female homosexual," or "any male homosexual."
- 1976. James Conrad and William More, "Lexical Codes and Sub-Cultures: Some Questions," *Anthropological Linguistics* 18, no. 1 (Jan. 1976): 22–26.
- 1986. Reinhold Aman, Unpublished study on gay slang, one question of which involved "Homosexual male, general terms."

ACADEMIC DISCUSSIONS OF GAY CODES AND CODED LANGUAGE
- 1976. Joseph Hayes, "Gayspeak," *Quarterly Journal of Speech* 62, no. 2 (Oct. 1976): 256–66. Includes sections on secret, social, and radical-activist settings. There is nothing on "friend of Dorothy" in either the secret setting or the discussion of Hollywood stars' names as metaphors, e.g., "A melodramatic loser . . . is a *Stella Dallas*."
- 1989. Joseph Goodwin, "It Takes One to Know One: Communication and Identification in the Gay Subculture," chapter 2 in *More Man Than You'll Ever Be: Gay Folklore and Acculturation in Middle America* (Bloomington: Indiana University Press). "Friend of Dorothy" would fit perfectly in Goodwin's discussion of "ambiguous signals . . . [the message of which] can be denied" (p. 14).
- 1996. Greg Jacobs, "Lesbian and Gay Male Language Use: A Critical Review of the Literature," *American Speech* 71, no. 1 (Spring 1996): 49–71.
- 1996. William Leap, "The Risk Outside: Gay English, 'Suspect Gays,' and Heterosexuals," chapter 4 in *Word's Out: Gay Men's English* (Minneapolis: University of Minnesota Press).
- 1997. Brett Beemyn, "A Queer Capital: Race, Class, Gender, and the Changing Social Landscape of Washington's Gay Communities, 1940–1955," in *Creating a Place for Ourselves: Lesbian, Gay, and Bisexual Community Histories*, ed. Brett Beemyn (New York: Routledge).
- 2006. Martin Meeker, *Contacts Desired: Gay and Lesbian Communications and Community, 1940–1970s* (Chicago: University of Chicago Press).

REFERENCE SOURCES ON LANGUAGE
- *American Speech* (yearly indexes, 1938–2000).
- *The Dictionary of American Regional English*. When I spoke to editors there in 1999 or 2000, nobody had heard of the expression.
- *A Dictionary of English Phrases, Phraseological Allusions, Catchwords, Stereotyped Modes of Speech and Metaphors, Nicknames, Sobriquets,*

Derivations from Personal Names, etc., by Albert Montefiore Hyamson (Detroit, MI: Gale Research, 1970).
- *Notes and Queries* (yearly and cumulative indexes, 1898–2000).
- *Words and Phrases Index* (1969–70, covering eight sources, mostly 1940s to 60s, but some earlier as well).

PERSONAL CORRESPONDENCE

The following LGBT researchers have told me they haven't come across the expression in interviews or research:
- Genny Brett Beemyn (editor of *Creating a Place for Ourselves: Lesbian, Gay, and Bisexual Community Histories*).
- George Chauncey (*Gay New York*): "I don't believe I've ever come across someone using the expression 'a friend of Dorothy' in all the letters and diaries I've gone through."
- Martin Meeker (*Contacts Desired: Gay and Lesbian Communications and Community, 1940–1970s*).
- Randy Riddle (interviewed pre-Stonewall gay night club performers).

Notes

The sources provided here are keyed to the text by chapter, page number, first words of the paragraph (in bold), and key phrase (underlined). For each work cited, complete bibliographic information is given at the first citation in each chapter; subsequent citations are in "author's last name, short title" format.

Introduction

6 **It turned out that quite a few people**
   thesis on the music of Oz: Ryan Bruce Bunch, "'Over the Rainbow': Difference, Utopia, and *The Wizard of Oz* in Queer Musical Experience" (master's thesis, University of Maryland at College Park, 2001).
   a few were analytic: Patrick Horrigan, *Widescreen Dreams: Growing Up Gay at the Movies* (Madison: University of Wisconsin Press, 1999).

7 **I also began to look at writings**
   Hometowns: John Preston, ed., *Hometowns: Gay Men Write About Where They Belong* (New York: Dutton, 1991).

7–8 **The session itself**
   about sixty people: Tonya Maxwell, "Revisiting the Land of Oz: Fans Flock to Bloomington to Celebrate the Classic Book's 100th Anniversary," *Indianapolis Star*, July 23, 2000, p. B7.

9–10 **A narrative work of art**
   give rise to the themes of the work: Jerome Bruner, *Actual Minds, Possible*

Worlds (Cambridge, MA: Harvard University Press, 1986).

symbols and images: See, for example, Alice Byrnes, *The Child: An Archetypal Symbol in Literature for Children and Adults* (New York: Peter Lang, 1995); Don Fredericksen, "Jung/Sign/Symbol/Film," chap. 1 in *Jung and Film: Post-Jungian Takes on the Moving Image*, ed. Christopher Hauke and Ian Alister (Philadelphia: Taylor & Francis; London: Brunner-Routledge, 2001); Richard Sugg, ed., *Jungian Literary Criticism* (Evanston, IL: Northwestern University Press, 1992); Elizabeth Wright, *Psychoanalytic Criticism: A Reappraisal*, 2nd ed. (New York: Routledge, 1998).

readers' or viewers' interactions: Elizabeth Freund, *The Return of the Reader* (New York: Methuen, 1987); Steven Mailloux, *Interpretive Conventions* (Ithaca, NY: Cornell University Press, 1982).

a particular setting: John Izod, "Active Imagination and the Analysis of Film," *Journal of Analytical Psychology* 45 (April 2000): 267–85.

10 **Effects of the interaction**
readers or viewers get something they need: Byrnes, *The Child*; Izod, "Active Imagination"; Phyllis Berdt Kenevan, *Paths of Individuation in Literature and Film* (Lanham, MD: Lexington Books, 1999); Susan Rowland, *C. G. Jung and Literary Theory* (New York: St. Martin's Press, 1999).

11 **Perhaps more controversially**
characteristics . . . are more salient: David Nimmons, *The Soul Beneath the Skin: The Unseen Hearts and Habits of Gay Men* (New York: St. Martin's Press, 2002); Will Fellows, *A Passion to Preserve: Gay Men as Keepers of Culture* (Madison: University of Wisconsin Press, 2004).

CHAPTER 1. Gay Men and Oz

17 **"I always wanted to be Dorothy"**
"I always wanted": "Rufus Wainwright, 23, Musician," Generation Q: The Arts, *The Advocate*, no. 739/740 (Aug. 19, 1997), p. 36.

17–18 **It's not just the appeal of Judy Garland**
Greg Louganis: Greg Louganis, *Breaking the Surface* (New York: Random House, 1995), p. 1.
Clive Barker: Randy Conner et al., *Cassell's Encyclopedia of Queer Myth, Symbol and Spirit: Gay, Lesbian, Bisexual, and Transgender Lore* (London: Cassell, 1997), s.v. "Clive Barker."

18–19 **The connection between gay men**
Ben Brantley: Ben Brantley, "Why Oz Is a State of Mind in Gay Life and

Drag Shows," *New York Times*, June 28, 1994, pp. B1, B5 (quote on p. B1); reprinted in *The Gay Rights Movement: The New York Times 20th Century in Review*, ed. Vincent J. Samar (Chicago: Fitzroy Dearborn, 2001).
"a gay landmark": Sheridan Morley and Ruth Leon, *Judy Garland: Beyond the Rainbow* (New York: Arcade, 1999), p. 47.
dictionaries and encyclopedias: Philip Brett and Elizabeth Wood, "Gay and Lesbian Music," in *The New Grove Dictionary of Music and Musicians*, vol. 9, ed. Stanley Sadie (London: Macmillan, 2001); Conner et al., *Cassell's Encyclopedia of Queer Myth*, q.v. "The Wizard of Oz."
Michael Ford: Michael Thomas Ford, *The World Out There: Becoming Part of the Lesbian and Gay Community* (New York: New Press, 1996), p. 73.

20 **Some gay men have also written**
"In the mid-'60s": Julie Bookman, "The Great and Powerful 'OZ': 1939 Movie Still Whisks Its Fans 'Somewhere Over the Rainbow,'" *Atlanta Constitution*, Nov. 9, 1998, p. 01C.

20 **In his book *Sissyphobia***
"I was even a big Barbra Streisand fan . . .": Tim Bergling, *Sissyphobia: Gay Men and Effeminate Behavior* (New York: Harrington Park Press, 2001), p. 45.
Fred Barton: questionnaire response.
Rufus Wainwright: "Rufus Wainwright, 23, Musician."
Patrick Horrigan: Patrick Horrigan, *Widescreen Dreams: Growing Up Gay at the Movies* (Madison: University of Wisconsin Press, 1999).
Gregory Maguire: Peter Galvin, "A Wizard with Words," *The Advocate*, no. 692 (Oct. 17, 1995), pp. 56–59.
Ian Young: Ian Young, *The Stonewall Experiment: A Gay Psychohistory* (New York: Cassell, 1995).
Tomie dePaola: Tomie dePaola, "Future Classics," *Horn Book Magazine*, Nov./Dec 2000, pp. 740–41.
Derek Jarman: Derek Jarman, *Dancing Ledge* (New York: Overlook Press, 1993).
Waters: Raymond Murray, *Images in the Dark: An Encyclopedia of Gay and Lesbian Film and Video* (New York: Plume/Penguin, 1996), s.v. "John Waters."
Vidal: Gore Vidal, "The Oz Books," in *The Second American Revolution and Other Essays, 1976–1982* (New York: Random House, 1982).
Clive Barker: Brandon Judell, "Hell's Angel: Clive Barker, Stephen King's Heir Apparent, Discusses AIDS, Horror, Homosexuality—and,

Of Course, His Upcoming Film," *10 Percent* 3, no. 13 (Mar./Apr. 1995): 52–55, 73; Gayle Kidder, "Fascinated by Fiction of Fear; Barker: Even Good Things Can Be Scary," *San Diego Union-Tribune*, Mar. 1, 1990, p. C-1.

20–21 **One direct piece of evidence**
lists of favorite gay movies: Donald Reuter, "15 Gay-Fave Movies," in *Gaydar: The Ultimate Insider Guide to the Gay Sixth Sense* (New York: Crown, 2002); "50 Fabulous Films," accessed Jan. 2001, Roughcut, http://roughcut.com/main/godzilla_1gp.html; "Fifty Motion Pictures Worth Saving," Popcorn Q, Badpuppy Gay Today, July 28, 1997, accessed June 2017, http://gaytoday.badpuppy.com/garchive/entertain/072897en.htm; Steve Greenberg, "Fasten Your Seat Belts: The Ten Gayest Straight Movies Ever," *Genre* 28 (May 1995), p. 71; "Saturday Night at the Movies: Eighteen Films Every Gay Man Should See," in Kevin DiLallo and Jack Krumholtz, *The Unofficial Gay Manual: Living the Lifestyle, or At Least Appearing To* (New York: Main Street/Doubleday, 1994), p. 180; *High Camp: A Gay Guide to Camp and Cult Films*, vol. 1, ed. Paul Roen (San Francisco: Leyland Publications, 1994), p. 241; Michael Bronski, "Gay Men and Movies: Reel to Real," in *Gay Life: Leisure, Love and Living for the Contemporary Gay Male*, ed. Eric Rofes (Garden City, NY: Doubleday/Dolphin, 1986), p. 228.

22–23 **Oz imagery is frequently seen**
Mr. Potato Head: Fred Kuhr, "Providence Lights Up for 'Nighttime Pride' Parade," *in newsweekly* 10, no. 44 (June 27, 2001): 1, 28.

25–26 **Oz shows up in a gay context**
Dead Boys' Club: The film is part of a compilation called *Boys' Shorts: The New Queer Cinema* (1993).

26 **Documentaries on gay topics**
Bérubé recounts: *Neighborhoods: The Hidden Cities of San Francisco*, 1997, KQED, written, directed, and produced by Peter L. Stein.
British television series: *Over the Rainbow* was created by the collective Testing the Limits; it was shown on Channel 4 in the United Kingdom in 1995 and in the United States as *The Question of Equality* the same year. The companion book to the series is *Over the Rainbow: Lesbian and Gay Politics in America Since Stonewall*, ed. David Deitcher (London: Boxtree, 1995).
"Something in Oz": *Tongues Untied*, 1990, produced and directed by Marlon Riggs.

27   Still more examples can be found
      novels and short stories: Some examples are Joe Babcock's *The Tragedy of Miss Geneva Flowers* (New York: Carroll & Graf, 2005); David Levithan's *Boy Meets Boy* (New York: Knopf, 2003); J. G. Hayes's *This Thing Called Courage* (New York: Harrington Park Press, 2002); Armistead Maupin's *The Night Listener* (New York: Perennial, 2001); Sal Iacopelli's *Love, Sal: Letters from a Boy in the City* (Emeryville, CA: Greenery/Grass Stain Press, 2000); Jonathan Wald's "My Nazi Summer," in *Kosher Meat*, ed. Lawrence Schimel (Santa Fe, NM: Sherman Asher, 2000); Jack Fritscher's "Rainbow County," in *Rainbow County and Other Stories* (San Francisco: Palm Drive/Alamo Square Press, 1998); Clive Barker's *Sacrament* (New York: Harper Paperbacks, 1996); Robert Thomson's "The Traveling Companion" and jem coones's "Alister's Adventures," in *Happily Ever After: Erotic Fairy Tales for Men*, ed. Michael Ford (New York: Masquerade Books, 1996).

27   Discussions of the Oz–gay connection
      "serves as a social allegory": Jim Boin, "Follow the Yellow Brick Road, Follow the Yellow Brick Road," *OutNow: The Gay & Lesbian Newsmagazine for the Peninsula & Silicon Valley*, Sept. 2001, pp. 10–12.

28–29 But does Oz appeal to lesbians
      "is cherished for the line": Wayne N. Bryant, *Bisexual Characters in Film: From Anaïs to Zee* (New York: Harrington Park Press, 1997), p. 131.
      many critics have commented: Most notably Osmond Beckwith, "The Oddness of Oz," *Children's Literature* 5 (1976): 74–91.

29   The phenomenon of the Oz–gay connection
      "like my Wizard of Oz": Billy Porter interviewed in *Fabulous: The Story of Queer Cinema*, directed by Lisa Ades and Lesli Klainberg (Orchard Films, 2006).

29   Oz's appeal transcends national boundaries
      more than forty languages: Wikipedia, http://en.wikipedia.org/wiki/The_Wonderful_Wizard_of_Oz, accessed Nov. 2007.

30   I am looking at the connection
      1902 musical version: David L. Greene and Dick Martin, *The Oz Scrapbook* (New York: Random House, 1977), p. 128. See also Allen Eyles, *The World of Oz* (Tucson, AZ: HP Books, 1985), pp. 42–44.

32–33 Many other lovers of Oz
      tradition of being written for children: See, for example, Atticus

Gannaway, *Sinister Gases in Oz* (Corpus Christi, TX: Ozian Seahorse Press, 1991/1995); Bill Campbell and Irwin Terry, *The Lavender Bear of Oz* (New York: Emerald City Press, 1998); Gina Wickwar, *The Hidden Prince of Oz* (Kalamazoo, MI: International Wizard of Oz Club, 2000).

33 **Other narrative formats**
"Friends of Dorothy": http://eu.nifty.org/nifty/gay/celebrity/friends-of-dorothy.html, accessed Aug. 2014.

33–34 **Oz has also been depicted on the theatrical stage**
seven Tony awards: Eyles, *The World of Oz*, p. 75, citing *Variety*.

35 ***The Land of Oz*, a television version**
Return to Oz . . . much darker: Peter David, *But I Digress* (Iola, WI: Krause, 1994).

35–36 **Oz is also kept alive by fan clubs**
objects with images and quotes: See, for example, Greene and Martin, *The Oz Scrapbook*; Eyles, *The World of Oz*; Jay Scarfone and William Stillman, *The Wizard of Oz Collector's Treasury* (West Chester, PA: Schiffer, 1992); John Fricke, *100 Years of Oz: A Century of Classic Images from The Wizard of Oz Collection of Willard Carroll* (New York: Stewart, Tabori & Chang, 1999).
annexed by the folk: Jerry Griswold, "There's No Place but Home: *The Wizard of Oz*," *Antioch Review* 45, no. 4 (Fall 1987): 462–75 (see specifically p. 465).
transmedia storytelling: J. L. Bell, "The original transmedia storyteller?" Oz and Ends blog, Mar. 19, 2010, http://ozandends.blogspot.com/2010/03/original-transmedia-storyteller.html, accessed June 2017; Marc Lougee, "The Wizard of Oz: Transmedia pioneer?" Marclougee.com blog, Sept. 4, 2010, http://marclougee.com/2010/09/04/transmedia-oz/, accessed June 2017.

36 **Of course, an analysis of the story**
symbolism of the color red: Larry Hermsen, "Over the Rainbow, Into Our Hearts: *The Wizard of Oz* and the Gay Experience," *White Crane Newsletter*, no. 8 (circa 1990), pp. 1, 4–6, 10; also in *Sex and Spirit: Exploring Gay Men's Spirituality*, ed. Robert Barzan (San Francisco: White Crane Press, 1995).
MGM Dorothy . . . less assertive: Suzanne Rahn, *"The Wizard of Oz": Shaping an Imaginary World* (New York: Twayne, 1998), and also Todd Gilman, "'Aunt Em: Hate You! Hate Kansas! Taking the Dog.' Dorothy': Conscious and Unconscious Desire in *The Wizard of Oz*," *Children's*

Literature Association Quarterly 20, no. 4 (Winter 1995–96): 161–67 (see specifically p. 166).
"flesh and blood": Carol Billman, "'I've Seen the Movie': Oz Revisited," in *Children's Novels and the Movies*, ed. Douglas Street (New York: Frederick Ungar, 1983), p. 97.
purists may not like: Billman, "I've Seen the Movie."

36–37 **The changes from printed page to screen**
book . . . more frightening: Gilly Bar-Hillel, participant in "*The Wizard of Oz* Baum birthday show," The Connection, WBUR radio talk show hosted by Tovia Smith, May 15, 1998 (cassette tape).
three jolly farmhands: Billman, "I've Seen the Movie," p. 97.
movie is more terrifying: Rahn, *Shaping an Imaginary World*; Douglas Street, "The Wonderful Wiz That Was: The Curious Transformation of *The Wizard of Oz*," *Kansas Quarterly* 16, no. 3 (Summer 1984): 91–98.

37 **The illustrations in *The Wonderful Wizard***
their own mental images: Victor Nell, *Lost in a Book: The Psychology of Reading for Pleasure* (New Haven, CT: Yale University Press, 1988); Francis Spufford, *The Child That Books Built: A Life in Reading* (New York: Metropolitan Books/Holt, 2002).
generate visceral reactions: Christopher Hauke and Ian Alister, introduction to *Jung and Film: Post-Jungian Takes on the Moving Image* (Philadelphia: Taylor & Francis; London: Brunner-Routledge, 2001).
visual aspects of the Hollywood *Wiz*: Horrigan, *Widescreen Dreams*, chap. 4.
"A little girl falls asleep": Griswold, "There's No Place but Home," p. 474.

CHAPTER 2: Surface Explanations

41 **Loving Judy Garland because of her performance**
special relationship with her audience: Michael Bronski, "Judy Garland and Others: Notes on Idolization and Derision," in *Lavender Culture*, ed. Karla Jay and Allen Young (New York: Harcourt Brace Jovanovich, 1978); Richard Dyer, "Judy Garland and Gay Men," chap. 3 in *Heavenly Bodies: Film Stars and Society* (New York: St. Martin's Press, 1986), reprinted in *Rainbow: A Star-Studded Tribute to Judy Garland*, ed. Ethlie Ann Vare (New York: Boulevard Books, 1998).
Garland's appearance and performing: Dyer, "Judy Garland," p. 156.

42 **Other reasons for loving Judy Garland**
manipulated by society: Larry Hermsen, "Over the Rainbow, Into

Our Hearts: *The Wizard of Oz* and the Gay Experience," *White Crane Newsletter*, no. 8 (circa 1990), pp. 1, 4–6, 10, reprinted in *Sex and Spirit: Exploring Gay Men's Spirituality*, ed. Robert Barzan (San Francisco: White Crane Press, 1995).

her appeal to gay men began: Dyer, "Judy Garland," p. 142; Charles Kaiser, *The Gay Metropolis, 1940–1996* (Boston: Houghton Mifflin, 1997), pp. 192–93.

Judy's resilience: Michael Bronski, "Judy Garland and Others."

list of idols: Michael Bronski, *Culture Clash: The Making of Gay Sensibility* (Boston: South End Press, 1984), p. 103.

Castro Theatre: George Chauncey, *Gay New York: Gender, Urban Culture, and the Making of the Gay Male World, 1980–1940* (New York: Basic Books, 1994), p. 288.

43   **Third, gay diva worship**
diva worship was declared over: Damien Cave, "Descent of the Divas," *Salon.com*, Jan. 10, 2000, http://www.salon.com/2000/01/10/divas/, accessed June 2017; Timothy Lee, "Parental Punishment," review of *Minnelli on Minnelli* by Liza Minnelli (Broadway Angel Records, 2000), *Lavender* 5, issue 125 (Mar. 10–23, 2000): 26–27; Keith Orr, "Where Have All the Gay Icons Gone?" *Bay Windows*, Aug. 8–14, 2002, section 2, p. 1; Anne Taubeneck, "Diva Worship: Why Are Gay Men Devoted to Judy and Liza and Madonna and Bette?" *Chicago Tribune*, Tempo section, May 23, 2000, pp. 1, 3; Steve Weinstein, "The Gay Generation Gap," *Out*, Oct. 2001, pp. 90–91, 108–9.

"Young gay men have ditched": Michael Joseph Gross, "The Queen Is Dead: Once a Gay Icon, Judy Garland Has Become an Embarrassment," *Atlantic Monthly*, Aug. 2000, pp. 62–70 (quote on p. 69).

Judy Garland in particular: Gross, "The Queen Is Dead"; David Plunket, "Farewell, Judy; Hello, Madonna," *New York Times*, June 19, 1994, Arts section, p. 23.

45–46   **"IT'S A MUSICAL."**
gay men love musicals: For gay love of stage musicals, see, for example, John Clum, *Something for the Boys: Musical Theater and Gay Culture* (New York: St. Martin's Press, 1999); David Halperin, "Homosexuality's Closet," *Michigan Quarterly Review* 41, no. 1 (Winter 2002): 21–54; John Kenrick, "Our Love Is Here to Stay: Gays and Musicals," web essay, http://www.musicals101.com/ourlove.htm, accessed June 2017; D. A. Miller, *Place for Us: Essay on the Broadway Musical* (Cambridge, MA: Harvard University Press, 1998); Mark

Steyn, "The Fags," in *Broadway Babies Say Goodnight: Musicals Then and Now* (New York: Routledge, 1999). For gay love of film musicals, see John Clum, "Musical Theater and Film," in *The Queer Encyclopedia of Music, Dance and Musical Theater*, ed. Claude Summers (San Francisco: Cleis, 2004); Paul Roen, *High Camp: A Gay Guide to Camp and Cult Films*, vol. 1 (San Francisco: Leyland Publications, 1994).

46 "GAY PEOPLE CREATED THE MOVIE."
gay designers: William J. Mann, "The Yellow Brick Road," in *Gay Pride: A Celebration of All Things Gay and Lesbian* (New York: Citadel Press/Kensington, 2004), p. 166.
Edgar Allan Woolf: Milton Rexford (a.k.a. Boze Hadleigh) quotes Samuel Marx as saying that Woolf was a homosexual ("The Lavender Wizard of Oz," *Torso Magazine* [date unknown], pp. 8–13; quote on p. 13).
George Cukor: William J. Mann, *Behind the Screen: How Gays and Lesbians Shaped Hollywood, 1910–1969* (New York: Viking, 2001).
Roger Edens: Mann, *Behind the Screen*; Linda Rapp, "Roger Edens," in *glbtq: An Encyclopedia of Gay, Lesbian, Bisexual, Transgender, and Queer Culture*, http://www.glbtqarchive.com/arts/edens_r_A.pdf, accessed June 2017.
Billie Burke: Anthony Slide, "The Silent Closet," *Film Quarterly* 53, no. 4 (Summer 1999): 24–32 (see specifically p. 32); Mann, *Behind the Screen*, pp. 73–74.
Judy Garland: David Shipman, *Judy Garland: The Secret Life of an American Legend* (New York: Hyperion, 1993), pp. xi, 138, 180, 351, 488–89; Sheridan Morley and Ruth Leon, *Judy Garland: Beyond the Rainbow* (New York: Arcade, 1999), p. 68; Gerald Clarke, *Get Happy: The Life of Judy Garland* (New York: Random House, 2000), pp. 169, 345.

49 Despite its street language
Boykin has described: Keith Boykin, *One More River to Cross: Black and Gay in America* (New York: Anchor/Doubleday, 1996).
Horrigan's identity: Patrick Horrigan, *Widescreen Dreams: Growing Up Gay at the Movies* (Madison: University of Wisconsin Press, 1999).

CHAPTER 3: Gay Boys

55 Kids are aware of their sexual orientation
coming out earlier: Caitlin Ryan and D. Futterman, "Lesbian and Gay Adolescents: Identity Development," *Prevention Researcher* 8, no. 1

(2001): 1–5; Jennifer Egan, "Lonely Gay Teen Seeking Same," *New York Times Magazine*, Dec. 10, 2000, pp. 110–17, 128–31; Kathy Jesse, "Gay Teens Are Revealing Their Sexual Orientation Earlier Than Ever," *in newsweekly* 10, no. 52 (Aug. 22, 2001): 34; Etelka Lehoczky, "Young, Gay and OK," *The Advocate*, Feb. 1, 2005, pp. 24–25, 29, 31; Patricia Nell Warren, foreword to *Being Different: Lambda Youths Speak Out*, by Larry Dane Brimmer (New York: Grolier/Frank Watts, 1995).

activists . . . surprisingly quiet: Ken Corbett, "Homosexual Boyhood: Notes on Girlyboys," chap. 5 in *Sissies and Tomboys: Gender Nonconformity and Homosexual Childhood*, ed. Matthew Rottnek (New York: New York University Press, 1999); Julia Reischel, "Queer in the Crib: Gay Adults Like to Say They Were Born That Way," *Village Voice*, June 19, 2007, pp. 81–82, 84, 87.

55–56 **There are at least two reasons**
appear long before sexual expression: Claude Summers, "Forster, E. M," in *The Gay and Lesbian Literary Heritage: A Reader's Companion to the Writers and Their Works, from Antiquity to the Present*, ed. Claude Summers, rev. ed. (New York: Routledge, 2002).
showing an interest: Reischel, "Queer in the Crib," p. 87.

56 **Writings by and interviews with**
gay celebrities: David Bahr, "A Chip off the Old Blockbuster: Christopher Rice Talks About Writing His First Book," *The Advocate*, Aug. 29, 2000, pp. 38–41; Colin Campbell, "Vows: Janis Ian and Patricia Snyder," *New York Times*, Sept. 7, 2003, section 9, p. 15; Lawrence Ferber, "Gay Director Adam Shankman Is the Real *Wedding Planner*," *in newsweekly* 10, no. 23 (Jan. 31, 2001): 25–26; R. J. Grubb, "This Boy's Life," *Bay Windows*, Oct. 14–20, 2004, Arts Plus section, p. 1.
retrospective accounts: Ritch Savin-Williams, *Gay and Lesbian Youth: Expressions of Identity* (New York: Hemisphere, 1990), p. 2; J. Michael Bailey, "Gender Identity," chap. 3 in *The Lives of Lesbians, Gays, and Bisexuals: Children to Adults*, ed. Ritch Savin-Williams and Kenneth Cohen (Fort Worth, TX: Harcourt Brace, 1996), p. 77.
parents' descriptions: For mothers' stories, see, for example, Jean Baker, *Family Secrets: Gay Sons, A Mother's Story* (New York: Haworth, 1998); Mary Borhek, *My Son Eric: A Mother Struggles to Accept Her Gay Son and Discovers Herself* (New York: Pilgrim Press, 1979); Mary Ann Cantwell, *Homosexuality: The Secret a Child Dare not Tell* (San Rafael, CA: Rafael Press, 1996); Robb Forman Dew, *The Family Heart: A Memoir of When Our Son Came Out* (Reading, MA: Addison-Wesley, 1994). One memoir

written by both mother and son is Marlene Fanta Shyer and Christopher Shyer, *Not Like Other Boys: Growing Up Gay: A Mother and Son Look Back* (Boston: Houghton Mifflin, 1996). For fathers' stories, see Andrew R. Gottlieb, *Out of the Twilight: Fathers of Gay Men Speak* (New York: Harrington Park/Haworth Press, 2000) and Bryce McDougall, ed., *My Child Is Gay: How Parents React When They Hear the News* (Crows Nest, NSW, Australia: Allen & Unwin, 1998). For parents who knew their sons were gay at a young age, see, for example, Shyer and Shyer, *Not Like Other Boys*, p. 225; Peter Cassells, "This Lady Has Her Act Togethur [*sic*]," *Bay Windows*, June 7–13, 2001, pp. 3, 20, 21.

56 **The best information**
later identify as gay: Bailey, "Gender Identity"; Corbett, "Homosexual Boyhood," p. 112; Richard Green, *The "Sissy Boy Syndrome" and the Development of Homosexuality* (New Haven, CT: Yale University Press, 1987); Edgardo Menvielle and Catherine Tuerk, "An Outreach Program for Children with Gender-Variant Behaviors," handout from a PowerPoint presentation by the Children's National Medical Center (n.d.); Reischel, "Queer in the Crib"; Eric Rofes, "Making Our Schools Safe for Sissies," *High School Journal*, Oct./Nov. 1993 and Dec./Jan. 1994), pp. 337–40.

56–57 **In the 1970s and 80s**
Outreach Program: Edgardo Menvielle, "Children's Hospital Reaches Out to Gender-Variant Children and Their Families," *Social Work News Report* (Washington, DC: National Association of Social Workers, Metropolitan Washington Chapter, Aug./Sept. 2002), pp. 4–5; Catherine Tuerk, Edgardo Menvielle, and James de Jesus, *If You Are Concerned About Your Child's Gender Behaviors: A Guide for Parents* (Washington, DC: Outreach Program for Children with Gender-Variant Behaviors and Their Families, Children's National Medical Center, 2003).
the child was gay then: Nicole Crawford, "Understanding Children's Atypical Gender Behavior," *Monitor on Psychology*, Sept. 2003, pp. 40–42 (see p. 42).

57–58 **Many gay adults report**
when they were young: Menvielle and Tuerk, "An Outreach Program," p. 5.
"I must have been three": Bryce McDougall, "My Story," in McDougall, *My Child Is Gay*, p. 169.
Saul: Green, *The "Sissy Boy Syndrome,"* p. 192.
Craig: Adam Mastoon, *The Shared Heart: Portraits and Stories Celebrating Lesbian, Gay, and Bisexual Young People* (New York: Morrow, 1997), p. 38.

58–59 **Being excited by seeing another male**
Vernon: Michael Zambotti (compiler), *Born Gay: Mom Should Have Known When . . . ; Recollections of Childhood Memories* (San Francisco: Alamo Square Press, 1998), p. 102.
Clark: Zambotti, *Born Gay*, p. 96.
Otto: Zambotti, *Born Gay*, p. 110.
Cyril: Zambotti, *Born Gay*, p. 9.
"He was a young man": Don Clark, "A Path of Mirrors," in *Charmed Lives: Gay Spirit in Storytelling*, ed. Toby Johnson and Steve Berman (Brooklyn, NY: White Crane Books, 2006), p. 205.

59–60 **Young boys can also fantasize**
Mike McGinty: Mike McGinty, "Peristalsis," in *From Boys to Men: Gay Men Write About Growing Up*, ed. Robert Williams and Ted Gideonse (New York: Carroll & Graf, 2006).
"I looked down at Steve": Michael McAllister, "Sleeping Eros," in Williams and Gideonse, *From Boys to Men*, p. 5.
"I remember when": Green, *The "Sissy Boy Syndrome,"* p. 88.

60 **Because affection and fantasy are not observable**
John Selig: John Selig, "Gay Students Graduate, but Our Memories Don't," in *Telling Tales Out of School: Gays, Lesbians, and Bisexuals Revisit Their School Days*, ed. Kevin Jennings (Los Angeles: Alyson Books, 1998), p. 35.
Horehound Stillpoint: Horehound Stillpoint, "The Boy with the Questions and the Kid with the Answers," in *Growing Up Gay: A Literary Anthology*, ed. Bennett Singer (New York: New Press, 1993).
Wayne: Zambotti, *Born Gay*, p. 85.
Mark: Zambotti, *Born Gay*, p. 100.
Harry: Zambotti, *Born Gay*, p. 95.
Jonathan Caouette: Grubb, "This Boy's Life."

60–61 **When the radical priest Malcolm Boyd**
"I stretched full length": Malcolm Boyd, "From *Take Off the Masks*," in Singer, *Growing Up Gay*, p. 100.

61 **Many adults and teens say**
"grew up that way": Eric, quoted in Brimmer, *Being Different*, p. 35; Kevin Jennings, "American Dreams," in Singer, *Growing Up Gay*, p. 4; James Morrison, *Broken Fever: Reflections of a Gay Boyhood* (New York: St. Martin's Press, 2001), p. 7; Bryce McDougall, "My Story," p. 170.

61–62 **What are the lives of gay boys like?**
feelings of isolation and confusion: Adam Mastoon, introduction to Mastoon, *The Shared Heart*.

62 **Kids perceived as gay**
teased and bullied: Rofes, "Making Our Schools Safe"; Kathleen Kelleher, "More Boys Are Reporting Sexual Harassment at School," *Los Angeles Times*, Mar. 4, 2002, p. E2; Laura Kiritsy, "Chasnoff Finds Bullying Widespread," *Bay Windows*, Feb. 26–Mar. 3, 2004, pp. 3, 12, 17; Margie Mason, "Bullying of Gay Kids Common, Says Study," *Long Beach Press Telegram*, Dec. 13, 2002, p. A25.
"Lucky is the gay man": Richard Goldstein, "The Myth of Gay Macho," *Village Voice*, June 26–July 2, 2002.
"As I got older": Will, quoted in Mastoon, *The Shared Heart*, p. 22.

62 **Parents often disapprove of their gay sons**
Adam Shankman's parents: Ferber, "Gay Director Adam Shankman."
Chris: Mastoon, *The Shared Heart*, p. 56.
conceal . . . and repress them entirely: Brian Pronger, *The Arena of Masculinity: Sports, Homosexuality, and the Meaning of Sex* (New York: St. Martin's Press, 1990), pp. 112–13; John Allen, "Working Out: SCSU Professor George Appleby," *Metroline* 29, no. 13 (early July 2002): 20–21.
"with the development of self-consistency": Kenneth Cohen and Ritch Savin-Williams, introduction to Savin-Williams and Cohen, *The Lives of Lesbians, Gays, and Bisexuals*, p. 4.

62–63 **Why are gay boys perceived**
"I discovered Mother's jewelry box": Lew, in Zambotti, *Born Gay*, p. 85.

63–64 **Do gay boys have a different way of being**
Samuel: Zambotti, *Born Gay*, p. 30.
Justin: Zambotti, *Born Gay*, p. 103.
Alan: Zambotti, *Born Gay*, p. 31.
empirical research: David Nimmons, "Our Peaceable Kingdom," chap. 2 in *The Soul Beneath the Skin: The Unseen Hearts and Habits of Gay Men* (New York: St. Martin's Press, 2002).

64 **Imagination and creativity seem to be hallmarks**
social stigma: Menvielle, "Children's Hospital Reaches Out," p. 4.
Eric Karl Anderson: Eric Karl Anderson, "Barbie Girls," in Williams and Gideonse, *From Boys to Men*.

64 **There is also anecdotal evidence**
Adam Shankman: Ferber, "Gay Director Adam Shankman," p. 26.
Justin: Zambotti, *Born Gay*, p. 103.
Earl: Zambotti, *Born Gay*, p. 59.
Luke: Zambotti, *Born Gay*, p. 108.

64–65 **Similarly, many gay adults report**
Clint: Zambotti, *Born Gay*, p. 51.
Nick: Zambotti, *Born Gay*, p. 89.
Austin: Zambotti, *Born Gay*, p. 54.
Kerry: Zambotti, *Born Gay*, p. 98.
Brad: Zambotti, *Born Gay*, p. 103.
Timothy: Zambotti, *Born Gay*, p. 100.
careers in the theater: Green, *The "Sissy Boy Syndrome,"* p. 257.

65 **Even before they label themselves as gay**
outside the mainstream: Brimmer, *Being Different*, p. 26; Richard Isay, *Being Homosexual: Gay Men and Their Development* (New York: Farrar, Straus & Giroux, 1989).
"different": Kevin Berrill, preface to *Understanding Sexual Identity: A Book for Gay Teens and Their Friends*, by Janice Rench (Minneapolis, MN: Lerner, 1990).
"deviant": Patrick Horrigan, *Widescreen Dreams: Growing Up Gay at the Movies* (Madison: University of Wisconsin Press, 1999), p. xviii.
not understand what makes them so: Edgardo Menvielle and Catherine Tuerk, "A Support Group for Parents of Gender-Nonconforming Boys," supplement to *Journal of the American Academy of Child and Adolescent Psychiatry* 41, no. 8 (Aug. 2002): 1010–13.
not limited to the United States: George Appleby, ed., *Working-Class Gay and Bisexual Men* (New York: Harrington Park/Haworth Press, 2001), also published as *Journal of Gay & Lesbian Social Services* 12, no. 3/4 (2001); and personal correspondence with George Appleby, May 2008.

66 **Once you believe you are different**
sense of not belonging: Bahr, "A Chip off the Old Blockbuster"; Jay Blotcher, "Returning the Lifeline Offered to a Boy by a Powerful Amazon," *Bay Windows*, Dec. 7–13, 2000, pp. 1, 4–5 (quote on p. 4); Mastoon, *The Shared Heart*, p. 2; Zambotti, *Born Gay*, p. 73; Green, *The "Sissy Boy Syndrome"*; Peter Cassells, "Men's Event Honoree Lauds Fenway's Role in His Road to Recovery and Self-Acceptance," *Bay Windows*, Mar. 14–20, 2002, pp. 1, 19.
lack of support from their parents: Rik Isensee, *Growing Up Gay in a*

Dysfunctional Family: A Guide for Gay Men Reclaiming Their Lives (New York: Simon & Schuster/Fireside, 1991).
avoid being teased: Isay, *Being Homosexual.*
"special friend": See, for example, J. R. Ackerley, *My Father and Myself* (New York: New York Review of Books, 1999; orig. pub. 1968); Will Roscoe, *Queer Spirits: A Gay Men's Myth Book* (Boston: Beacon Press, 1995), p. xv; Aaron Hamburger, "Whatever Happened to . . . ," in Williams and Gideonse, *From Boys to Men.* Eric Jon Nones's *Caleb's Friend* (New York: Farrar, Straus & Giroux, 1993), a beautiful story about a boy who makes friends with a mer-boy, contains all the yearning for a special friend that many gay men write about.

66 **Gay youth themselves experience**
being gay itself is bad: Corbett, "Homosexual Boyhood"; Menvielle, "Children's Hospital"; Douglas Sadownick, "To Be Gay and Young in L.A.," *LA Weekly,* July 12–18, 2002, pp. 24–26.
internalize society's homophobia: Menvielle and Tuerk, "An Outreach Program"; Isensee, *Growing Up Gay.*
become ashamed: Alan Downs, *The Velvet Rage: Overcoming the Pain of Growing Up Gay in a Straight Man's World* (Cambridge, MA: Da Capo Press, 2005); Isensee, *Growing Up Gay.*
"I hate myself": Menvielle and Tuerk, "A Support Group," p. 1012.

66–67 **When kids (and adults) are ashamed**
won't discover their secret: Pronger, *The Arena of Masculinity,* pp. 112–13.
feeling of being a phony: Allen, "Working Out"; Ritch Savin-Williams, "Memories of Childhood and Early Adolescent Sexual Feelings Among Gay and Bisexual Boys," chap. 4 in Savin-Williams and Cohen, *The Lives of Lesbians, Gays, and Bisexuals.*
want to escape: Downs, *The Velvet Rage,* p. 27.
"best little boy in the world" syndrome: Andrew Tobias (writing as John Reid), *The Best Little Boy in the World* (New York: Ballantine, 1973).
academic achievement: Tobias, *Best Little Boy*; Joseph Harry, *Gay Children Grown Up: Gender Culture and Gender Deviance* (New York: Praeger, 1982).

67 **Of course, not every gay boy**
Morris Kight: Al Martinez, "L.A. Gay Rights Icons Loud, Proud, Moving On," *Los Angeles Times,* July 22, 2002, p. E1; see also Joseph, in Green, *The "Sissy Boy Syndrome,"* p. 362.

68 There are, then, clusters of feelings
different internal life: Savin-Williams and Cohen, preface to *The Lives of Lesbians, Gays, and Bisexuals*.

CHAPTER 4: Escaping to Oz

73–74 Why would gay fans, young or old
"The safest place to hide": Mark Thompson, *Gay Body: A Journey Through Shadow to Self* (New York: St. Martin's Press, 1997), pp. 24–25.

74 But gay Oz fans don't retreat
joyful experiences: Dorothy Singer and Jerome Singer, *The House of Make-Believe: Children's Play and the Developing Imagination* (Cambridge, MA: Harvard University Press, 1990).

75 Gay kids might be attracted to Oz
Growing up: Roger C. Aden, *Popular Stories and Promised Lands: Fan Cultures and Symbolic Pilgrimages* (Tuscaloosa: University of Alabama Press, 1999).

75–76 For many adult fans
helps you remember: Anne Fadiman, "On Rereading," foreword to *Rereadings*, ed. Anne Fadiman (New York: Farrar, Straus & Giroux, 2005). See Robert Brockway, *Myth from the Ice Age to Mickey Mouse* (Albany: State University of New York Press, 1993), for a discussion of Disneyland's nostalgic appeal for adults.
recollect them playfully: Singer and Singer, *House of Make-Believe*, pp. 238–39.

79 The fantasy and play that arise from stories
cognitive and emotional growth: Singer and Singer, *House of Make-Believe*, especially p. 34 and chap. 6; James Hillman, "A Note on Story," *Children's Literature* 3 (1974): 9–11.

80 Having a story read to you again
comfort: Fadiman, "On Rereading"; Emily Yoffe, "Play It Again, Mom (Again and Again . . .)," *New York Times*, July 13, 2003, Arts and Leisure section, pp. 9, 16.
pleasure: Fadiman, "On Rereading"; David Galef, "Observations on Rereading," in *Second Thoughts: A Focus on Rereading* (Detroit, MI: Wayne State University Press, 1998).
safety and mastery: Galef, "Observations on Rereading"; Singer and Singer, *House of Make-Believe*, p. 64; Aden, *Popular Stories*.

miniaturized into a more controllable one: Singer and Singer, *House of Make-Believe*, p. 151.

integrated into existing schemas: Singer and Singer, *House of Make-Believe*, p. 180; Galef, "Observations on Rereading"; Yoffe, "Play It Again, Mom."

80–81 **In early childhood, the very youngest fans**
Andre: Michael Zambotti (compiler), *Born Gay: Mom Should Have Known When . . . ; Recollections of Childhood Memories* (San Francisco: Alamo Square Press, 1998), pp. 34–35. Andre may or may not be an adult Oz fan.

81 **It is also very common for fans in middle childhood**
Gregory Maguire: Peter Galvin, "A Wizard with Words," *The Advocate*, Oct. 17, 1995, p. 56.

82–83 **Adults can play with Oz in a more deliberate way**
two Oz novels: *Leprechauns in Oz* (Protea, 2000) and *The Medicine Man of Oz* (Protea, 2001).
Derek Jarman: Derek Jarman, *Dancing Ledge* (New York: Overlook Press, 1993); Steve Nallon, "Could Even Van Damme Be a Friend of Dorothy?" www.stevenallon.com/Dorothy.html, accessed Mar. 2001.

84–85 **The gay Oz fan's immersion**
a life of its own: Andrew Samuels, Bani Shorter, and Fred Plaut, *A Critical Dictionary of Jungian Analysis* (New York: Routledge & Kegan Paul, 1986); John Izod, "Active Imagination and the Analysis of Film," *Journal of Analytical Psychology* 45 (Apr. 2000): 267–85; Susan Rowland, *C. G. Jung and Literary Theory* (New York: St. Martin's Press, 1999).
symbolically live another life: Robert Johnson, *Inner Work: Using Dreams and Active Imagination for Personal Growth* (New York: Harper & Row, 1986), p. 138.

85–86 **The rich visual symbols of film**
process akin to active imagination: Christopher Hauke and Ian Alister, introduction to *Jung and Film: Post-Jungian Takes on the Moving Image* (Philadelphia: Taylor & Francis; London: Brunner-Routledge, 2001), p. 2.
turn these aspects into strengths: Johnson, *Inner Work*, p. 207.
fuses imagery: Izod, "Active Imagination," pp. 271–72.
Baum, who encouraged his readers: Suzanne Rahn, *"The Wizard of Oz": Shaping an Imaginary World* (New York: Twayne, 1998), p. 130.

86   **We all have unfulfilled aspects of ourselves**
   such as fantasies: K. M. Soehnlein's "The Story I Told Myself," in *From Boys to Men*, ed. Robert Williams and Ted Gideonse, is a particularly elaborate example of a fantasy based on repressed aspects of the personality.
   try on different identities: Aden, *Popular Stories*, p. 255; Fadiman, "On Rereading."
   experience unlived parts of yourself: Johnson, *Inner Work*, pp. 207–8.
   vicarious experience: Maurice Saxby, "The Gifts of Wings: The Value of Literature to Children," and Gordon Winch, "The Light in the Eye: On Good Books for Children," in *Give Them Wings: The Experience of Children's Literature*, ed. Maurice Saxby and Gordon Winch (South Melbourne/Crows Nest, NSW, Australia: Macmillan, 1987); Francis Spufford, *The Child That Books Built: A Life in Reading* (New York: Metropolitan Books/Holt, 2002); D. W. Harding, "What Happens When We Read? (1)," in *The Cool Web: The Pattern of Children's Reading*, ed. Margaret Meek, Aidan Warlow, and Griselda Barton (New York: Atheneum, 1978), p. 70.
   fantasy also moves inward: Ursula Le Guin, "Do-It-Yourself Cosmology (1977)," in *The Language of the Night: Essays on Fantasy and Science Fiction*, edited and with introductions by Susan Wood; rev. ed. edited by Ursula Le Guin (London: Women's Press, 1989). See also Spufford, *The Child That Books Built*; Susan Cooper, "Escaping into Ourselves," in *Celebrating Children's Books: Essays on Children's Literature in Honor of Zena Sutherland*, ed. Betsy Hearne and Marilyn Kaye (New York: Lothrop, Lee & Shepard, 1981).

88   **Many fantasy stories**
   recreation of an entire world: Malcolm Edwards and Robert Holdstock, *Realms of Fantasy: An Illustrated Exploration of Ten of the Most Famous Worlds in Fantasy Fiction* (Garden City, NY: Doubleday, 1983); Karl Beckson and Arthur Ganz, "Fantasy," in *Literary Terms: A Dictionary*, rev. 3rd ed. (New York: Noonday/Farrar, Straus & Giroux, 1989); Ann Swinfen, *In Defence of Fantasy: A Study of the Genre in English and American Literature Since 1945* (Boston: Routledge & Kegan Paul, 1984); J. R. R. Tolkien, "On Fairy Stories," the first part of *Tree and Leaf*, in *The Tolkien Reader* (New York: Ballantine, 1966).

89   **By and large, the Land of Oz**
   not allowed to fight: S. J. Sackett, "The Utopia of Oz," in *The Wizard of Oz: The Critical Heritage*, ed. Michael Patrick Hearn (New York: Schocken

Books, 1983), p. 209.
Ozma refuses to fight: L. Frank Baum, *The Emerald City of Oz* (Chicago: Reilly & Britton, 1910), p. 268.
excellent message for children: Edward Wagenknecht, *Utopia Americana* (Folcroft, PA: Folcroft Press, 1970), p. 33; reprint of 1929 edition, University of Washington Book Store, Seattle, 1929.
Gay men . . . much less likely to be violent: Nimmons, *The Soul Beneath the Skin: The Unseen Hearts and Habits of Gay Men* (New York: St. Martin's Press, 2002), p. 24.

90 **But Oz is not all utopian goodness**
certain amount of conflict: Elizabeth Cook, *The Ordinary and The Fabulous: An Introduction to Myths, Legends and Fairy Tales for Teachers and Storytellers* (Cambridge: Cambridge University Press, 1969).
communities under threat: Neil Earle, *"The Wonderful Wizard of Oz" in American Popular Culture: Uneasy in Eden* (Lewiston, NY: Edwin Mellen Press, 1993), p. 70.

90 **Luckily for readers of the books**
"civilized": Sackett, "The Utopia of Oz," p. 208.
identify with Dorothy: Ben Indick, "Utopia, Allegory, and Nightmare," *Baum Bugle* 18 (Spring 1974): 14–19.

90 **One thing that makes a journey**
Scarecrow twists the necks of crows: Indick, "Utopia, Allegory, and Nightmare."
MGM Oz is even scarier: Rahn, *Shaping an Imaginary World*, p. 122.

91–92 **Adventure and conflict**
allow for exploration: Singer and Singer, *House of Make-Believe*, p. 74.
cruel side of play: Brian D'Amato, "The Wooden Gargoyles: Evil in Oz," in *Hard Road: A Cat Marsala Mystery* by Barbara D'Amato (New York: Scribner, 2001), p. 273.

92 **Magic gives one power**
conflict is created: Jack David Zipes, "L. Frank Baum and the Utopian Spirit of Oz," in *When Dreams Came True: Classical Fairy Tales and Their Tradition* (New York: Routledge, 1999), p. 176.

92–93 **Small characters mirror**
alternative to adult importance: Jerry Griswold, *Feeling Like a Kid: Childhood and Children's Literature* (Baltimore, MD: Johns Hopkins University Press, 2006), p. 106.

93 **Fantasy in general and myths**
generate wonder and awe: Tolkien, "On Fairy Stories"; Jack Zipes, introduction to *Spells of Enchantment: The Wondrous Fairy Tales of Western Culture*, ed. Jack Zipes (New York: Viking, 1991); Ellen Datlow, "Introduction, Red as Blood: Fairy Tales and Horror," in *Snow White, Blood Red*, ed. Ellen Datlow and Terri Windling (New York: Morrow/AvoNova, 1993).
L. Frank Baum was alert: Gore Vidal, "The Oz Books," in *The Second American Revolution and Other Essays, 1976–1982* (New York: Random House, 1982); Wagenknecht, *Utopia Americana*.

93–94 **Home is most commonly thought of**
the family you grew up in: See Christopher Carrington, *No Place Like Home: Relationships and Family Life Among Lesbians and Gay Men* (Chicago: University of Chicago Press, 1999).
can also mean a refuge: Griswold, *Feeling Like a Kid*, p. 9; Will Brooker, "A Sort of Homecoming: Fan Viewing and Symbolic Pilgrimage," in *Fandom: Identities and Communities in a Mediated World*, ed. Jonathan Gray, Cornel Sandvoss, and C. Lee Harrington (New York: New York University Press, 2007); Fadiman, "On Rereading"; Galef, "Observations on Rereading"; Yoffe, "Play It Again, Mom."
escape to Oz: Joel Chaston, "If I Ever Go Looking for My Heart's Desire: 'Home' in Baum's 'Oz' Books," *The Lion and the Unicorn* 18, no. 2 (Dec. 1994): 209–19.

94 **The arc of Dorothy's feelings**
ambivalent feelings: Patrick Horrigan, *Widescreen Dreams: Growing Up Gay at the Movies* (Madison: University of Wisconsin Press, 1999); John Preston, ed., *Hometowns: Gay Men Write About Where They Belong* (New York: Dutton, 1991); Mark Thompson, *Gay Soul: Finding the Heart of Gay Spirit and Nature with Sixteen Writers, Healers, Teachers, and Visionaries* (San Francisco: HarperSanFrancisco, 1995).

94–95 **Dorothy's yearning to go home**
conditions . . . have not: Todd Gilman, "'Aunt Em: Hate You! Hate Kansas! Taking the Dog. Dorothy': Conscious and Unconscious Desire in *The Wizard of Oz*," *Children's Literature Association Quarterly* 20, no. 4 (Winter 1995–96): 161–67.

95 **In the third, fourth, and fifth Oz books**
free from the obligations: Chaston, "If I Ever Go Looking," pp. 216–17.

Rushdie: Salman Rushdie, *The Wizard of Oz* (London: BFI Publishing, 1992), p. 57.

95 **When a gay male goes off**
new gay friends who become: Clive Barker, *Sacrament* (New York: Harper Paperbacks, 1996).
build a new family in Oz: Julian Fleisher, *The Drag Queens of New York: An Illustrated Field Guide* (New York: Riverhead Books, 1996).
later Thompson book: Ruth Plumly Thompson, *Ojo in Oz* (Chicago: Reilly & Lee, 1933).
Tin Woodman finds a brother: L. Frank Baum, *The Tin Woodman of Oz* (Chicago: Reilly & Britton, 1918).
Scarecrow . . . family tree: L. Frank Baum, *The Scarecrow of Oz* (Chicago: Reilly & Britton, 1915).

96 **In general, Baum represents**
home . . . to escape from: Chaston, "If I Ever Go Looking."

96 **Like Salman Rushdie**
places of refuge: John D'Emilio, *Sexual Politics, Sexual Communities: The Making of a Homosexual Minority in the United States, 1940–1970* (Chicago: University of Chicago Press, 1983).
transformation of identity: Peter Berger, *Invitation to Sociology: A Humanistic Perspective* (Garden City, NY: Anchor Books/Doubleday, 1963), p. 58.
New York and . . . Greenwich Village: Tina Landau's play *1969* compares both New York City and Greenwich Village to Oz and the Emerald City, as Ronald Zank mentions in "'Come Out, Come Out, Wherever You Are,'" chap. 4 in *The Universe of Oz: Essays on Baum's Series and Its Progeny*, ed. Kevin Durand and Mary Leigh (Jefferson, NC: McFarland, 2010), p. 73. A character in Christopher Bram's novel *Exiles in America* (New York: William Morrow, 2006) talks of Manhattan as Oz (p. 159). New York is equated with the Emerald City in Michael Arlen's "Eros in the Emerald City: The Low Spark of High-Rise Towns," *Rolling Stone*, Oct. 6, 1977, pp. 43–44.
San Francisco and its Castro: Les Wright, "San Francisco," in *Queer Sites: Gay Urban Histories*, ed. David Higgs (New York: Routledge, 1999), p. 173; Sal Iacopelli, *Love, Sal: Letters from a Boy in the City* (Emeryville, CA: Greenery/Grass Stain Press, 2000), p. 14. Marlon Riggs and Allan Bérubé also characterize San Francisco as Oz, as mentioned earlier.

CHAPTER 5: Gender Roles in Oz

97 **Science fiction, with its ray guns**
Fantasy . . . being for girls: Beverly Lyon Clark, *Kiddie Lit: The Cultural Construction of Children's Literature in America* (Baltimore, MD: Johns Hopkins Press, 2003); Mary Rouse, "We're Off to See the Wizard," unknown newspaper (probably from New York, the *Daily News* or *Post*), ca. 1975.

98 **In Oz, adult males are often weak**
Walter Murch: Interviewed in Michael Ondaatje, *The Conversations: Walter Murch and the Art of Editing Film* (New York: Knopf, 2002), p. 290.
girls and women rule: Alison Lurie, "The Oddness of Oz," *New York Review of Books* 48, no. 20 (Dec. 21, 2000): 16–24. See also Salman Rushdie, *The Wizard of Oz* (London: BFI Publishing, 1992).

98 **Gender-atypical behavior usually begins to manifest**
same time . . . fandom strikes: Edgardo Menvielle, "Children's Hospital Reaches Out to Gender-Variant Children and Their Families," *Social Work News Report* (Washington, DC: National Association of Social Workers, Metropolitan Washington Chapter, Aug./Sept. 2002), pp. 4–5.
put off by a human character: Harry Benshoff and Sean Griffin, *Queer Images: A History of Gay and Lesbian Film in America* (Lanham, MD: Rowman & Littlefield, 2006), p. 11.
identify with animals: Ellen Handler Spitz, *Inside Picture Books* (New Haven, CT: Yale University Press, 1999); Jerry Griswold, *Feeling Like a Kid: Childhood and Children's Literature* (Baltimore, MD: Johns Hopkins University Press, 2006); Anthony Storr, *Solitude* (London: Flamingo/Fontana/Collins, 1989).
indulge in behavior: Judith Goldstein, "Realism Without a Human Face," in *Spectacles of Realism: Body, Gender, Genre*, ed. Margaret Cohen and Christopher Prendergast (Minneapolis: University of Minnesota, 1995); Edward Hudlin, "The Mythology of Oz: An Interpretation," *Papers on Language and Literature* 24, no. 4 (Fall 1989): 443–62.

98–99 **In middle childhood**
seek approval: Laurie Brady, "Children and Their Books: The Right Books for the Right Child, 1," in *Give Them Wings: The Experience of Children's Literature,* ed. Maurice Saxby and Gordon Winch (South Melbourne/Crows Nest, NSW, Australia: Macmillan, 1987).

99–100 **The character gay fans most commonly cite**
early strong female: Susan J. Douglas, *Where the Girls Are: Growing*

Up Female with the Mass Media (New York: Times Books/Random House, 1994); Laura Sessions Stepp, "Hollywood's Material Girls," *Washington Post*, Aug. 3, 2003, Arts section, pp. N1, N4; Mark West, "The Dorothys of Oz: A Heroine's Unmaking," in *Stories and Society: Children's Literature in Its Social Context*, ed. Dennis Butts (London: Macmillan, 1992).

100–101 **Dorothy's companions**
traditionally male qualities: Robert Hopcke, *Jung, Jungians and Homosexuality* (Boston: Shambala, 1989); Suzanne Rahn, *"The Wizard of Oz": Shaping an Imaginary World* (New York: Twayne, 1998); Gita Dorothy Morena, *The Wisdom of Oz* (San Diego, CA: Inner Connections Press, 1998).
"inner masculinity": Hopcke, *Jung, Jungians*, p. 144.
"destructive power": Hopcke, *Jung, Jungians*, p. 145.
feel better about both male and female aspects: Mark Thompson, *Gay Body: A Journey Through Shadow to Self* (New York: St. Martin's Press, 1997), p. 253, fn. 2.

101 **In the Oz books two powerful practitioners**
Glinda is described: L. Frank Baum, *The Wonderful Wizard of Oz*, chap. 18 (any edition).
Dorothy first sees her: Baum, *The Wonderful Wizard*, chap. 23.

101–102 **The MGM Glinda**
"femme allure": Alexander Doty, "'My Beautiful Wickedness': *The Wizard of Oz* as Lesbian Fantasy," in *Flaming Classics: Queering the Film Canon* (New York: Routledge, 2000), p. 66.
"cotton candy" outfit: George Keating interviewed in "Sing Out, Dorothy!" *Next Magazine* 10, no. 48 (June 6, 2003): 12.
caricature of femininity: Rushdie, *The Wizard of Oz*; Doty, "'My Beautiful Wickedness.'"

102 **In her role as Dorothy's helper**
mother or grandmother figure: Jordan Brotman, "A Late Wanderer in Oz," in *Only Connect*, ed. Sheila Egoff, 1st ed. (New York: Oxford University Press, 1969).
Kristin Chenoweth: Andy Humm, "Kristin Chenoweth's Gospel Journey," *Gay City News* 4, no. 16 (Apr. 21–27, 2005), http://gaycitynews.nyc/gcn_416/kristinchenowethsgospel.html, accessed June 2017.

102 **The benevolent Princess Ozma**
"most beautiful girl": L. Frank Baum, *The Magic of Oz*

(Chicago: Reilly & Lee, 1919), p. 241.
"From the couch arose": L. Frank Baum, *The Marvelous Land of Oz* (Chicago: Reilly & Britton, 1904), p. 275.

102–103 **Although sometimes appearing quite young**
"a merry little girl": S. J. Sackett, "The Utopia of Oz," in *The Wizard of Oz: The Critical Heritage*, ed. Michael Patrick Hearn (New York: Schocken Books, 1983), p. 210.

103 **As a fairy, Ozma**
spiritual companion: Thompson, *Gay Body*, p. 25.

103–104 **Fans also identify with the Witch**
camp value: Doty, "'My Beautiful Wickedness,'" p. 51.
Miss Gulch Returns: Fred Barton, *Miss Gulch Returns: A Wicked Musical* (Fab Music, 1999), CD liner notes, p. 2.

105 **Jinjur is another strong female character**
"The City glitters": Baum, *Marvelous Land*, pp. 87–89.

106 **Traditionally, masculinity is associated**
weak, ineffectual losers: The adjectives—"weak" and "ineffectual"—are from Osmond Beckwith, "The Oddness of Oz," *Children's Literature* 5 (1976): 74–91; "losers" is a term used by a questionnaire respondent.

107 **The Cowardly Lion as portrayed by Bert Lahr**
"one of filmdom's professional sissies": Parker Tyler, *Screening the Sexes: Homosexuality in the Movies* (New York: Da Capo Press, 1993), p. 341.
"cinema's best-loved nelly character": Richard Smith, "Daring to Dream: On the Centenary of the Birth of Yip Harburg," *Gay Times* (London), no. 211 (Apr. 1996), pp. 60–61 (quote on p. 60).
Zen of Oz: Joey Green, *The Zen of Oz: Ten Spiritual Lessons from Over the Rainbow* (Los Angeles: Renaissance Books, 1998), pp. 83–85.

107 **When Dorothy and her companions come across**
"Hah, put 'em up" and other quotations from the screenplay: Noel Langley, Florence Ryerson, and Edgar Allan Woolf, *The Wizard of Oz: The Screenplay*, edited and with an introduction by Michael Patrick Hearn (New York: Delta/Dell, 1989), pp. 79–80.

107–108 **Later the four travelers**
socially constructed, masculinity: Reid Davis, "What WOZ: Lost Objects, Repeat Viewings, and the Sissy Warrior," *Film Quarterly* 55, no. 2 (Winter 2001–02): 2–13.

109 **Learning about camp**
   Reid Davis: Davis, "What WOZ," p. 10.

110 **In the MGM film the mannerisms**
   "This is his Majesty's day": Baum, *The Marvelous Land*, p. 123.

110 **Even children notice**
   "a bit fey": Maguire's questionnaire response.

110–111 **The Tin Woodman also stands for sensitivity**
   "No one comes round": Christopher John Treacy, "What Time Is It, 'Tin Man'?" *in newsweekly* 15, no. 15 (Nov. 30, 2005), p. A17.
   courtesy, kindness: L. Frank Baum, *The Patchwork Girl of Oz* (Chicago: Reilly & Britton, 1913), p. 323.
   empathizes with bugs: Baum, *The Wonderful Wizard*, chap. 6.
   and flowers: Baum, *The Patchwork Girl*, chap. 26.
   inexpressive male: Doty, "'My Beautiful Wickedness,'" p. 49.

112 **Two other citizens of Oz**
   Wogglebug . . . dresses like a dandy: L. Frank Baum, *The Emerald City of Oz* (Chicago: Reilly & Britton, 1910), chap. 5.
   Frogman . . . dresses in fancy clothing: L. Frank Baum, *The Lost Princess of Oz* (Chicago: Reilly & Britton, 1917), chap. 17.

113–114 **The Wizard of Oz in the main story**
   no real power: Joel Chaston, "If I Ever Go Looking for My Heart's Desire: 'Home' in Baum's 'Oz' Books," *The Lion and the Unicorn* 18, no. 2 (Dec. 1994): 212.
   stand for fathers: Rahn, *Shaping an Imaginary World*, p. 70.

114 **Gay men who feel alienated**
   patriarchal values: Michael Bronski, "*The Wizard of Oz* Baum Birthday Show," The Connection, WBUR radio talk show hosted by Tovia Smith, May 15, 1998 (cassette tape).
   fathers who distanced themselves: Bruce Shenitz, ed., *The Man I Might Become: Gay Men Write About their Fathers* (New York: Marlowe, 2002), especially Douglas Sadownick, "My Father, My Self," and James Saslow, "Daddy Was a Hot Number"; Richard Isay, *Being Homosexual: Gay Men and Their Development* (New York: Farrar, Straus & Giroux, 1989).

114 **Billina, the Yellow Hen, began life**
   Billina: L. Frank Baum, *Ozma of Oz* (Chicago: Reilly & Britton, 1907), chap. 2.

114–115 **Perhaps the most startling**
"'Yes,' said the old Witch": Baum, *The Marvelous Land*, pp. 269–72.
Kenneth Anger: Bill Landis, *Anger: The Unauthorized Biography of Kenneth Anger* (New York: HarperCollins, 1995), p. 11.
transgender child: Maximillian Potter, "Second Nature," *5280: Denver's Magazine*, March 2008, http://www.5280.com/2010/08/second-nature/, accessed June 2017.

116 **The typical girls' story**
modeling gender nonconformity: Hopcke, *Jung, Jungians*, p. 141.

CHAPTER 6: Difference in Oz

117 **Writers of fantasy aren't bound**
subgenre of fantasy: Rosemary Jackson, *Fantasy: The Literature of Subversion* (New York: Methuen, 1981); Kathleen Morner and Ralph Rausch, *NTC's Dictionary of Literary Terms* (Lincolnwood, IL: National Textbook Co., 1991); Ann Swinfen, *In Defence of Fantasy: A Study of the Genre in English and American Literature Since 1945* (Boston: Routledge & Kegan Paul, 1984).
Baum created Oz: Suzanne Rahn, *"The Wizard of Oz": Shaping an Imaginary World* (New York: Twayne, 1998), p. 43.
considered a utopia: The first serious critical writing about Oz was Edward Wagenknecht's *Utopia Americana*, published in 1929 by University of Washington Book Store, Seattle (reprinted Folcroft, PA: Folcroft Press, 1970). See also Andrew Karp, "Utopian Tension in L. Frank Baum's Oz," *Utopian Studies* 9, no. 2 (1988): 103–21; S. J. Sackett, "The Utopia of Oz," in *The Wizard of Oz: The Critical Heritage*, ed. Michael Patrick Hearn (New York: Schocken Books, 1983); Ben Indick, "Utopia, Allegory, and Nightmare," *Baum Bugle* 18 (Spring 1974): 14–19; Jack David Zipes, "L. Frank Baum and the Utopian Spirit of Oz," in *When Dreams Came True: Classical Fairy Tales and Their Tradition* (New York: Routledge, 1999).

117–118 **Friendship is a strong theme**
"caught the Scarecrow": L. Frank Baum, *The Marvelous Land of Oz* (Chicago: Reilly & Britton, 1904), p. 124.

118 **Friendship and caretaking**
aspects of gay male sensibility and culture: Christian De la Huerta, *Coming Out Spiritually: The Next Step* (New York: Tarcher/Putnam, 1999); David Nimmons, *The Soul Beneath the Skin: The Unseen Hearts and Habits of Gay Men* (New York: St. Martin's Press, 2002); David Nimmons,

"Manifest Love," in *Charmed Lives: Gay Spirit in Storytelling*, ed. Toby Johnson and Steve Berman (Brooklyn, NY: White Crane Books, 2006); Don Clark, *Someone Gay: Memoirs* (Maple Shade, NJ: Lethe Press, 2007).
"special friend": J. R. Ackerley, *My Father and Myself* (New York: New York Review of Books, 1999; orig. pub. 1968); Will Roscoe, *Queer Spirits: A Gay Men's Myth Book* (Boston: Beacon Press, 1995), pp. xiii–xvi.
"circle of loving companions": Roscoe, *Queer Spirits*, pp. 303–4. See also Nimmons, *The Soul Beneath the Skin*, chap. 6.

118–119 **Lonely children often turn**
native inhabitants: Zipes, "Baum and the Utopian Spirit," p. 174.

119 **Living in harmony**
communal feelings: Zipes, "Baum and the Utopian Spirit," pp. 176, 182.

119 **While cooperation is valued**
Ozma is a hands-off ruler: Sackett, "The Utopia of Oz," p. 209.
drive many plots: Karp, "Utopian Tension," p. 116.
lesson Baum teaches: Karp, "Utopian Tension," p. 118.

120 **But Oz itself is made up of**
country defined by its own customs: Rahn, *Shaping an Imaginary World*, p. 101.

121 **Oz's government**
values of the Land are democratic: Indick, "Utopia, Allegory, and Nightmare"; Sackett, "The Utopia of Oz."
Ozma often plays merrily: Sackett, "The Utopia of Oz," p. 210.

122 **The traditional power differential**
children become . . . prominent: Gary Westfahl, "Giving Horatio Alger Goosebumps," chap. 4 in *Science Fiction, Children's Literature, and Popular Culture: Coming of Age in Fantasyland* (Westport, CT: Greenwood, 2000), p. 39.

122 **Upon closer inspection**
unique individuals are considered superior: Karp, "Utopian Tension," p. 109.
humans . . . never seem to do work: Karp, "Utopian Tension," p. 108.

122 **The most important utopian value**
judged by their behavior: Willard Carroll, preface to *The 100 Years of Oz: A Century of Classic Images from The Wizard of Oz Collection of Willard Carroll* (New York: Stewart, Tabori & Chang, 1999); Andrew Karp,

"Utopian Tension"; Rahn, *Shaping an Imaginary World*; Katherine Rogers, *L. Frank Baum: Creator of Oz* (New York: St. Martin's Press, 2002); Cathleen Schine, "America as Fairyland," *New York Times Book Review*, July 7, 1985, p. 13; Zipes, "Baum and the Utopian Spirit."

123 **The way Dorothy befriends**
society populated by eccentrics: Schine, "America as Fairyland."

124 **There is nothing objectively wrong**
Oz's celebrities: L. Frank Baum, *Ozma of Oz* (Chicago: Reilly & Britton, 1907), p. 20.
"You have the pleasure of knowing": L. Frank Baum, *The Tin Woodman of Oz* (Chicago: Reilly & Britton, 1918), p. 116.

124–125 **Outsiders in other versions**
Boykin: Keith Boykin, *One More River to Cross: Black and Gay in America* (New York: Anchor/Doubleday, 1996), p. 7.

126 **Adult gay fans also respond**
archetypal outsiders: Robert H. Hopcke, interviewed in *Gay Soul: Finding the Heart of Gay Spirit and Nature with Sixteen Writers, Healers, Teachers, and Visionaries*, by Mark Thompson (San Francisco: HarperSanFrancisco, 1995), p. 215.
the "other": Harry Hay, "A Separate People Whose Time Has Come," in *Gay Spirit: Myth and Meaning*, ed. Mark Thompson (New York: St. Martin's Press, 1987), p. 89.
strangers in a heterosexual world: Michael Bronski, participant in "*The Wizard of Oz* Baum birthday show," The Connection, WBUR radio talk show hosted by Tovia Smith, May 15, 1998 (cassette tape); Anita Gates, "Festival of Short Gay Plays About Seeking Acceptance," *New York Times*, Dec. 21, 2001, section E, p. 4.

126 **Adult gay fans escape to Oz in their imaginations**
Vidal's claim: Gore Vidal, "The Oz Books," in *The Second American Revolution and Other Essays, 1976–1982* (New York: Random House, 1982).

CHAPTER 7: Messages and Uses of Oz

127 **Because heterosexuality is a societal norm**
conformity is . . . poignant: Mitch Walker, *Men Loving Men: A Gay Sex Guide and Consciousness Book*, rev. ed. (San Francisco: Gay Sunshine Press, 1994); Michael Zambotti (compiler), *Born Gay: Mom Should Have Known When . . . ; Recollections of Childhood Memories* (San Francisco: Alamo Square Press, 1998).

"false self": Andrew Tobias (writing as John Reid), *The Best Little Boy in the World* (New York: Ballantine, 1973).

pretend to be straight: Frontline, "Assault on Gay America: The Life and Death of Billy Jack Gaither," PBS/WGBH television show, originally aired Feb. 15, 2000.

period of hiding: Alan Downs, *The Velvet Rage: Overcoming the Pain of Growing Up Gay in a Straight Man's World* (Cambridge, MA: Da Capo Press, 2005); Rik Isensee, *Growing Up Gay in a Dysfunctional Family: A Guide for Gay Men Reclaiming Their Lives* (New York: Simon & Schuster/Fireside, 1991).

127 **Deceit and humbug**

Deceit and humbug are disparaged: Brian D'Amato, "The Wooden Gargoyles: Evil in Oz," in *Hard Road: A Cat Marsala Mystery* by Barbara D'Amato (New York: Scribner, 2001), p. 274.

"coming out from behind the screen": Linda Hansen, "Experiencing the World as Home: Reflections on Dorothy's Quest in *The Wizard of Oz*," *Soundings* 67, no. 1 (Spring 1984): 91–102 (quote on p. 100). This was not said in a gay context.

Purple Prince of Oz: Chicago: Reilly & Lee, 1932.

128 **Given parental assumptions**

symbols, fantasy literature, and myths: Robert Johnson, *Inner Work: Using Dreams and Active Imagination for Personal Growth* (New York: Harper & Row, 1986); Stephen Larsen, *The Mythic Imagination: The Quest for Meaning Through Personal Mythology* (Rochester, VT: Inner Traditions, 1996); Gary J. Stern, *A Few Tricks Along the Way: Daily Reflections for Gay Men, Queer Boys, Magnificent Queens and the People Who Love Them* (Freedom, CA: Crossing Press, 1994), page for Nov. 30.

help us see the reality: Northrop Frye, *The Educated Imagination*, The Massey Lectures, 2nd series (Toronto: CBC, 1963); J. R. R. Tolkien, "On Fairy Stories," the first part of *Tree and Leaf*, in *The Tolkien Reader* (New York: Ballantine, 1966); Ann Swinfen, *In Defence of Fantasy: A Study of the Genre in English and American Literature Since 1945* (Boston: Routledge & Kegan Paul, 1984).

follow their bliss: Joseph Campbell, with Bill Moyers, *The Power of Myth* (New York: Doubleday, 1988).

128 **But the message of Oz is deeper**

Dorothy finally understands the power: Jerry Griswold, "There's No Place but Home: *The Wizard of Oz*," *Antioch Review* 45, no. 4 (Fall 1987): 473.

129 For some, going to Oz

psychic life is unconscious: Frances Wickes, *The Inner World of Childhood* (Englewood Cliffs, NJ: Prentice-Hall/Spectrum, 1978), p. 16.

Symbols . . . tap into the unconscious: Johnson, *Inner Work*; John Izod, "Active Imagination and the Analysis of Film," *Journal of Analytical Psychology* 45 (April 2000): 267–85; Ursula Le Guin, "Myth and Archetype in Science Fiction (1976)," in *The Language of the Night: Essays on Fantasy and Science Fiction,* edited and with introductions by Susan Wood; rev. ed. edited by Ursula Le Guin (London: Women's Press, 1989); Kathleen Raine, "C. G. Jung: A Debt Acknowledged," chap. 13 in *Jungian Literary Criticism,* ed. Richard Sugg (Evanston, IL: Northwestern University Press, 1992); Phyllis Berdt Kenevan, *Paths of Individuation in Literature and Film* (Lanham, MD: Lexington Books, 1999); John Beebe, "The *Anima* in Film," chap. 11 in *Jung & Film: Post-Jungian Takes on the Moving Image,* ed. Christopher Hauke and Ian Alister (Philadelphia: Taylor & Francis; London: Brunner-Routledge, 2001).

access inner truths: Kenevan, *Paths of Individuation.*

accepted without gay fans' compromising: Kenevan, *Paths of Individuation.*

129–130 One type of self-discovery

in touch with early feelings: Larry Hermsen, "Over the Rainbow, Into Our Hearts: *The Wizard of Oz* and the Gay Experience," *White Crane Newsletter,* no. 8 (circa 1990), p. 10.

no longer heed authorities: Toby Johnson, "Straw into Gold: Storytelling and Self-Fulfilling Prophecy," introduction to *Charmed Lives: Gay Spirit in Storytelling,* ed. Toby Johnson and Steve Berman (Brooklyn, NY: White Crane Books, 2006).

see with gay eyes: Les Wright, "'Female' Trouble: Reading Symbolic Gender Dysphoria in Cult Films as Gay Male Coming Out Parables," paper presented at the Literature/Film Association Annual Conference, Towson State University, November 1994.

get rid of the false self: Isensee, *Growing Up Gay.*

quests are metaphors: Gerald Clarke, *Get Happy: The Life of Judy Garland* (New York: Random House, 2000), pp. 106–9.

Dorothy is on a journey: Mary Ann Horenstein et al., *Reel Life, Real Life: A Video Guide for Personal Discovery* (Kendall Park, NJ: Fourth Write Press, 1994); Edward Hudlin, "The Mythology of Oz: An Interpretation," *Papers on Language and Literature* 24, no. 4 (Fall 1989): 443–62; Cynthia Richmond, "Gee Wiz, Dorothy! Envisioning 'Oz' as a Journey to the Self as the Classic Is Released," *Los Angeles Times,* Nov. 6, 1998, p. E2; Richard Tuerk, "Dorothy's Timeless Quest," *Mythlore* 63 (Autumn 1990): 20–24.

parallels that of gay men: Clarke, *Get Happy*; Jeff Buhrman, "Artistic Director's Message," in program to *The Wizard of Oz*, March 22–24, 2002, Gay Men's Chorus of Washington, DC, p. 11; Richmond, "Gee Wiz, Dorothy!"; Horenstein et al., *Reel Life*.
shamanic journey: Hermsen, "Over the Rainbow."

130 **Many gay boys and adolescents**
poor self-esteem: Richard Isay, *Being Homosexual: Gay Men and Their Development* (New York: Farrar, Straus & Giroux, 1989).
and shame: Downs, *The Velvet Rage*; Isensee, *Growing Up Gay*.
like the Wizard: Richard Eder, "There's No Place That's Home," *New York Times Book Review*, Mar. 19, 2000, p. 9.
free to be who they really are: Andrew Karp, "Utopian Tension in L. Frank Baum's Oz," *Utopian Studies* 9, no. 2 (1988): 106, 113; Darren John Main, *Spiritual Journeys Along the Yellow Brick Road* (Tallahassee, FL: Findhorn Press, 2000), p. 62.

131 **Because we rarely encounter**
identity question: Harry Hay, "A Separate People Whose Time Has Come," in *Gay Spirit: Myth and Meaning*, ed. Mark Thompson (New York: St. Martin's Press, 1987), p. 281; Peter Sweasey, *From Queer to Eternity: Spirituality in the Lives of Lesbian, Gay and Bisexual People* (London: Cassell, 1997), p. 215; Will Roscoe, *Queer Spirits: A Gay Men's Myth Book* (Boston: Beacon Press, 1995), p. xv.
ask ourselves who we are: Sweasey, *From Queer to Eternity*, p. 215; Elizabeth Kastor, "The Lure of Creating an Identity," *Los Angeles Times*, Aug. 8, 1997, p. E3.
Myths... establish... identities: David Feinstein and Stanley Krippner, *Personal Mythology: The Psychology of Your Evolving Self: Using Ritual, Dreams and Imagination to Discover Your Inner Story* (Los Angeles: Tarcher, 1988); Roger C. Aden, *Popular Stories and Promised Lands: Fan Cultures and Symbolic Pilgrimages* (Tuscaloosa: University of Alabama Press, 1999), pp. 6, 99.
reinvent themselves: Wright, "'Female' Trouble."

131 **The Scarecrow lacks brains**
metaphors for creating... identity: Schine, "America as Fairyland."
individuation: Richard Sugg, ed., *Jungian Literary Criticism* (Evanston, IL: Northwestern University Press, 1992), p. 422.
comfortable with their identities: Jack David Zipes, "L. Frank Baum and the Utopian Spirit of Oz," in *When Dreams Came True: Classical Fairy Tales and Their Tradition* (New York: Routledge, 1999), p. 177.

journey of individuation: Robert Hopcke, *Jung, Jungians and Homosexuality* (Boston: Shambala, 1989).

131 **Becoming whole**
integrate aspects of our earlier lives: John Preston, ed., *Hometowns: Gay Men Write About Where They Belong* (New York: Dutton, 1991); Wright, "'Female' Trouble."
integrate our gay identities: Marie Mohler, *Homosexual Rites of Passage: A Road to Visibility and Validation* (New York: Harrington Park Press, 2000).
companions can also represent aspects: Hopcke, *Jung, Jungians*; Rahn, *Shaping an Imaginary World*; Gita Dorothy Morena, *The Wisdom of Oz* (San Diego, CA: Inner Connections Press, 1998).
Dorothy becoming whole herself: Christine Downing, Prologue to *Mirrors of the Self: Archetypal Images That Shape Your Life*, ed. Christine Downing (Los Angeles: Tarcher, 1991); Larsen, *The Mythic Imagination*.

131–132 **The process of gay males understanding themselves**
Dorothy's journey . . . as allegory: Ben Brantley, "Why Oz Is a State of Mind in Gay Life and Drag Shows," *New York Times*, June 28, 1994, pp. B1, B5 (reprinted in *The Gay Rights Movement: The New York Times 20th Century in Review*, ed. Vincent J. Samar [Chicago: Fitzroy Dearborn, 2001]); Julian Fleisher, *The Drag Queens of New York: An Illustrated Field Guide* (New York: Riverhead Books, 1996); Hermsen, "Over the Rainbow"; Brian Finnegan, "Homosexual Tendencies: *The Wizard of Oz*," *In Dublin* 25, no. 5 (Mar. 9–22, 2000): 78; Wright, "'Female' Trouble."
patriarchy and heterocentrism: Wright, "'Female' Trouble"; Gerard Sullivan and Robert Reynolds, "Homosexuality in Midlife: Narrative and Identity," in *Getting It! Gay Men's Sexual Stories*, ed. Robert Reynolds and Gerard Sullivan (New York: Harrington Park/Haworth Press, 2003).

132 **Dorothy's adventure without supervising adults**
coming out on your own terms: Finnegan, "Homosexual Tendencies."
small town to a big city: Preston, *Hometowns*; John D'Emilio, *Sexual Politics, Sexual Communities: The Making of a Homosexual Minority in the United States, 1940–1970* (Chicago: University of Chicago Press, 1983); Ryan Bunch, "Program Notes," in program for *The Wizard of Oz*, March 22–24, 2002, Gay Men's Chorus of Washington, DC, pp. 19, 21.
city-full-of-possibilities: Patrick Horrigan, "Like Home," chap. 4 in *Widescreen Dreams: Growing Up Gay at the Movies* (Madison: University of Wisconsin Press, 1999).

132–133 **A myth tells a story for an individual**
tells a story: Aden, *Popular Stories*; Robert Brockway, *Myth from the Ice Age to Mickey Mouse* (Albany: State University of New York Press, 1993); Frederick Turner, "Tempest, Flute, and Oz," in *Tempest, Flute, and Oz: Essays on the Future* (New York: Persea Books, 1991); Dan McAdams, *Stories We Live By: Personal Myths and the Making of the Self* (New York: Morrow, 1993).
characters are often archetypes: Carl G. Jung, *Man and His Symbols* (New York: Doubleday, 1964).
experience the transcendent: McAdams, *Stories We Live By*, p. 34.
such questions: Feinstein and Krippner, *Personal Mythology*; Larsen, *The Mythic Imagination*; Christian De la Huerta, *Coming Out Spiritually: The Next Step* (New York: Tarcher/Putnam, 1999); Campbell, *The Power of Myth*; Maurice Saxby, "The Gifts of Wings: The Value of Literature to Children," in *Give Them Wings: The Experience of Children's Literature*, ed. Maurice Saxby and Gordon Winch (South Melbourne/Crows Nest, NSW, Australia: Macmillan, 1987); Brockway, *Myth from the Ice Age*; Warren Blumenfeld and Diane Raymond, *Looking at Gay and Lesbian Life* (New York: Philosophical Library, 1988), pp. 352–54.

133 **The Wonderful Wizard and its MGM movie incarnation**
understood as, and experienced as, myths: Neil Earle, *"The Wonderful Wizard of Oz" in American Popular Culture: Uneasy in Eden* (Lewiston, NY: Edwin Mellen Press, 1993); Paul Nathanson, *Over the Rainbow: "The Wizard of Oz" as a Secular Myth of America* (Albany: State University of New York Press, 1991); Turner, "Tempest, Flute, and Oz"; John Clute and John Grant, *The Encyclopedia of Fantasy* (New York: St. Martin's Press, 1997), s.v. "The Wizard of Oz."
going through the stages: Joseph Campbell, *Hero with a Thousand Faces* (Princeton, NJ: Princeton University Press, 1968), p. 30; Larsen, *The Mythic Imagination*.
aided by companions: Earle, *Uneasy in Eden*; William Lindsay Gresham, "The Scarecrow to the Rescue," *Baum Bugle* 39, no. 2 (Autumn 1995): 21.
Dorothy as questing hero: Brockway, *Myth from the Ice Age*; Elliott Gose, *Mere Creatures: A Study of Modern Fantasy Tales for Children* (Toronto: University of Toronto Press, 1988); Hudlin, "The Mythology of Oz"; Richmond, "Gee Wiz, Dorothy!"; Richard Tuerk, "Dorothy's Timeless Quest"; Earle, *Uneasy in Eden*.
conveying universal truths: Main, *Spiritual Journeys*; Gresham, "The Scarecrow to the Rescue."

133 Stories set in Oz
mythic imagery and archetypal symbolism: Gresham, "The Scarecrow to the Rescue"; Main, *Spiritual Journeys*; Ann Bedford Ulanov, *The Feminine in Jungian Psychology and in Christian Theology* (Evanston, IL: Northwestern University Press, 1971); Hermsen, "Over the Rainbow."
whose authority is undermined: Hudlin, "The Mythology of Oz."
Wizard . . . a humbug: Michael Bronski, participant in "*The Wizard of Oz* Baum Birthday Show," The Connection, WBUR radio talk show hosted by Tovia Smith, May 15, 1998 (cassette tape); Osmond Beckwith, "The Oddness of Oz," *Children's Literature* 5 (1976): 74–91; Earle, *Uneasy in Eden*.
"bad mother" . . . "good mother": Ulanov, *The Feminine*; Bronski, "Baum Birthday Show"; John Fricke, *100 Years of Oz: A Century of Classic Images from The Wizard of Oz Collection of Willard Carroll* (New York: Stewart, Tabori & Chang, 1999); Griswold, "There's No Place but Home"; Madonna Kolbenschlag, *Lost in the Land of Oz: Befriending Your Inner Orphan and Heading for Home* (New York: Harper & Row, 1988).
symbolize archetypal friendship: Christine Downing, introduction to part IV of *Mirrors of the Self: Archetypal Images That Shape Your Life*, ed. Christine Downing (Los Angeles: Tarcher, 1991), p. 202.
intelligence, compassion, and courage: Richmond, "Gee Wiz, Dorothy!"; Ulanov, *The Feminine*; Hopcke, *Jung, Jungians*.
mythogems: Larsen, *The Mythic Imagination*.
the Ork: Gresham, "The Scarecrow to the Rescue."
trickster: Gose, *Mere Creatures*.

133 **Mythology offers many transcendental messages**
messages: Campbell, *The Power of Myth*.

134 **Life and death**
becoming: Campbell, *The Power of Myth*, p. 70.
death is an end or a beginning: Maurice Saxby, "The Wonder of Myth and Legend," in Saxby and Winch, *Give Them Wings*.

134 **Like Dorothy's trip to Oz**
coming out has the form of a hero's journey: Wilfrid Koponen, *Embracing a Gay Identity: Gay Novels as Guides* (Westport, CT: Bergin & Garvey, 1993), p. 10.
"mythical lives": Roscoe, *Queer Spirits*, p. xv.
gay people don't have myths: David Groff, editor's note in *Sanctuary*, by Paul Monette (Los Angeles: Alyson Books, 1997), p. 8.

mainstream writers: Roscoe, *Queer Spirits*, p. xv.
gay myth . . . would help give meaning: Christine Downing, *Myths and Mysteries of Same-Sex Love* (New York: Continuum, 1989); Robert Hopcke, Karin Lofthus Carrington, and Scott Wirth, eds., *Same-Sex Love and the Path to Wholeness* (Boston: Shambala, 1993).
find out who we are: Mark Thompson, "Making a New Myth," in *Gay Men at the Millennium*, ed. Michael Lowenthal (New York: Tarcher, 1997), p. 141. See also Bertram Cohler, *Writing Desire: Sixty Years of Gay Autobiography* (Madison: University of Wisconsin Press, 2007); Sullivan and Reynolds, "Homosexuality in Midlife."

134–135 **When a culture lacks significant myths**
personal myths and mythologies: Larsen, *The Mythic Imagination*; Feinstein and Krippner, *Personal Mythology*; McAdams, *Stories We Live By*.
basis for one's identity: McAdams, *Stories We Live By*.

135–136 **The process of developing a personal myth**
"myth-making material": Wickes, *The Inner World of Childhood*, p. 244.
preschool child: McAdams, *Stories We Live By*, pp. 35–36. See also Oz references on pp. 55 and 68–69 of McAdams.
Wicked Witch . . . particularly potent: McAdams, *Stories We Live By*.

136 **The tone and general form of a personal myth**
narrative tone: McAdams, *Stories We Live By*.

136 **Characters who began as simple images**
characters might stand for: Rollo May, *The Cry for Myth* (New York: Norton, 1991); Jerome Bruner, "Myth and Identity," in *Myth and Mythmaking*, ed. Henry Murray (New York: Braziller, 1960); Downing, *Mirrors of the Self*; Feinstein and Krippner, *Personal Mythology*; Larsen, *The Mythic Imagination*; Mary Watkins, *Waking Dreams* (New York: Harper Colophon, 1976).

137 **Different life stages**
life stages: Eric Erikson, *Childhood and Society*, 2nd ed. (New York: Norton, 1963); Daniel Levinson et al., *The Seasons of a Man's Life* (New York: Knopf, 1978).

138 **Arnie Kantrowitz structures an entire memoir**
Under the Rainbow: New York: St. Martin's Press, 1996.

CHAPTER 8: The Subcultural Phenomenon

144 **But other young fans**
sleep, breathe, and eat: Paraphrase of one respondent describing himself.

145–146 **The adult fan's impulse**
Son of a Witch: Michael Blanding, "Oz in the Family: A Conversation with *Wicked* Author Gregory Maguire, G90," *Tufts Magazine*, Fall 2005, pp. 38–40; Regina Marler, "Back to Oz," *The Advocate*, Sept. 27, 2005, p. 72.

147–148 **There are also established ways**
Reid Davis . . . at the Castro: Reid Davis, "What WOZ: Lost Objects, Repeat Viewings, and the Sissy Warrior," *Film Quarterly* 55, no. 2 (Winter 2001–02): 2–13.

149 **As gay fans share and boost Oz**
knowledge gets passed along: Steve Greenberg, "Fasten Your Seat Belts: The Ten Gayest Straight Movies Ever," *Genre* 28 (May 1995): 36, 71–72.

153 **Fans can go further**
factors outside our control: Elizabeth Long, "Textual Interpretation as Collective Action," in *The Ethnography of Reading*, ed. Jonathan Boyarin (Berkeley: University of California Press, 1993).

154 **The social context of gay fandom**
Rufus Wainwright: "Rufus Wainwright, 23, Musician," Generation Q: The Arts, *The Advocate*, no. 739/740 (Aug. 19, 1997), p. 36.

157 **When heterosexuals find out**
"And then came the tallest": Jeannine Athens, "A Strange, Wonderful Trip on the Yellow Brick Road," *Gary (Indiana) Post Tribune*, Sept. 19, 1999, Region section, p. 1.
"I was Glinda": Catherine Saint Louis, "The Way We Live Now: 1-30-00: What They Were Thinking," *New York Times Magazine*, Jan. 30, 2000, p. 24.

158 **In 2005, my exhibit of Oz items**
"I think it's wrong": James Marino quoted in Shaun Moriarty, "Library Officials React to Marino's Remarks," *Southbridge Evening News*, June 2, 2006, p. A1.

159 **And not everyone thinks the Chicago dragsters**
letter to the editor: Heather Lloyd, letter to *Chesterton Tribune*, Sept. 23, 1999, "Voice of the People" column, p. 2.

159 **Homophobic straight individuals**
Draper, Utah: Celia Baker and Scott Morgan, "'Oz' Director Quits amid Colored-Flag Flap in Draper," *Salt Lake City Tribune*, Oct. 15, 2002; also personal correspondence with and questionnaire responses from Dolce.

CHAPTER 9: Oz and Judy in Gay Folklore

162 **When did the Oz–gay connection begin?**
Some writers assert: Steve Nallon, "Could Even Van Damme Be a Friend of Dorothy?" www.stevenallon.com/Dorothy.html, accessed Mar. 2001.

163 **Documented references to and uses of Oz**
"a hallucinatory musical": Julian Fleisher, *The Drag Queens of New York: An Illustrated Field Guide* (New York: Riverhead Books, 1996), pp. 38–39.
"Oz as a cult": Ethan Mordden, "Welcome to Middle-Earth," *Christopher Street* 8, no. 1 (1984): 52–54 (quote on p. 53).
"gay national anthem": Michael Bronski, "Gay Men and Movies: Reel to Real," in *Gay Life: Leisure, Love and Living for the Contemporary Gay Male*, ed. Eric Rofes (Garden City, NY: Doubleday/Dolphin, 1986). This was confirmed in an email I got from Near.
"gay story": Judy Grahn, "Flaming Without Burning: Some of the Roles of Gay People in Society," in *Gay Spirit: Myth and Meaning*, ed. Mark Thompson (New York: St. Martin's Press, 1987), p. 8.

164–165 **Garland probably became a gay icon**
"dazzling" concerts: Rawley Grau, "Why Was Judy Garland So Important to Gays?" *in newsweekly* 10, no. 43 (June 20, 2001): 56.
comeback part of her appeal: Ethan Mordden, "A Critic at Large: I Got a Song," *New Yorker*, Oct. 22, 1990, 110–42; Doris Grumbach, "Neurosis and Rainbows: The Garland Legend Grows," op-ed, *New York Times*, Aug. 17, 1975, p. 93.
members of the audiences: Richard Dyer, "Judy Garland and Gay Men," chap. 3 in *Heavenly Bodies: Film Stars and Society* (New York: St. Martin's Press, 1986), reprinted in *Rainbow: A Star-Studded Tribute to Judy Garland*, ed. Ethlie Ann Vare (New York: Boulevard Books, 1998).
Seeing one another: George Chauncey, *Gay New York: Gender, Urban Culture, and the Making of the Gay Male World, 1890–1940* (New York: Basic Books, 1994); Charles Kaiser, *The Gay Metropolis, 1940–1996* (Boston: Houghton Mifflin, 1997).

165 **The second most often mentioned**
gay men admired her: David Bianco, *Gay Essentials: Facts for Your Queer*

Brain (Los Angeles: Alyson Books, 1999); William Stewart, *Cassell's Queer Companion: A Dictionary of Lesbian and Gay Life and Culture* (London: Cassell, 1995).

married . . . had warm relationships: Marion Meade, *Dorothy Parker: What Fresh Hell Is This?* (New York: Villard Books, 1988); Leslie Frewin, *The Late Mrs. Parker* (New York: Macmillan, 1986).

165 **There are two eras when Parker**
gay admirers: Meade, *What Fresh Hell*, p. 396.
put them down: Meade, *What Fresh Hell*; Frewin, *The Late Mrs. Parker*.

165–166 **Another minority candidate**
Dorothy King: Amanda Tyrrell, Correction to Origin of "A Friend of Dorothy" (FOD), Alt.showbiz.gossip Anti-FAQ, https://groups.google.com/forum/#!topic/alt.showbiz.gossip/Hi4qw4LgfZ8, accessed June 2017; Mr. Right, columns in the *Isthmus* (July 19, 2002; Aug. 9, 2002; Sept. 6, 2002).
Dorothy Dean: Hilton Als, "Downtown Chronicles: Friends of Dorothy," *New Yorker*, Apr. 24, 1995.

166 **Pinning down when the expression**
soldiers in World War II: John Kenrick, "Our Love Is Here to Stay," web essay, http://www.musicals101.com/ourlove.htm; Rebecca K. Conn, "Gay History—Friends of DOROTHY," email post to PF-Gay-Straight Alliance, Dec. 12, 2000; Wikipedia, "Friend of Dorothy," http://en.wikipedia.org/wiki/Friend_of_Dorothy, Feb. 7, 2008 (entry first appeared in 2004).
1940s: Ben Brantley, "Why Oz Is a State of Mind in Gay Life and Drag Shows," *New York Times*, June 28, 1994, pp. B1, B5; reprinted in *The Gay Rights Movement: The New York Times 20th Century in Review*, ed. Vincent J. Samar (Chicago: Fitzroy Dearborn, 2001).
1940s and 50s: Randy Shilts, *Conduct Unbecoming: Lesbians and Gays in the U.S. Military, Vietnam to the Persian Gulf* (New York: St. Martin's Press, 1993).
1950s and 60s: Michael Bronski, "*The Wizard of Oz* Baum Birthday Show," The Connection, WBUR radio talk show hosted by Tovia Smith, May 15, 1998 (cassette tape).

166–167 **"Friend of Dorothy" does not appear**
not until 2002: Paul Baker, *Fantabulosa: A Dictionary of Gay Slang* (London: Continuum, 2002).

168–169 **Judy Garland's funeral took place**
Many associate: Stewart, *Cassell's Queer Companion*; Stephen Maddison, "Fags, Female Icons and Stonewall," in *Fags, Hags and Queer Sisters: Gender Dissent and Heterosocial Bonds in Gay Culture* (New York: St. Martin's/Scholarly Press, 2000); Simon Gage, Lisa Richards, and Howard Wilmot, *Queer* (New York: Thunder's Mouth Press, 2002), pp. 46, 87; Brantley, "Why Oz Is a State of Mind."
"The woman and the movie": Brent Bambury, "Gay Community's Love Affair with Judy Garland and *The Wizard of Oz*," interview with Bill Richardson and Alan Conter on Canadian Broadcasting Corporation's *Infoculture*, June 25, 2000.

169 **Others go beyond simply associating the funeral**
reaching a breaking point: Michael Bronski, *Culture Clash: The Making of Gay Sensibility* (Boston: South End Press, 1984); Smith Galtney, "Music," chap. 3 in *Mondo Homo: Your Essential Guide to Queer Pop Culture*, ed. Richard Andreoli (Los Angeles: Alyson Books, 2004); Christopher Guly, "The Judy Connection," *The Advocate*, June 28, 1994, p. 49; Kaiser, *The Gay Metropolis*; Robert Nesti, "A Look at 'the Dailies,'" *Bay Windows*, June 6–12, 2002, Arts Plus section, p. 1; Neil Schlager, ed., *St. James Press Gay and Lesbian Almanac* (Detroit, MI: Gale, 1998), s.v. "film"; Robert Stein, producer, "The Judy Connection," *In the Life* (TV show), originally broadcast June 1999.
"I was at the Riots": Stein, "The Judy Connection" (TV show); Guly, "The Judy Connection."
historians of the riots discount: Martin Duberman as quoted in Guly, "The Judy Connection"; David Carter, *Stonewall: The Riots That Sparked the Gay Revolution* (New York: St. Martin's Press, 2004).
street youths: Carter, *Stonewall*, p. 261.
contemporary accounts: Carter, *Stonewall*, p. 260.

169 **Garland's death can also be seen**
symbolic of the change: Carter, *Stonewall*, p. 261. See also Tom Burke, "The New Homosexuality," *Esquire*, Dec. 1969, pp. 178, 304–18; Neil Miller, *Out of the Past: Gay and Lesbian History from 1869 to the Present* (New York: Vintage/Random House, 1995); Dennis Altman, *Homosexual: Oppression and Liberation* (New York: Avon, 1971), p. 118.
myth of the gay subculture: Ryan Bruce Bunch, "'Over the Rainbow': Difference, Utopia, and *The Wizard Of Oz* in Queer Musical Experience" (master's thesis, University of Maryland at College Park, 2001); Guly,

"The Judy Connection"; Maddison, "Fags, Female Icons and Stonewall"; Conter in Bambury, "Gay Community's Love Affair with Judy Garland."
has to be true: Maddison, "Fags, Female Icons and Stonewall."

170 **Judy Garland's performance**
signature piece: Gerald Clarke, *Get Happy: The Life of Judy Garland* (New York: Random House, 2000).
gay anthem: Bronski, *Culture Clash*; Robert J. Nishikawa, "The Top 100 Songs of Popular Gay Culture," *Washington Blade*, August 2, 2002 ("Over the Rainbow" was #2, after Madonna's "Vogue"); Bunch, "'Over the Rainbow'"; Ethan Mordden, *The Hollywood Musical* (New York: St. Martin's Press, 1981); Philip Brett and Elizabeth Wood, "Gay and Lesbian Music," in *The New Grove Dictionary of Music and Musicians*, vol. 9, ed. Stanley Sadie (London: Macmillan, 2001).
master's thesis: Bunch, "'Over the Rainbow.'"

170 **"Over the Rainbow" is perhaps**
expression of longing: Salman Rushdie, *The Wizard of Oz* (London: BFI Publishing, 1992).
"hometown" songs: William L. Leap, "Claiming Gay Space: Songs About Cities," chap. 5 in *Word's Out: Gay Men's English* (Minneapolis: University of Minnesota Press, 1996); Eve Kosofsky Sedgewick, *Epistemology of the Closet* (Berkeley: University of California Press, 1990).
contributed to . . . gay male following: Bronski, *Culture Clash*, p. 56.

170–171 **In 1978 Gilbert Baker designed**
more colorful: John O'Brien, "The Prideful Story of Our Rainbow Flag," *IGLA Bulletin*, 1994, pp. 4–5.
symbol of the gay community: Hank Stuever, "Rainbows," *The Stranger* 9, no. 40 (June 22–29, 2000), http://www.thestranger.com/seattle/rainbows/Content?oid=4263, accessed June 2017. See also Tom Orr's song "I'm So Over the Rainbow," from his revue *Dirty Little Showtunes* (1997).
associate the flag with "Over the Rainbow": Ian Young, *The Stonewall Experiment: A Gay Psychohistory* (New York: Cassell, 1995); "50 Fabulous Films," Roughcut, http://www.roughcut.com/main/godzilla_igp.html (Jan. 30, 2001); Nishikawa, "The Top 100 Songs."
Galindo draped himself: Bunch, "'Over the Rainbow.'"
assume that Baker was thinking: Les Wright, "San Francisco," in *Queer Sites: Gay Urban Histories*, ed. David Higgs (New York: Routledge, 1999), p. 173; Robert Hopcke, *Jung, Jungians and Homosexuality* (Boston: Shambala, 1989), p. 137; Kenrick, "Our Love Is Here to Stay"; National Museum and Archive of Gay and Lesbian History, "Rainbow Flag," in

The Gay Almanac (New York: Berkley Books, 1996); Tim Timan, Review of "Rufus Wainwright: Live at Carnegie Hall," *The Times* (London), Jan. 19, 2008, http://entertainment.timesonline.co.uk/tol/arts_and_ entertainment/music/cd_reviews/article3192262.ece.

conjures up Oz: Celia Baker and Scott Morgan, "'Oz' Director Quits amid Colored-Flag Flap in Draper," *Salt Lake City Tribune*, Oct. 15, 2002.

171–172 **What is going on with these widespread beliefs**

developed their own subculture: Martin Levine, introduction to *Gay Men: The Sociology of Male Homosexuality*, ed. Martin Levine (New York: Harper & Row, 1979), p. 11; Deborah Blincoe and John Forrest, "The Dangers of Authenticity" (editorial essay), *New York Folklore* 19, no. 1–2 (1993): 1–14; Joseph Goodwin, "Coming Out, Coming Home: Reclaiming a Place to Belong," *New York Folklore* 19, no. 1–2 (1993): 15–26 (see specifically p. 16).

answering questions such as: David Feinstein and Stanley Krippner, *Personal Mythology: The Psychology of Your Evolving Self: Using Ritual, Dreams and Imagination to Discover Your Inner Story* (Los Angeles: Tarcher, 1988); Stephen Larsen, *The Mythic Imagination: The Quest for Meaning Through Personal Mythology* (Rochester, VT: Inner Traditions, 1996); Christian De la Huerta, *Coming Out Spiritually: The Next Step* (New York: Tarcher/Putnam, 1999); Joseph Campbell, with Bill Moyers, *The Power of Myth* (New York: Doubleday, 1988); Maurice Saxby, "The Gifts of Wings: The Value of Literature to Children," in *Give Them Wings: The Experience of Children's Literature*, ed. Maurice Saxby and Gordon Winch (South Melbourne/Crows Nest, NSW, Australia: Macmillan, 1987); Robert Brockway, *Myth from the Ice Age to Mickey Mouse* (Albany: State University of New York Press, 1993); Warren Blumenfeld and Diane Raymond, *Looking at Gay and Lesbian Life* (New York: Philosophical Library, 1988), pp. 352–54.

friends . . . as surrogate families: Levine, introduction to *Gay Men*.

passing along . . . practices: Andrew Sullivan, "The End of Gay Culture," *New Republic*, Oct. 24, 2005, pp. 16–21.

media: Eric Rofes, introduction to *Gay Life*, ed. Eric Rofes (Garden City, NY: Doubleday/Dolphin, 1986); Derek Cohen and Richard Dyer, "The Politics of Gay Culture," in *Homosexuality: Power and Politics*, ed. Gay Left Collective (London: Allison and Busby, 1980).

urban centers: Blumenfeld and Raymond, *Looking at Gay and Lesbian Life*.

172 **Folklore, which may or may not be "true,"**

may or may not be "true": Joseph Goodwin, personal communication.

forge a group's identity: Goodwin, "Coming Out," p. 10.
role in gay communities: Blincoe and Forrest, "The Dangers of Authenticity."

174 **As we saw in Chapter 7**
sense of identity and history: Bunch, "'Over the Rainbow,'" chap. 2.

174–175 **Gay men feel the need to be connected**
Gay men feel the need: Robert Barzan, introduction to *Sex and Spirit: Exploring Gay Men's Spirituality*, ed. Robert Barzan (San Francisco: White Crane Newsletter, 1995); Randy Conner, introduction to *Cassell's Encyclopedia of Queer Myth, Symbol and Spirit: Gay, Lesbian, Bisexual, and Transgender Lore* (London: Cassell, 1997); De la Huerta, *Coming Out Spiritually*; Peter Sweasey, *From Queer to Eternity: Spirituality in the Lives of Lesbian, Gay and Bisexual People* (London: Cassell, 1997).
Folklore can give us a feeling: Goodwin, "Coming Out," p. 21.
shape identity: Cohen and Dyer, "The Politics of Gay Culture"; Blumenfeld and Raymond, *Looking at Gay and Lesbian Life*.
reinforces our gay identities: Blincoe and Forrest, "The Dangers of Authenticity," p. 9.

175 **Beliefs about Judy Garland**
myth becomes history: Bunch, "'Over the Rainbow,'" p. 20.

176 **Many traditional myths are origin stories**
origin stories: Elizabeth Cook, *The Ordinary and the Fabulous: An Introduction to Myths, Legends and Fairy Tales for Teachers and Storytellers* (Cambridge: Cambridge University Press, 1969); David Leeming and Jake Page, *Myths, Legends, and Folktales of America* (New York: Oxford University Press, 1999); Maurice Saxby, "The Wonder of Myth and Legend," in Saxby and Winch, *Give Them Wings*; Brockway, *Myth from the Ice Age*.

CHAPTER 10: The Oz-Gay Connection Now and in the Future

179 **There is abundant evidence**
"I'm proud to be a friend": Margaret Gray, "Paying Close Attention to the 'Wizard,'" *Los Angeles Times*, Sept. 21, 2013, p. D4; Paul Hodgins, "Revamp Creates a 'Wizard' of Flaws," *Orange County Register*, Sept. 22, 2013, Arts & Entertainment section, p. 3.

179–180 **The travel section of the Sunday *New York Times***
Melbourne: Nic Price, "Life-Size Lion Statue a Symbol of Courage for Yarra's Gay and Lesbian Community," *Melbourne Leader*, July 18, 2004,

Central section, pp. 9C–15C, http://www.heraldsun.com.au/leader/central/lifesize-lion-statue-a-symbol-of-courage-for-yarras-gay-and-lesbian-community/story-fngnvlpt-1226993478078?nk=d6fc897c120d340 38a750beea9cd94f8, accessed June 2017.

180–181 **Gregory Maguire's novel** *Wicked*
venerated by gay bookstores: Daniel Handler, "Hey, Watch Who You're Calling Wicked," *New York Times*, June 29, 2003, Arts and Leisure section, p. 5.
had a field day: Mark Carmien, "Hot Flash, 10/15/05," Northampton's Pride and Joy, email; J. S. Hall, "Bewitched: Gregory Maguire's *Wicked* Sequel Is the Gayest of Them All," *Bay Windows*, Oct. 27–Nov. 1, 2005, Arts Plus section, p. 5; Regina Marler, "Back to Oz," *The Advocate*, Sept. 27, 2005, p. 72.
queer love story: Stacy Wolf, "'Defying Gravity': Queer Conventions in the Musical *Wicked*," *Theatre Journal* 60, no. 1 (Mar. 2008): 1–21.

181–182 *Wicked* **the musical has been taken**
fervor by some gay men: Brandon Voss, "Friends of Elphaba," *The Advocate*, Nov. 20, 2007, p. 15; Brandon Voss, "The Enchantress," *in newsweekly* 17, no. 25 (Feb. 6, 2008): A13; Romeo San Vincente, "Deep Inside Hollywood," *New England Blade* 17, no. 51 (Aug. 6, 2008): 21.
gay icon: Scott Kearnan, "Hear Him Roar," *Bay Windows*, Oct. 16–22, 2008, pp. 19, 21; Voss, "Friends of Elphaba"; Voss, "The Enchantress."
"Green is so the new gay": Voss, "Friends of Elphaba."
"Defying Gravity": Laura Kiritsy, "'All by Herself' with *I Stand*, Idina Menzel Relishes Return to the Stage," *Bay Windows*, Apr. 3–9, 2008, pp. 1, 24.
embraced by gay fans: Kearnan, "Hear Him Roar."

183 **Oz allusions continue to appear**
"Breeder's Digest": blog entry, Mar. 26, 2009, https://breedersdigest.wordpress.com/category/signs-symbols/, accessed June 2017.

183–184 **Pop singers from a younger generation**
young gay bloggers: "The WIZARD of OZ . . . is Gay!" flickr group, https://www.flickr.com/groups/530982@N25/, accessed June 2017; Rantasm, "The Wizard of Oz Needs More Gay," Channel Awesome, https://channelawesome.com/the-wizard-of-oz-needs-more-gay/, accessed June 2017; Joseph Sciambra, "Over the Rainbow: The Gay Male Obsession with *The Wizard of Oz*," http://josephsciambra.com/over-the-rainbow-the-gay-male-obsession-with-the-wizard-of-oz/, accessed June 2017.

184 **There are, however, some signs**
sing-alongs: Karen Barker Crowley, "Oz and Ends: A Behind-the-Scenes Guide to the World's Gayest Movie," *Queue Press* 2, no. 5 (July 2003): 8; "Sing Out, Dorothy!" *Next Magazine* 10, no. 48 (June 6, 2003), p. 12; Cathy Crimmins, *How the Homosexuals Saved Civilization* (New York: Tarcher/Penguin, 2004), Tony Giampetruzzi, "Chamber of Commerce Sponsors *Wizard of Oz* Sing-a-long in Ogunquit," *in newsweekly* 11, no. 8 (Oct. 17, 2001): 34.
make fun: Howard Kurtzman, personal communication.

184–185 **The Wicked Witch may be replacing Dorothy**
replacing Dorothy: Someone made this suggestion when I gave a talk at the Library of Congress in September 2000.
not . . . on every gay reading list: Dave White, "Literature," chap. 4 in *Mondo Homo: Your Essential Guide to Queer Pop Culture*, ed. Richard Andreoli (Los Angeles: Alyson Books, 2004).
outlast Judy: Brent Bambury, "Gay Community's Love Affair with Judy Garland and *The Wizard of Oz*," interview with Bill Richardson and Alan Conter on Canadian Broadcasting Corporation's *Infoculture*, June 25, 2000.
"Gays and lesbians have come": Hank Stuever, "Rainbows," *The Stranger* 9, no. 40 (June 22–29, 2000), http://www.thestranger.com/seattle/rainbows/Content?oid=4263, accessed June 2017.

185–186 **Similar patterns of behaviors**
Recent research: Glenn Wilson and Qazi Rahman, *Born Gay: The Psychobiology of Sex Orientation* (London: Peter Owen, 2005).
ways of being: Will Fellows, *A Passion to Preserve: Gay Men as Keepers of Culture* (Madison: University of Wisconsin Press, 2004); Robert Williams and Ted Gideonse, eds., *From Boys to Men: Gay Men Write About Growing Up* (New York: Carroll & Graf, 2006); David Nimmons, *The Soul Beneath the Skin: The Unseen Hearts and Habits of Gay Men* (New York: St. Martin's Press, 2002).
gay sensibility itself will change: Andrew Sullivan, "The End of Gay Culture," *New Republic*, Oct. 24, 2005, pp. 16–21; Daniel Harris, *The Rise and Fall of Gay Culture* (New York: Hyperion, 1997).

186 **Other aspects of being gay**
have given way: Gerard Sullivan and Robert Reynolds, "Homosexuality in Midlife: Narrative and Identity," in *Getting It! Gay Men's Sexual Stories*, ed. Robert Reynolds and Gerard Sullivan (New York: Harrington Park/Haworth Press, 2003); Bertram Cohler, *Writing Desire: Sixty Years of Gay Autobiography* (Madison: University of Wisconsin Press, 2007; Laura

Kiritsy, "Scissor Sisters Versus Show Tunes," *Bay Windows*, Jan. 4–10, 2006, pp. 1, 12.

187 **The environment with respect to gay-positive information**
environment . . . has changed greatly: Jennifer Egan, "Lonely Gay Teen Seeking Same," *New York Times Magazine*, Dec. 10, 2000, pp. 110–17, 128–31.

187–188 **What about a replacement**
small fraction: Jacob Stockinger, "Reading Across Orientations," in *The Gay and Lesbian Literary Heritage: A Reader's Companion to the Writers and Their Works, from Antiquity to the Present*, ed. Claude Summers, rev. ed. (New York: Routledge, 2002).
more widely distributed: Ellen Bosman and John Bradford, *Gay, Lesbian, Bisexual, and Transgendered Literature: A Genre Guide* (Westport, CT: Libraries Unlimited, 2008); Michael Ford, "Gay Books for Young Readers," *Publishers Weekly*, Feb. 21, 1994, pp. 24–27.
avoid disapproval: Ford, "Gay Books for Young Readers."
likely to choose: Harry Benshoff and Sean Griffin, *Queer Images: A History of Gay and Lesbian Film in America* (Lanham, MD: Rowman & Littlefield, 2006); Will Roscoe, *Queer Spirits: A Gay Men's Myth Book* (Boston: Beacon Press, 1995), p. 22.

188–189 **There are also several textual reasons**
reaches into subconscious: Bruno Bettelheim, *The Uses of Enchantment* (New York: Vintage, 1977); Ellen Siegelman, *Metaphor and Meaning in Psychotherapy* (New York: Guilford Press, 1990); Carl G. Jung, *Man and His Symbols* (New York: Doubleday, 1964); Ritch Savin-Williams, "Memories of Childhood and Early Adolescent Sexual Feelings Among Gay and Bisexual Boys," chap. 4 in *The Lives of Lesbians, Gays, and Bisexuals*, ed. Ritch Savin-Williams and Kenneth Cohen; Andrew Tobias (writing as John Reid), *The Best Little Boy in the World* (New York: Ballantine, 1973); Richard Isay, *Being Homosexual: Gay Men and Their Development* (New York: Farrar, Straus & Giroux, 1989).
lasting: Melynda Huskey, "Queering the Picture Book," *The Lion and the Unicorn* 26, no. 1 (Jan. 2002): 66–77; Ellen Handler Spitz, *Inside Picture Books* (New Haven, CT: Yale University Press, 1999).
appropriation: Patrick Horrigan, *Widescreen Dreams: Growing Up Gay at the Movies* (Madison: University of Wisconsin Press, 1999); Andy Medhurst, "Batman, Deviance and Camp," in *The Many Lives of the Batman: Critical Approaches to a Superhero and His Media*, ed. Roberta Pearson and William Uricchio (New York: Routledge; London: BFI Publishing, 1991); Brett Farmer, *Spectacular Passions: Cinema, Fantasy,*

Gay Male Spectatorships (Durham, NC: Duke University Press, 2000); Alan Sinfield, *Cultural Politics—Queer Reading* (Philadelphia: University of Pennsylvania Press, 1994); David Van Leer, *The Queening of America: Gay Culture in Straight Society* (New York: Routledge, 1995).

189–190 **Any work that replaces**
Fantasy can . . . tap into the imagination: Roscoe, *Queer Spirits*.

190 **The protagonists of Disney films**
Disney films: Sean Griffin, *Tinker Belles and Evil Queens: The Walt Disney Company from the Inside Out* (New York: New York University Press, 2000); Akash Nikolas, "It's Not Just *Frozen*: Most Disney Movies Are Pro-Gay," *The Atlantic*, Apr. 23, 2014, http://www.theatlantic.com/entertainment/archive/2014/04/its-not-just-frozen-disney-has-always-been-subtly-pro-gay/361060/, accessed June 2017.
Frozen . . . lambasted: Kierran Petersen, "Disney's *Frozen* and the 'Gay Agenda,'" BBC News Echo Chambers, Mar. 27, 2014, http://www.bbc.com/news/blogs-echochambers-26759342.
Frozen . . . positive themes: Gina Luttrell, "7 Moments That Made *Frozen* the Most Progressive Disney Movie Ever," Arts.Mic, Jan. 20, 2014, http://mic.com/articles/79455/7-moments-that-made-frozen-the-most-progressive-disney-movie-ever, accessed June 2017.

191 **Even very young children know Oz**
tickets sold: John Fricke, Jay Scarfone, and William Stillman, *The Wizard of Oz: The Official 50th Anniversary Pictorial History* (New York: Warner Books, 1989).
most widely seen: Fricke, Scarfone, and Stillman, *The Wizard of Oz: The Official 50th Anniversary Pictorial History*.

192 **Oz's appeal to the population at large**
appeal . . . is timeless: Leonard Everett Fisher, "Future Classics," *Horn Book Magazine*, Nov./Dec. 2000, p. 739; Richard Tuerk, "Dorothy's Timeless Quest," *Mythlore* 63 (Autumn 1990): 20–24; Warren Hollister, "Oz and the Fifth Criterion," in *The Wizard of Oz: The Critical Heritage*, ed. Michael Patrick Hearn (New York: Schocken Books, 1983), orig. pub. in *Baum Bugle*, Christmas 1971, pp. 5–8.
sick son: Jeanne Schinto, "In the Land of Oziana," *Maine Antique Digest*, Dec. 2008, pp. 38B–39B (both quotes on 39B).

192–193 **Maybe love of Oz can be passed along**
pass on their values: Spitz, *Inside Picture Books*; Glenn Miller, "Becoming Little Red Riding Hood," *Wall Street Journal*, May 10–11, 2008, p. W12.

Fantasy and science fiction fans: Bruce Campbell, director, *Fanalysis* (Campbell Entertainment, 2002), documentary short.

193 **When we are little**
everyday sensory reality: R. L. Gregory, "Ways Forward for the Psychologist: Alternative Fictions," in *The Cool Web*, ed. Margaret Meek, Aidan Warlow, and Griselda Barton (New York: Atheneum, 1978).
shape who we are: David Leeming and Jake Page, *Myths, Legends, and Folktales of America* (New York: Oxford University Press, 1999); Bertram Cohler, *Writing Desire: Sixty Years of Gay Autobiography* (Madison: University of Wisconsin Press, 2007); Toby Johnson, "Straw into Gold: Storytelling and Self-Fulfilling Prophecy," introduction to *Charmed Lives: Gay Spirit in Storytelling*, ed. Toby Johnson and Steve Berman (Brooklyn, NY: White Crane Books, 2006); Dan McAdams, *Stories We Live By: Personal Myths and the Making of the Self* (New York: Morrow, 1993).

194 **Oz is full of magic**
more than escape . . . also about play: John Fricke, personal communication.

APPENDIX B: Methodology

212 **This is not to say that members of other groups**
immigrants: Salman Rushdie, *The Wizard of Oz* (London: BFI Publishing, 1992).
female readers: Alison Lurie, "The Oddness of Oz," *New York Review of Books* 48, no. 20 (Dec. 21, 2000): 16–24; Noah Seaman and Barbara Seaman, "Munchkins, Ozophiles, and Feminists Too," *Ms.* 11, no. 7 (Jan. 1974): 93.

216 **Another possibility for future research**
retellings of fairy tales: Peter Cashorali, *Fairy Tales: Traditional Stories Retold for Gay Men* (San Francisco: HarperSanFrancisco, 1995); Peter Cashorali, *Gay Fairy and Folk Tales: Traditional Stories Retold for Gay Men* (Boston: Faber and Faber, 1997).
erotic fairy tales: Michael Ford, *Happily Ever After: Erotic Fairy Tales for Men* (New York: Masquerade Books, 1996).

APPENDIX C: Was Baum Gay?

219–220 **There is no question that Baum**
Baum had . . . strange fears: Osmond Beckwith, "The Oddness of Oz," *Children's Literature* 5 (1976): 74–91.

220 **But it doesn't take much imagination**
Newsweek article: David Bahr, "Wonder Boy Michael Chabon Talks About *The Amazing Adventures of Kavalier & Clay* and His Affinity for Gay Characters," *The Advocate*, Dec. 19, 2000.
"Although Lagerlof's work": Rawley Grau, "Who Was Selma Lagerlof?" Past Out column, *in newsweekly* 10, no. 31 (Mar. 28, 2001): 39.

220–221 **Here's what we know about Baum**
hated military school: Angelica Shirley Carpenter, *L. Frank Baum: Royal Historian of Oz* (Minneapolis, MN: Lerner Publications, 1992).
design window displays: Jack David Zipes, "L. Frank Baum and the Utopian Spirit of Oz," in *When Dreams Came True: Classical Fairy Tales and Their Tradition* (New York: Routledge, 1999); William Leach, *Land of Desire: Merchants, Power, and the Rise of a New American Culture* (New York: Pantheon Books, 1993).
window dressing . . . book: *The Art of Decorating Dry Goods Windows and Interiors* (Chicago: Show Window Publishing, 1900).
spanking his son: Carpenter, *L. Frank Baum*.

APPENDIX E: Early Allusions to Oz in Gay Contexts

227 **In 1973, on his first visit**
"The lights were glittering": "The Castro," written, directed, and produced by Peter L. Stein, an episode of *Neighborhoods: The Hidden Cities of San Francisco* (KQED, 1997).

Index

"Abby" (Shanower short story) 153
acceptance 12, 96, 124, 125, 132, 150, 174
active imagination 84–86
actors 49, 65, 102, 105, 128, 182
  see also individual actors, e.g., Bette Davis
actualization 131
  see also being yourself
adolescents *see* young adults
adult characters 122, 132
adult fans 75, 82–83, 87, 126, 145–46
adult vs. childhood fandom 74–75, 87, 109, 148
adventure in Oz 36, 90–92, 98, 104, 116, 122
advertising 21–22, 27, 135, 152
  see also images of Oz in gay contexts
affection 57–58
  see also friendship; love
African Americans 29 note f
  see also race
AIDS 138, 146, 180
  see also specific AIDS organizations, e.g., Outreach Zone
AIDS Educational Theatre (Chicago) 34
Algonquin Round Table 165
Alice (Carroll character) 219 note a
Alice books (Carroll) 77, 189
alienation 124, 125, 131
All About Eve (film) 105 note j, 152 note g
All American Boy (Mann) 80 note e
All in Good Time (Anthony Whitaker album) 83

allegory 27, 130, 132, 138–39
Almanza, Aaron 78, 156
aloneness, feeling of 62, 66, 186, 118–19
Andersen, Brian 183, 191 note t
Anderson, Eric Karl 64
anecdotal accounts 6
animals 120, 122 note g, 133
  see also individual animals, e.g., Cowardly Lion
animated versions of Oz stories 35, 78, 190
Annotated Wizard of Oz, The 51–52 note n
appearance, personal 62, 105, 106, 108, 110
  see also dandies
appropriation 10, 79–80, 135, 149, 152, 188, 193
  see also resonance
approval, need for 67
  see also self-esteem
archetypes 102, 126, 132, 133, 135
  see also Jungian theory
Arlen, Harold 34, 45 note g, 170
armies 89, 105
art inspired by Oz 84, 174
artificiality 102, 152
assumptions
  about heterosexuality 135 note d, 215
  about homosexuality 62–63, 154–56, 219–21
Atlanta Constitution 20
attraction, sexual 57
Auckland, New Zealand 21
audience for Oz stories 32–33, 74 note b, 97, 191

283

284 · Index

Aunt Em (character in MGM film) 35, 37, 94, 95
Auntie Mame (film) 105 note j, 152 note g
authenticity 128, 130
  see also being yourself
"Awaken your heart, be connected" 134
awe 93, 194
  see also wonder

baby boomers 10, 151, 186, 187, 208, 216
Bachardy, Don 165
"bad mother" archetype 133
BAGLY (Boston youth group) 182
Baker, Gilbert 170–71
Barbie dolls 63, 64
Barker, Clive 17, 20
Barnstormer in Oz, A (Farmer) 32
Barton, Fred 20, 83, 87, 104, 114
baseline for research 215
Baum, Kenneth 221
Baum, Lyman Frank 85–86, 191, 192, 220
  gender issues and 3, 97 note b, 99, 106, 116, 219–20
  possible homosexuality of 153, 219–21
  pseudonyms 3, 116
  values and messages 117, 122, 126, 134, 220
  as writer 32, 33–34
Baum Bugle 86, 113 note t
beauty 105–6
Beckwith, Osmond 99 note d, 219
becoming whole 131
Beeman, Bill 75
being yourself 125, 127–32
  see also coming out; "Follow your bliss"
belonging *see* acceptance
Best Little Boy in the World, The (Tobias) 66 note i
Betsy Bobbin (Baum character) 102–3, 120, 122
Betty Boop 184
Big Gay Musical, The (film) 25
Billina, the Yellow Hen (Baum character) 114, 120, 133
Billy DeFrank Lesbian and Gay Community Center of San Jose (CA) 27
Billy Elliot (film) 99 note e
Bisexual Characters in Film: From Anaïs to Zee (Bryant) 28
bisexuals 28, 213
black-and-white vs. color (MGM film) 3, 26, 132, 135

bloggers 184
  see also online information
Bogdan, Brian 146 note b
Bonanza (TV series) 65
book collecting 144
Bookey, Seth 62, 63
boomers *see* baby boomers
Boop, Betty 184
Born Gay: The Psychobiology of Sex Orientation (Wilson and Rahman) 11 note e, 58, 60
Bortman, Camo 94, 147
"Bosom Buddies" (song in *Mame*) 181 note f
Boston Youth Pride 182
boy characters 106
  see also male characters
boys *see* gay boys
Brace, Clement 165
Brantley, Ben 18, 166
BraveStarr action figures/dolls 156
Breeder's Digest blog 183
Brothers and Sisters (TV series) 182
Brown University Library 5
bubble, Glinda's 37, 92
bullying *see* harassment; violence: in gay lives
Bunch, Ryan 6, 146 note b
Bungle, the Glass Cat (Baum character) 111 note s, 120, 122 note g, 123
Burke, Billie 34, 46
butch vs. femme 105
Butterworth Farm (Orange, MA) 24
Button-Bright (Baum character) 81, 111, 120, 122

C-3PO (*Star Wars* character) 110 note q
Cabaret (film) 45 note g
Calamity Jane (film) 105
Cambridge, MA 165
camp 24, 27, 42, 63, 152
  current attitudes toward 184, 193
  MGM characters as 102, 103–4, 108, 109
Campbell, Alan 165
Cantlin, J 145
Capote, Truman 165
career choices 65, 82–84, 137
"Castro, The" (TV episode) 26
Castro neighborhood (San Francisco) 26, 51 note n, 96, 126
Castro Theatre (San Francisco) 42, 94, 109, 148, 149, 151
categories vs. concepts 11 note d

causality vs. correlation 215
celebrities in Oz 116, 120, 122–25, 126, 128, 130, 134
    see also individuals, e.g., Tin Woodman
censorship 107, 188
characters 9, 74, 106, 120, 136
    adults vs. children 122, 132
    animals 120, 122 note g, 133; see also individuals, e.g., Cowardly Lion
    child characters 122, 132
    humans 120, 123; see also individuals, e.g., Tip
    independent characters 104–5
    military characters 89, 105, 120
    non-humans 98, 120, 133, 134; see also individuals, e.g., Patchwork Girl
    as role models 20, 98, 109, 128 note a, 194
    small characters 92–93
    strong females 98, 104–5, 212
    see also identification; male characters
Chesterton Oz festival 147, 157, 159
child characters 122, 132
childhood 50–51, 76, 91, 93
    vs. adulthood 87, 122, 189
    developmental stages 68, 79, 135–37
    early childhood 79, 80–81, 135–36
    middle childhood 76, 79, 81, 98–99
    see also children's literature; gay boys; young adults
children's literature 74 note b, 97, 116, 188 note q, 189
    see also young adults: fiction
Children's National Medical Center (Washington, DC) 57
China Country 36, 88, 92–93, 120, 134
choices, reasons for 209, 211–12, 217
chosen families 95, 126, 171–72
Chronicles of Narnia, The (Lewis) 77
cities 96, 132
class issues 208
collecting 3, 6, 88, 128 note a, 144, 156–57
    see also expertise; Oz merchandise
Collins, Liz 171 note l
color coordination 88
Columbia University Library 3
"Come out, come out, wherever you are" 24, 101–2
comics 33, 82, 183, 191 note t
coming out 102, 115–16, 130, 131–32, 134
    see also being yourself; repression

communities/countries within Oz 36, 88, 119, 120, 134
    see also China Country; Emerald City; Munchkinland; Winkies
companions, Dorothy's
    deficiencies of 100, 106–7, 131, 133
    fans' relationship with 23, 106, 136, 152
    and friendship 117, 119, 131
    and masculinity 106–7, 137, 156, 164
    see also Cowardly Lion; Scarecrow; Tin Woodman
compassion 119 note d, 134
concepts vs. categories 11 note d
conflict 90, 92, 134
conformity 124, 127
    see also acceptance
Connection, The (radio show) 51
connection between gay men and Oz
    see Oz–gay connection
control 77, 80, 145
control groups 213
conventions 35, 144, 147, 149, 159
cooperation 116, 119, 137, 151
core story see main story
corresponding/being in touch 87
costumes see cross-dressing; dressing up
counter-myths 134 note d
Courderc, Pierre 114
Cowardly Lion 8, 34, 107–10
    and aggression 107, 137
    as animal in books 120, 121 note f, 122, 133
    camp and flamboyance 108, 109, 111, 135, 152
    gay aspects of 108–9, 152, 179, 180
    sissy aspects of 20, 107, 109–10, 153, 214
    FAN RESPONSE TO THE LION
    fans acting the role of 82, 83
    as favorite character 106, 109, 209
    identifying with 93, 99 note f, 106, 109
    reactions before vs. after coming out 109, 110, 116
    see also companions, Dorothy's
creating your own Oz story see fan-created stories
creativity 64, 67 note j, 88, 190, 220
cross-dressing 64, 114, 223–25
    see also dressing up as Oz characters
crushes/infatuation 59
crystal ball, Wicked Witch's 37, 92
Cukor, George 46
culture 161 note a, 171
    gay culture 7, 11, 27, 71, 149

mainstream 25, 134, 139, 187 note n
responses to Oz as personal vs. cultural 31, 148, 153
transmitting 145 note a, 149, 171
cyclone in MGM film 132

Dana, Paul 107 note m, 111–12 note s, 144, 155
dandies 106, 107 note m, 110, 112
"dandy-lion" 20, 107 note m, 109 note p, 152, 214
danger 90
Dark Oz (comic books) 33
Dashemoff Daily, Sir (Oz stage character) 114
Davis, Bette 105, 145, 218 note d
Davis, Reid 109, 146 note b, 148
Day, Doris 65, 105
daydreams 73, 79, 85 note g
Dead Boys' Club (short film) 26
Dean, Dorothy 165, 168
death 134, 138, 168–69, 209
deceit 127
Defense of Marriage Act 179
"Defying Gravity" (song in *Wicked*) 181
democratic values 121
demographic issues 27–31, 208
  bisexuals 28, 213
  class 208
  geography 29, 65
  lesbians 18, 27, 28, 213–16
  minorities 181, 186–87, 212–13
  race 29, 120, 121 note f, 208
  transgender people 28, 115, 213
  see also gender; history
Denslow, W. W. 32, 51 note n
dePaola, Tomi 20
depression 62
De Shields, Andre 49 note j
design expertise 64, 67 note j, 88, 190, 220
desire 57, 61
developmental stages 79, 68, 135–37
difference 122–26, 130
  feeling different 49, 65, 67, 123
  see also acceptance
"Ding Dong, the witch is dead" 23, 179
  parodies of 84, 227
Disney films 35, 190
distribution/publishing 34, 187, 188, 189, 190
divas 43, 102, 182, 185, 193
  see also gay icons
diversity 7, 123
  see also acceptance

Dolce, Jesse 84, 159
dolls 63, 64, 65, 156
Dorothy 29, 135, 164–68, 219 note a
  adventures of 120, 131
  agency of 51, 128, 132
  companions *see* companions, Dorothy's
  journey/quest of 130, 132, 134, 137
  and Kansas/home 94, 100 note g, 124 note j, 137
  as outsider 124, 136
  in particular works 25, 36, 49, 77
  relationship to companions 107, 113, 117, 123
  relationship to other characters 92, 102, 114, 122, 133
  FAN RESPONSE TO DOROTHY
  dressing up as 23, 24, 83, 147, 159, 183
  as favorite character 42, 99–100
  identifying with 49, 90, 99–100, 125, 184, 194
  use in gay contexts 21, 25, 26, 146, 154
  wanting to be 80 note e, 99, 154
  see also "friend of Dorothy"; Judy Garland
"Dorothy and Toto" (slang expression) 166 note f
drama *see* theater
dramatic versions *see* stage versions
Draper, UT 159
dream ending of MGM film 36, 44, 48 note i, 94–95, 209
dressing up as Oz characters 22–23, 24, 101, 146–47, 179, 184
  Chesterton Festival contest 147, 157, 159
  young boys 64, 80
  see also cross-dressing
"drunk as Cooter Brown" (slang expression) 166 note e
DuBois Library (UMass) 158
Duffy, Mike 151

early childhood 79, 80–81, 86, 135–36
Earthsea books (Le Guin) 77
eccentric characters 120, 122–25, 126, 128, 130, 134
Edens, Roger 46
education 61–62
effeminacy 62, 105, 106, 108, 110
elementary school 62
  see also early childhood; middle childhood
elitism 122
Elphaba (*Wicked* character) 181, 184, 124–25

Emerald City
   as celebrities' residence 90, 95, 102, 105, 120, 136
   in gay contexts 21, 22, 24, 148, 179, 180
   as metaphor for escape 96, 132, 138
   in MGM film 107, 117 note a
   visual aspects of 22, 24, 37, 44, 106, 135

Emerald City (TV series) 191

Emerald City Guard (character in MGM film) 111

Emerald City of Oz, The (Baum) 89, 95, 120

Enchanted Apples of Oz, The (Shanower) 33

equality 121–22

escape 12, 66–67, 73, 78–79
   see also fantasy; going to Oz; imaginary worlds; negative messages

Eureka, the Pink Kitten (Baum character) 122 note g

evil 90, 101, 103, 119 note e, 133, 184

"Experience the rapture of being alive" 133

expertise 5, 6–7, 51, 87, 128 note a, 157

exploring Oz 36, 90–92, 98, 104, 116, 122

"false self" 127, 130

families 171, 219 note b
   creating new 95, 126, 171–72
   fans' relationship with 124, 145, 17,
   gay kids and 56, 67
   Oz fandom and 62, 135, 144, 154–57
   see also home; mothers; parents

fan clubs 35
   see also IWOC

fan-created films 26, 35, 81

fan-created stories 32, 33, 35, 79–80, 82–83, 191 note t

fan fiction 32, 33, 191

fandom 53, 151, 186
   adult fans 75, 82–83, 87, 126, 145–46
   adult vs. childhood 74–75, 87, 109, 148
   becoming a fan 74–75, 78, 98, 193
   book vs. film fans 43, 51
   definition of 10
   degree of 207, 208
   gay fandom 11–12, 145, 147–48, 216, 217–18
   gender and 97 note a
   manifesting *see* manifesting fandom
   organizations 86–87
   reactions to 7–8, 98, 128, 144–45, 154–59
   sharing 10, 143, 144, 145, 150–51, 209

fantasies, sexual 59

fantasy 73–74
   as genre 77 note c, 88, 128, 190, 192–93
   play *see* make-believe
   unconscious and 86, 190
   see also escape; imagination

farmhands (MGM characters) 36, 37, 94 note q

Farrier, Van 99

fathers 56 note a, 64, 67, 95, 138
   father figures 114, 133
   Martin Michel 3, 6, 8, 162
   negative responses to gay sons 80 note e, 154, 155, 156
   see also parents

feelings
   hiding feelings *see* secrecy
   about home 7, 93–94, 170
   about homosexuality 159–60, 218
   about Patchwork Girl 93, 194
   about Wicked Witch *see* Wicked Witch: FAN RESPONSE TO
   see also specific feelings, e.g., shame

female characters 99–106, 116
   strength of 98, 104–5, 212

female singers *see* singers, female

Ferrari, Brian 83

festivals, Oz 35–36, 147, 157, 159

fiction 118–19, 146, 187 note n, 191 note t
   see also individual works, e.g., *All American Boy*; fan fiction; fantasy: as genre; gay fiction; graphic novels; series books; short stories

fictional places 96 note t, 163
   see also China Country; Emerald City; Munchkinland

field mice (*Wiz* characters) 34

film versions of Oz stories 26, 34, 35, 78, 114, 190
   see also individual films, e.g., MGM *Wizard*; *Return to Oz*

film versions of *Wonderful Wizard* 34, 35, 114
   see also MGM *Wizard*

filmmaking *see* movie-making

films created by fans 26, 35, 81

Finnegan, Brian 84, 145, 147

"First Date with the D.J." (Pearlberg poem) 28 note e

fitting in *see* acceptance

Fiyero (*Wicked* character) 181

folklore 171–76, 187 note m
   needs met by 174, 176

"Follow your bliss" 128, 134
  see also being yourself
formats of Oz stories *see* Oz stories
Forster, E. M. 165
Fort Lauderdale, FL 21
Four Dorothys, The (Ruditis) 183
Frank, Barney 18
free will 153, 211–12
Freudian theory 209, 110, 219 note b
friend archetype 133
Friend of Dorothy (Brian Andersen comic books) 183, 191 note t
"friend of Dorothy" (slang expression)
  history/origin of 150, 164–68, 176 note q, 229–33
  in names of gay businesses 22, 179 note a
  referring to people/creatures 25, 33, 108 note n, 146 note b, 179, 183, 191 note t
Friend of Dorothy's (online clothing store) 22
"Friends of Dorothy" (Kanefsky short story) 33
Friends of Dorothy® (San Francisco business) 22
Friends of Dorothy Travel (Australian business) 22
friends of fans 144, 186 note l
  gay friends as chosen family 95, 126, 171–72
friendship 117–19, 123, 137
  see also companions, Dorothy's
Frogman (Baum character) 112
Frozen (film) 190

Gage, Matilda 98 note c
Galves, Victoria 26
Gannaway, Atticus 82, 156
Garland, Judy 18, 42, 43, 46, 164, 165, 172
  as Dorothy Gale 41, 167, 172, 173
  as singer/concerts of 41, 65, 96, 100 note g, 164–65
  GAY CONNECTION/FANDOM
  cult of Judy as explanation for Oz–gay connection 17, 41–45, 164
  "friend of Dorothy" origin 229–30
  funeral and Stonewall 168–69
  and gay culture 24, 28 note e, 44 note c, 145, 162, 172–73, 183
  gay fans of 10, 42, 151, 165, 216 note c
  as gay icon 41–42, 44 note c, 65, 149–50, 168, 185

gay appeal of MGM *Wizard* 18, 41, 52
gay culture 50, 143, 161–71, 184–85, 193
  interpretations/meanings/messages 27, 106, 130, 132, 138–39
  knowledge of 6, 46–47, 149
  lists of gay movies 20, 43, 148, 184, 193
  see also Oz–gay connection
gay artists 81, 82, 119, 146, 165, 187 note n
  see also Eric Shanower
gay bars 20–21, 89
gay bookstores 25, 51 note n, 181
gay boys 12, 73, 186 note l, 193–94
  documentation about 6–8, 55–56
  evidence for 55–61, 67
  families of *see* families
  internal life of 61–67, 190
  social and school environment 61, 62, 125, 143, 155–56, 186–87
  as young adults 8, 12, 55, 65, 187 note n, 216
  see also gay sensibility; gender: atypicality
gay businesses 20–22, 148, 207
  see also specific businesses, e.g., Hungry Tiger Press
gay celebrities 17, 26, 171
  see also individuals, e.g., Rufus Wainwright
gay choruses 24, 149, 170
gay community 20, 120, 132, 143, 149, 172, 208
  see also gay culture
gay contexts, Oz in 21–27, 148, 149, 163, 227
gay culture 7, 11, 27, 71, 149
  see also Judy Garland: and gay culture
gay dance events/clubs 20–21, 24, 179
gay documentaries 26
gay events 27, 147
  see also gay pride events
gay fabulousness 152
gay fandom 11–12, 145, 147–48, 216, 217–18
gay fiction 183, 187 note n, 188
  see also fan fiction
gay film festivals 147, 180
gay filmmakers 26, 46, 84
  see also individuals, e.g., Derek Jarman
gay gift shops 22, 24, 25, 51–52, 148, 181 note c, 184
"gay gifts" 67 note k
gay health events 22
gay icons 23–24, 35, 92, 181, 182
  see also Judy Garland: and gay culture
gay identity 7, 11, 152, 208
  see also identity

gay images 7, 10, 67 note k, 120, 179, 186, 187
  lack of 61–62
gay issues, literature on 10
gay language 164, 166, 231–32
gay life 132
  see also coming out
gay media 26, 163, 166–67, 171–72, 181
gay myths 18, 134, 174–77
gay oppression 63 note g, 119 note e, 125, 130, 169 note j, 172, 185–86, 194
  see also heterocentrism; homophobia
gay organizations, names of 20 note c, 22–24, 148, 163, 179, 207
  see also names of specific organizations, e.g., BAGLY
gay–Oz connection *see* Oz–gay connection
gay Oz fans *see* fandom; gay appeal of MGM *Wizard*; gay boys; gay culture; Oz–gay connection; Oz stories: FAN RESPONSE TO
gay people 126, 192, 186–87
gay press 163, 166–67, 171–72, 181
gay pride events 22–24, 25, 146, 148, 169, 170, 171 note l
gay sensibility 11, 12, 89, 118, 152
  in Baum 221
  in boys 63–64, 67, 68
  in MGM film 46, 52, 152
  inborn 63–64 note g, 185–86, 191–92
  see also camp; gay stereotype; gentleness; nonviolence; performing arts
gay singers 29
  see also Fred Barton; Rufus Wainwright
gay space 42, 96
gay stereotype 18, 55–56, 61, 63–64, 108, 151, 153–54
gay–straight alliances 55, 186
gay writers 20, 51, 80, 96 note t, 207, 220
  see also individuals, e.g., Clive Barker
gender
  atypicality 56, 57, 63, 98, 116
  Baum and 97–99, 219–20
  boundaries 28, 106, 114–16, 223–25
  fandom and 97 note a
  politics 98, 99, 137
  roles 12, 99, 110, 114, 209
  see also female characters; male characters; masculinity
General Jinjur (Baum character) 105, 115, 120
Genova, Ted 146
Gentlemen Prefer Blondes (film) 45 note g

gentleness
  in gay boys 64, 89, 116
  in Oz characters 106, 111, 112, 119, 185, 192
geography
  as demographic issue 29, 65
  of Oz 88–93, 120, 136; *see also* China Country; Emerald City; Munchkinland; Winkies
GI Joe action figures 65
Gigi (film) 45 note g
Gillikins (Baum characters) 88
girl, wanting to be a 63
girls' stories 97, 116, 156
Glass Cat (Baum character) 111 note s, 120, 122 note g, 123
GLENDA (Pittsburgh organization) 22
Glinda 24, 34, 44, 101–2, 121 note f, 147, 194
  bubble of 37, 92
  as camp 102, 116, 152
  dressing up as 23, 147, 152, 157
  magic/power of 92, 101, 114–15, 116, 131
  mythic aspects of 133, 136
Glinda of Oz (Baum) 32
Gnome King of Oz, The (Thompson) 49
going to Oz 73–88, 103, 126, 129, 132, 192
  reasons for 73–76, 194
Goldstein, Richard 62
good vs. evil 90, 92
  see also evil
Gone with the Wind (film) 215
Goodnight Moon (Brown) 189 note s
Gorlinda (Brian Andersen comic character) 183
Gott, Dave 62
government of Oz 105, 121, 125
Grahn, Judy 163
graphic novels 33, 82
Green, Richard 56–57
Greenwich Village (NYC) 96, 147, 168
greeting cards 25, 36, 150, 184
Griffin, Mark 62, 81, 138, 144, 217
Griffo, Michael 152, 154
Griswold, Jerry 91 note n
Growing Up Gay (Singer) 60
GSAs 55, 186

Haas, Mark 82
Haley, Jack 34, 110
Hall, Todrick 182
Haller, Ken 58

Halloween 147, 157
Hamburger, Aaron 75
Hamilton, Margaret 34, 35, 44 note e, 103 note h, 146
   fans' contact with 82–83, 87–88, 104
   see also Wicked Witch
Hammerheads (Baum characters) 36
handing down culture 171–72
handing down love of Oz 145, 192–93
Handy Mandy (Thompson character) 104
hanky code 183
happy endings 92, 194
harassment 62, 66, 96, 118–19, 125, 188 note o
   see also violence: in gay lives
Harburg, E. Y. 34, 45 note g, 170
Harry Potter 190
He-Man action figures 156
Health Education Resource Organization (Baltimore) 22
Heintz, James 146
Hermsen, Larry 146 note b
hero's journey 100, 130, 133, 134, 137
heterocentrism 61 note c, 66, 135 note d, 186–87, 215
heterosexuality 127, 128
   assumptions about 135 note d, 215
   images of 128, 218
heterosexuals 19, 61, 157
   boys 57, 68
   fans 30–31, 158, 213–16
   reactions to Oz–gay connection 7, 157–59, 218
High Priest Colender (Baum character) 88
high school 55, 62, 84, 183
   see also young adults
history 30 note h, 162 note b, 186
   twentieth century 30
   World War II 166, 167
   1960s 126 note l
   pre-Stonewall gay life 176 note q, 186
   post-Stonewall generations 163, 172
   younger generations 53, 182–84
   see also baby boomers
Hitchcock, Alfred 91 note m
Hobbit, The (Tolkien) 77 note c
Hollywood 48 note i, 151
Hollywood Palace (TV series) 42
home 131, 212, 219 note b
   gay feelings about 7, 93–94, 170
   Kansas as 96, 131, 132, 138, 212
   Oz as 93–96
   theme in Oz and gay lives 7, 12, 49, 50–51, 209
   see also families; Kansas
"Home" (song in *The Wiz*) 130
Hometowns (Preston) 7
Homo Heights (film) 26
homophobia 61 note c, 126, 157, 186
   internalized homophobia 66, 98, 130, 149 note e, 217
   see also gay oppression; heterocentrism
homosexuality 12, 61–63, 156–57
   assumptions about 62–63, 154–56, 219–21
   feelings about 159–60, 218
honesty 127
Hot Peaches (NYC theater group) 163
Hottentot (Baum character) 121 note f
hourglass timer, Wicked Witch's 135
humans 120, 123
   see also individuals, e.g., Dorothy
Hungry Tiger (Baum character) 121 note f, 122 note g, 123
Hungry Tiger Press (San Diego) 84

I Was a Teenage Judy Garland Fan (play) 83
icons see gay icons
identification 74, 86, 93, 97, 102, 128 note a, 135, 136
   see also role models
identity 86, 96, 128, 131, 152, 212
   see also gay identity
"If I only had a brain" T-shirt 5
illustrations in Oz books 32, 49, 51 note n, 106, 135–36, 147
images of Oz in gay contexts 21–27, 149, 163, 227
imaginary friends 80, 81, 220
imaginary worlds 80, 88, 96 note t, 163
imagination 64, 153, 190
   see also fantasy
immigrants 212
independence 104–5, 119, 120, 137
individuation 131
infatuation 59
innate characteristics 63–64 note g, 185–86, 191–92
   see also gay sensibility
integration
   of identity 128, 131
   social integration 119–20
   see also acceptance

internalized homophobia 66, 98, 130, 149 note e, 217
see also homophobia
international issues 29, 65
International Wizard of Oz Club see IWOC
Internet see online information
introjection 129
irony 152, 184 note j, 193
see also camp
Isherwood, Christopher 165
Isle of Lesbos (film) 26–27
isolated fans 144
isolation 62, 66, 186, 118–19
It's Elementary (film) 62 note d
"It's sad, believe me, missy" 107
"I've a feeling we're not in Kansas anymore" 22, 27 note d, 148
variations 26, 149, 150, 179–80
IWOC 51, 84, 86–87, 157–58, 199
conventions 5, 7, 8, 145, 147, 159
gay men in 51, 149 note e, 150
members 5, 113 note t, 182 note i
as publisher 6, 32, 82

Jack Pumpkinhead (Baum character) 123, 131, 134
Jarman, Derek 20, 84
Jarrett, Conrad 84, 87, 103, 156
Jinjur (Baum character) 105, 115, 120
jobs 65, 82–84, 137
Johnny Tremain (Forbes) 156
Jones, Dean 59
Journey Back to Oz (film) 35
Judge Sifter (Baum character) 88
Jung, Jungians and Homosexuality (Hopcke) 6 note b
Jungian theory 84–85, 129, 130 note c, 131, 192, 210
active imagination 84–86
see also archetypes
junior high school 12, 55, 62

Kalidahs (Baum characters) 34, 90
Kanefsky, Bob 33, 191 note t
Kansas 37, 44, 50, 119, 124
as home 96, 131, 132, 138, 212
farmhands 36, 37, 94 note q
in questionnaire 9, 50
tornado 132, 135
visual aspects of 44, 159
wanting to return to 94–95, 132

see also home; "I've a feeling we're not in Kansas anymore"
Kantrowitz, Arnie 138
Keating, George 95 note s
Kenrick, John 146
Kight, Morris 67
King, Dorothy 165, 167
King Kleaver (Baum character) 88
Kovert, Frederick 114
Kriebel, Barry, Jr. 156

L.A. Shanti 22
labor 122
Lahr, Bert 34, 44 note e, 107–10
see also Cowardly Lion
Lance Loud! A Death in an American Family (film) 26
Land of Oz
adventuring/exploring in 36, 90–92, 98, 104, 116, 122
as benign place 89, 90, 92, 134, 209
communities/countries within Oz 36, 88, 119, 120, 134
geography of 88–93, 120, 136; see also China Country; Emerald City; Munchkinland; Winkies
government of 105, 121, 125
social values in 119, 121–22, 127
as utopia 117, 137, 194
visual splendor of 89
Land of Oz, The (Baum) see *Marvelous Land of Oz*
Land of Oz, The (TV special) 3, 35
language from Oz in gay contexts 21–27, 148, 149, 163, 227
Law of Oz and Other Stories, The (Dana) 111 note s
lesbians 18, 27, 28, 213–16
letter writing/corresponding 87
LGBT parents 188 note p, 193
libraries 5, 191
borrowing from 3, 77, 78, 155, 156, 191
exhibits 3, 158
refuge in 7, 144
see also specific libraries, e.g., DuBois Library
"Life and death are two aspects of the same thing" 134
Liir (*Wicked* character) 181
liking something, reasons for 209, 211–12, 217
Lion see Cowardly Lion

Lion Among Men, A (Maguire) 181 note d
"Lions and tigers and bears! Oh my!" 25
literature about gay issues and Oz 7
Little Me (Dennis) 152 note g
Little Women: LA (TV series) 180
live performances *see* stage versions
London 165
loneliness 62, 66, 186, 118–19
longitudinal studies 56 note b
Lord of the Rings, The (Tolkien) 77 note c, 216
Los Angeles 165
   Hollywood 48 note i, 151
   West Hollywood 18, 22, 24, 165
love 119 note d, 134
Love Bites (film) 18, 163
Love Bug, The (film) 59
Love Magnet 136 note e

Ma Vie en Rose (1997 film) 99 note e
MacMillan, Violet 114
Madama Butterfly (opera) 65
Maddox, John 83–84
magic 88, 92–93, 133
   of Wizard 113–14, 116, 131
   of others 101 103, 120, 131
   in Oz 80–81, 194
   objects 100, 103, 128, 134, 136 note e; *see also* Wicked Witch: magical objects
Magic Belt 100, 103
Magic of Oz, The (Baum) 48
Magic Picture 103
Magic Umbrella of Oz, The (Dana) 111 note s
Maguire, Gregory 76, 82
   childhood responses to MGM film 20, 81, 110
   gay connection and 50 note k, 65 note h, 149, 180 note b
   see also Wicked
Mailer, Norman 165
main story of *The Wizard of Oz* 6, 37, 38, 90, 113, 117, 133, 137
   stage versions of 148, 150–51, 159, 183; *see also* stage versions: of MGM *Wizard*, and of *Wonderful Wizard*
make-believe 64, 74, 79–81, 91, 128 note a
   imaginary friends 80, 81, 220
male characters 8, 106–14, 116
   weakness of 93 note o, 98, 106
male singers *see* singers, male

manifesting fandom 84, 87
   collecting 3, 6, 88, 128 note a, 144; *see also* Oz merchandise
   creating works *see* fan-created films; fan-created stories
   expertise 5, 6–7, 51, 87, 128 note a, 157
   letter writing/corresponding 87
   participating in events 51, 146, 158, 181; *see also* conventions; participating in an Oz story
   recreating works *see* recreating an Oz story
   using in life 10, 134–39
   see also sing-alongs of MGM film
map of Oz 136
   see also geography
marketing 20 note c, 22, 25, 191
Martin, Marvin 126
Marvelous Land of Oz, The (Baum) 32, 48, 105, 110, 112, 117, 148
   Tip in 28, 111, 114
   versions based on 3, 35
masculinity 108, 128, 219–20
mass media 187, 190
mastery 79, 80, 128 note a
Maxine, David 84, 87, 116 note v, 145
McAllister, Michael 59
McClellan, Mark 62
McClemont, Doug 84
McDougall, Bryce 57–58
McGinty, Mike 59
meaning of a work 9–10, 74, 209–10
Meet Me in St. Louis (film) 43
Mego Dorothy doll 156
Melbourne, Australia 180
Men from the Boys, The (Mann) 149 note d
Menvielle, Edgardo 57, 66
merchandise *see* Oz merchandise
Merry Go Round in Oz (McGraw and McGraw) 49
messages from Oz stories 128, 133–34, 137
metaphysical realm 93, 128, 132
methodology 210–18
MGM *Wizard* 34, 44–47, 120, 133, 144, 162–63, 191
   actors 34, 44 note e, 46, 84, 107–10, 114; *see also* Judy Garland; Margaret Hamilton
   advertising 27, 152
   creators 34, 45 note g, 46, 170
   merchandise 24, 36
   studio 45, 46, 164–65

CINEMATIC ASPECTS
black-and-white vs. color 3, 5, 26, 132, 135
other visual aspects of 44, 46, 89, 135, 152
dream ending 36, 44, 48 note I, 94–95, 209
lines from the film 20 note c, 24–25, 51, 101, 137, 144, 148; *see also particular lines*, e.g., "It's sad, believe me, missy"
scariness 91–92, 136
see also specific characters, e.g., Glinda; Wicked Witch
FAN RESPONSE TO THE FILM
fan involvement 82–84
gay appeal *see* gay appeal of MGM *Wizard*
public showing 42, 94, 109, 148, 149, 151
reenacting 81, 146
singing at piano/video bar 146, 181
VERSIONS AND COMPARISONS
compared with *Wonderful Wizard* 36–37, 43, 44, 48 note i, 51
compared with other Oz stories 35, 50, 124 note j
film allusions to 26
sing-alongs 21 fig 1.2, 27, 95 note s, 147, 174 note n, 184, 191
stage versions 27, 34, 108 note n, 179, 191
other versions 26, 33, 35
on television *see* television viewing of MGM *Wizard*
mice (*Wiz* characters) 34
Michel, Dee 1–12, 158
family 3, 7, 8, 162
IWOC talk 7–8, 158
Michel, Martin 3, 6, 8, 162
middle childhood 12, 76, 79, 81, 86, 98–99
Middle Earth (Tolkien) 163
middle school 55, 62, 186
military characters 89, 105, 120
military school 220
Milk (film) 25
Miller, Jeff 77, 156
Milton, James 78
minorities 181, 186–87, 212–13
Miss Gulch (character in MGM film) 36, 82–83, 94, 104, 114
Miss Gulch Returns (musical) 83, 104, 114, 147
see also Fred Barton
model of meaning 9–10, 74, 209–10
Mombi (Baum character) 32, 114–15
Mordden, Ethan 163
Morgan, Frank 111
mother figures 102, 133

mothers 8, 41, 63, 80, 115, 138
negative responses to fandom 62, 154, 192
positive responses to fandom 56 note a, 157
see also families; parents
movie villains 25, 103, 184
see also Wicked Witch
moviemaking 17, 44–45 note e, 84
see also films created by fans; MGM *Wizard*: CINEMATIC ASPECTS
Mr. Potato Head 24
Munchkinland 44, 88, 90, 99, 119 note e, 121 note f
Munchkins 111, 120, 159, 172
actors 84, 114
costumes/dressing up as 44, 84, 147, 159
size/stature of 88, 92–93, 120
Murch, Walter 98
"Murder in Oz, A" (Snow short story) 116
museums 35
musicals 11, 34, 35, 45–46, 181 note f
see also individual shows, e.g., *Wicked*; performing arts
My Favorite Martian (TV series) 58
My Fellow Americans (film) 19
mythogems 133
mythology 128, 132–35
gay myths 18, 134, 174–76
need for myths 171–77
Oz as myth 132–39
personal myths 134–37

name-calling 62, 118–19
names of gay organizations and businesses 20–22, 148, 163, 207
narrative tone of myths 136
National Gay and Lesbian History Month 182
Near, Holly 163
negative messages from society 61 note c, 66, 135 note d, 186–87, 215
Neher, Erick 86, 87, 186 note l
Neighborhoods: The Hidden Cities of San Francisco (TV series) 26
Neill, John R. 32, 51 note n, 106
Nell, Victor 79 note d
New Orleans, LA 21
New York City 35, 165, 168
New Yorker 19, 165
Newsweek 220
Nick Chopper *see* Tin Woodman
Nickolaus, John 155, 156

Night in the Emerald City, A (L.A. Shanti benefit) 22
Night on Bald Mountain (Mussorgsky orchestral piece) 25
Nightmare on Castro Street (film) 25
"No place like home" *see* "There's no place like home"
Nome King (Baum character) 91, 92
non-human characters 98, 120, 133, 134
  see also individual characters, e.g., Patchwork Girl
nonviolence 64, 89, 116, 137
Northwestern Connecticut Community College 182
nostalgia 74, 75–76, 137, 174, 192
novels *see* fiction

obsessive fans 144
oddballs 120, 122–25, 126, 128, 130, 134
Of Oz the Wizard (film) 26
"Off to see the Wizard" (lyric in MGM film) 138
Off to See the Wizard (TV series) 78
Ojo (Baum character) 11 note s, 95, 120, 122, 143, 194
  gender issues 111–12, 114
  as outsider 125, 136
Ojo in Oz (Thompson, 1933) 49
Oklahoma! (musical) 87
Once in a Lullaby (Breyette painting) 174
online information 35–36, 84, 143, 146 note b, 184, 186, 191
"Only bad witches are ugly" 121 note f, 148
Oppenheimer, George 165
oppression *see* gay oppression
"Optimistic Voices" (song in MGM film) 35 MGM
oral communication 173
origin of sexual orientation 10–11
origin stories 176
original Oz stories *see* fan-created stories
Ork (Baum character) 133
"other" archetype 126
other realm 93, 128, 132
Out of Oz (Maguire) 181 note d
Outreach Program for Children with Gender-Variant Behaviors and Their Families 57, 66
Outreach Zone (Chicago organization) 23
outsider archetype 126
outsider status of gay males 11, 50, 126

outsiders, Oz characters as 120, 122–25, 126, 128, 130, 134, 181
"Over the Rainbow" (song in MGM film) 25, 185
  as expression of yearning 44, 96, 132, 138, 164 note d, 170
  as gay anthem 27 note d, 163, 170
  as gay event theme 21, 24, 182
  in gay film/TV/ads 22, 25, 26
  as music 34, 35, 45 note g, 50, 103 note i, 170
  performances in gay context 26, 147, 149
  rainbow flag and 170–73, 176
Over the Rainbow (Minneapolis bar) 21
Over the Rainbow (UK TV series) 26
Over the Rainbow and Back (Butterworth Farm event) 24
Oxford English Dictionary 166 note g
Oz (imaginary place) *see* Land of Oz
"Oz" as name of club/bar 21
Oz Before the Rainbow (Swartz) 51–52 note n
Oz books 47–48, 50, 75, 77, 78, 136
  canon 32, 38
  gay males and 6, 20, 30, 162, 183–85, 186 note l
  illustrations 32, 49, 51 note n, 106, 135–36, 147
  plot points 114, 117, 122, 127
  as series 3, 32, 44, 76, 77, 118, 189, 191
  reading aloud 3, 135, 144
  reading as escape 73–74, 118–19
  by Thompson 8, 32, 38, 49, 95, 97 note b, 104, 127
  see also individual titles, e.g., *Marvelous Land of Oz*; Oz stories
Oz fandom *see* fandom
Oz Fantasy Parade (Chesterton, IN) 157
Oz Film Manufacturing Company 34
Oz–gay connection 8, 17, 20 note c, 30
  evidence for 18–27, 179
  origin of 143–48, 162–63, 212
  change in status 185–93
  learning about 149, 151, 163, 180 note b
  reactions to 6, 149–60
  see also gay appeal of MGM *Wizard*
Oz in gay contexts 21–27, 148, 149, 163, 227
Oz Kids (video series) 35
Oz merchandise 5, 36, 51 note n, 53, 155, 184, 191
  greeting cards 25, 36, 150, 184

poppers 25, 163
refrigerator magnets 24–25, 36, 51 note n
Oz on stage *see* stage versions
Oz phenomenon 3–6, 7, 32–39, 191, 210–12
Oz poppers 25, 163
Oz Squad (comic books) 33
Oz stories 32–35, 38–39, 47–52, 191
    availability of different versions of Oz stories 74, 189
    gay appeal of Oz stories across versions 6, 17, 18, 36, 143, 162
    VERSIONS
    animated versions 35, 78, 190
    film versions 26, 34, 35, 78, 114, 190; *see also individual films*, e.g., *Return to Oz*
    stage versions 34, 81, 82–84, 182
    television versions 3, 35, 78, 191
    see also main story of *The Wizard of Oz*; Oz books; *Wonderful Wizard*
    FAN RESPONSE TO OZ STORIES
    audience for 32–33, 74 note b, 97, 191
    fans and 50, 51, 53, 75, 78, 79
    see also appropriation; recreation
    THEMES
    gender 28, 116
    myth 132–39
    other themes across versions 28, 117, 124, 130
Oz the Great and Powerful (film) 35
Oz: The Hundredth Anniversary Celebration (Glassman) 51–52 note n
Ozma (Baum character) 102–3
    beauty of 102, 106
    court and palace 95, 120, 121 note f, 122, 126
    fans and 81, 143, 192
    friendships with girls 103, 121, 122
    magic and power of 92, 101, 103
    origin as Tip 32, 102, 114–16, 136
    as ruler 89, 95, 100, 112, 119
    see also Tip
Ozma of Oz (Baum) 35, 48, 114
Ozmapolitan Convention 51
Ozzo Unlimited (Houston company) 25, 163

parents
    control over kids 188, 193
    gay and gender issues 56 note a, 57, 62, 128
    love of Oz 3, 78, 145, 192–93
    reading aloud 3, 76, 192
    see also LGBT parents; mothers

Paris Is Burning (film) 29
Parker, Dorothy 165–67, 230
participating in an Oz story 82–84, 152
parties 148
passing along culture 171–72
passing along love of Oz 145, 192–93
Patchwork Girl (Baum character) 104, 112, 114, 122, 136
    fan response to 93, 194
    as humanoid 120, 134
Patchwork Girl of Oz, The (Baum novel) 34, 48, 111 note s, 121 note f
Patchwork Girl of Oz, The (film) 114
Peacock Lady (early Oz film character) 114
performativity/performing an identity 152
performing arts 64–65, 152, 220
    see also specific performing groups, e.g., Hot Peaches; musicals; stage versions
personal appearance *see* appearance, personal
personal mythology 134–37
Peter Pan (1904 play) 189
phenomenon of Oz 3–6, 7, 32–39, 191
phoniness *see* secrecy
piano bars 144, 146
Pirates in Oz (Thompson) 49
play *see* make-believe
play versions *see* stage versions
plays *see* theater
Polychrome (Baum character) 104, 122
pop singers 183–84
    see also singers, female; singers, male; singing groups
pop-up *Wizard* (Sabuda) 33, 51 note n, 181 note c
poppers 25, 163
poppy field 28 note 3, 34, 135–36
popular culture 135
post-Stonewall generations 163, 172
Potter, Harry 190
Powder of Life 92, 134
preschool *see* early childhood
pre-Stonewall gay life 176 note q, 186
Prince of Regalia (Baum character) 127
Princess Ozma *see* Ozma
print media 84, 173, 189
private fandom 144
products 51, 184, 191
Professor Marvel (character in MGM film) 36, 44 note e
projection 129

psychoanalytic theory 209, 110, 219 note b
  see also subconscious; unconscious
publishing 84, 173, 189

Quadlings (Baum characters) 88
qualitative vs. quantitative research 207, 209, 213–16
Queer Today, Gone Tomorrow (short film) 26
questionnaire 8–9, 31, 50, 199–205
quests 100, 130, 133, 134, 137
Quigley, Patrick 155, 156

Raabe, Meinhardt 84
race 29, 120, 121 note f, 208
Rainbow Center (University of Connecticut) 182
rainbow flag 51–52 note n, 159, 170–72
Randy (Thompson character) 127
Rape of Ganymede, The (film) 25–26
reactions to fandom 7–8, 98, 128, 144–45, 154–59
reader-response theory 210
readers 9, 79
reading
  aloud 3, 135, 144
  as escape 73–74, 118–19
  gay reading lists 185
  learning to read 77
  see also rereading
Realbad, the bandit chief (Thompson character) 95
reality behind illusion 93, 128, 132
recordings 35, 41 note a, 45 note g, 65, 78, 83, 215
recreating an Oz story 79, 81, 137, 146, 152
  see also appropriation
refrigerator magnets 24–25, 36, 51 note n
refuge 80, 93, 96, 125
Rent (musical) 182 note h
repeat readings and viewings 10, 78, 80, 136–37, 193
repression 62, 129–30
  see also coming out
rereading/reviewing 10, 78, 80, 136–37, 193
research, types of 6, 56, 207, 209, 213–16
research for this book 6–8, 11–12
  logic 7, 60, 68, 156–57, 209, 215
  methodology 210–18
  model 9–10, 74, 209–10
  questionnaire 8–9, 31, 50, 199–205
  results *see* themes in a work or a life

subjects 207–9
terminology 38–39
resonance 9–10, 78, 135, 173, 190, 192–93
  see also appropriation
retrospective accounts 56
Return to Oz (film) 35, 49, 78, 90
"Return to Oz" (Scissor Sisters song) 183–84
Rinkitink in Oz (Baum) 121 note f
Rivers, Rebecca 157
Road to Oz (Baum) 77, 81
Robinson, Scott 147
Rockshots greeting card 150
Rocky and His Friends (TV series) 189 note s
Rocky Horror Picture Show, The (film) 27, 45 note g
role models 98, 190
  gay men as 20, 43, 131, 187 note n
  Oz characters as 20, 109, 128 note a, 194
  see also identification
Royal Army of Oz 89
Royal Shakespeare Company version of MGM film 34 note j
Ruby Slippers (MGM film) 28 note e, 128, 137, 138–39
  in gay contexts 22, 24, 25, 27, 157, 182
  as plot device 95, 100, 102
  visual aspects of 37, 44, 92, 135
RuPaul's Drag Race (TV series) 180
Ryman, Geoff 32, 34, 49–50, 51 note n, 80 note e, 82, 146

Sabuda, Robert 33, 51 note n, 119, 181 note c
safety 80, 93, 96, 125
San Francisco 25, 179, 180
  Castro neighborhood 26, 51 note n, 96, 126
  Castro Theatre 42, 94, 109, 148, 149, 151
  Freedom Day Parade 25
  Friends of Dorothy® (San Francisco business) 22
  as a gay place 24, 26, 96
Sando, Steve 154
saturation 207
Sawhorse (Baum character) 93, 120, 122 note g, 123 note h, 134
Scarecrow 5, 28, 34, 95, 105, 117–18
  brains of 86, 131
  dressing up as/play character 81, 147
  as favorite character 99 note f, 103, 112, 113
  friendship/cooperation 119, 138
  as humanoid 120, 121 note f, 122, 133, 134
  identifying with 194

Lion and 107, 108
  recognizability of 136, 143
  strength and weakness of 89, 90, 93, 137
  Tin Woodman and 33, 110, 111, 117–18
  in *The Wiz* 35, 113
  see also companions, Dorothy's
scariness 37, 89 note l, 90–92, 128 note a, 136
Schiller, Justin 5
scholarly work 6–7, 157
Scholastic Books program 156
school environment 61–62, 66
  elementary school 62; *see also* early childhood; middle childhood
  middle school 55, 62; *see also* middle childhood
  high school 55, 62, 84, 183; *see also* young adults
  school plays 81, 82, 84, 191
  schoolmates 125, 143, 144, 155
  see also harassment
scope of Oz 32–39
Scraps, the Patchwork Girl *see* Patchwork Girl
Seattle 21
secrecy 62, 66–67, 127, 130
  see also being yourself; coming out
segregation 119–20
  see also acceptance
self-esteem 62, 67, 130
self-knowledge 12, 49, 128–30
  see also being yourself
self-reliance 128
Selig, John 60
sense-making 79, 80
series books 3, 32, 44, 76, 77, 118, 152 note g, 189, 191
  see also names of individual series, e.g., *Tales of the City*
sexual attraction 57
sexual excitement 58–59
sexual fantasies 59
sexual orientation 10–12, 55
Shaggy Man (Baum character) 122, 123, 136, 209
shame 127, 129, 130
Shanower, Eric 33, 75, 82, 84, 145, 153
shared fantasy play 81
sharing fandom 10, 143, 144, 145, 150–51, 209
shoes 26, 36
  see also Ruby Slippers; Silver Shoes
short stories 28 note e, 116, 124 note i, 146, 153

siblings 186 note l
  see also families
Silver Shoes (*Wonderful Wizard*) 36, 128, 158
Simmons, Nikita 186 note l
sing-alongs of MGM film 27, 95 note s, 147, 174 note n, 184, 191
singers, female 29 note g, 35, 151, 171
  see also Judy Garland; Barbra Streisand
singers, male 29, 34, 35, 113
  see also Fred Barton; Rufus Wainwright
Singin' in the Rain (film) 45 note g
singing at piano/video bar 146, 181
singing groups 111, 150, 183–84
Sir Dashemoff Daily (early Oz stage character) 114
sissies 20, 62, 63, 108
Sissy Boy Syndrome, The (Green) 56–57 note b, 65
"sissy"/"sissyboy" 63 note f
Sissyphobia (Bergling) 20
sixties (1960s) 126 note l
slang 164, 166, 231–32
slash fiction 191 note t
small characters 92–93
small presses 32, 187
social construction 10, 12, 108
social environment 11, 30 note h, 186, 191, 193–94, 212, 217
  see also gay boys: social and school environment
Soldier with the Green Whiskers (Baum character) 89
soldiers in World War II 166, 167
"Some people go both ways" 28
"Somewhere Over the Rainbow" *see* "Over the Rainbow"
Son of a Witch (Maguire) 51–52 note n, 146, 181
"Song for the Tin Man" (What Time Is It, Mr. Fox? song) 111, 184
Songs for the Tin Man (What Time Is It, Mr. Fox? EP) 184
Sound of Music, The (film) 45 note g, 105 note j
Southbridge Public Library 158
"special friend" 57, 66, 118
Spectrum Center (Marin, CA) 24
Speedy (Thompson character) 8, 214
Speedy in Oz (Thompson) 8
spirituality 7, 9, 74 note a, 84, 103, 190, 192
  reality behind illusion 93, 128, 132

Splash (NYC bar) 181
SpongeBob SquarePants (TV series) 189
    note s
Spoon Brigade (Baum characters) 88
Springfield, MA 21
St. Paul, MN 21
stage versions
    of main story 148, 150–51, 159, 183
    of MGM *Wizard* 27, 34, 108 note n, 179, 191
    of Oz stories 34, 81, 82–84, 182
    see also Was; *Wicked*; *Wizard of Oz* (1902 musical)
Star Is Born, A (1954 film) 43
Star Trek (TV series) 192
Star Wars (films) 192
Stillpoint, Horehound 60
Stonewall Riots
    Garland's funeral and 168–69, 175
    as historical turning point 43, 163, 175 note p, 176 note q
    plays about 168 note i
Stonewall Veteran's Association 169
stories *see* fiction; Oz stories; short stories
stories for girls 97, 116, 156
Storm, Earl 62
Straight Outta Oz (album and live performance) 182
strong female characters 98, 104–5, 212
"Stuck up here with a pole up your back" 148
subconscious 86, 132, 188
    see also unconscious
subjects, research 207–9
subterranean works 187–89, 190, 194
suicide 12
support groups 96, 186
    for parents of gender-atypical kids 57, 64, 66
Surrender Dorothy (film) 26
surrogate families 95, 171–72
Sutton, Roger 186 note l
symbols 9, 128, 129

Tales of the City (Maupin) 152 note g
tattoos 84
teachers 61–62, 66
teasing 62, 118–19
teenagers *see* young adults
television versions of Oz stories 3, 35, 78, 191
television viewing of MGM *Wizard* 27, 34, 41
    annual viewing by boomers 76–77, 163, 191
    black-and-white only 3, 44 note d

Temple, Shirley 3, 35
Ten Quart Kettle (Baum character) 88
terminology 38–39
Terrien, Brent 84, 151
Terry (dog who played Toto) 114
theater *see names of individual plays*, e.g., *Rent*; dressing up as Oz characters; performing arts; school environment: school plays; stage versions; Stonewall Riots: plays about
themes in a work or a life 9, 91
    in gay lives 187–88, 212–16
    in gay lives and Oz 7, 30–31, 209–10
    in many Oz stories 11–12, 53
    in Oz books 96, 118
    in *The Wiz* 49, 130
    in works competing with Oz 190, 192, 193, 194
    mythic themes 135, 137
    see also individual themes, e.g., gender; home; identity
themes, use of 88
theory 210
    see also Freudian theory; Jungian theory
"There's no place like home" (line in MGM film)
    in gay contexts 21 fig 1.4, 22, 23, 180
    sentiment 94, 100 note g, 138, 209
Thompson, Mark 73–74, 135, 144, 156
Thompson, Ruth Plumly 8, 32, 38, 49, 95, 97 note b, 104, 127
three-dimensionality of Land of Oz 88
Tik-Tok (Baum character) 122
time, changes over *see* history
Time Hotel (Manhattan) 22
Tin Man (TV miniseries) 128, 191
Tin Woodman 34, 95, 107
    appearance of 110
    emotions, sensitivity 110–11, 134
    as humanoid 120, 121 note f, 122
    lacking heart 5, 111
    and Scarecrow 33, 111, 117–18
    strength/weakness 89, 90, 137
    see also companions, Dorothy's
Tinman (*Wiz* character) 81
Tip (Baum character) 105, 111, 123 note h, 136
    becoming Ozma 28, 32, 102, 114–16, 136
    Shirley Temple as 3, 35
    see also Ozma
Tommy Kwikstep (Baum character) 124
Tongues Untied (film) 26

tornado 132, 135
Toronto 21
Toto 96 note q, 114, 133
　gay slang 166 note f
　in gay context 22, 26
　size of 92, 122
"Toto, I've a feeling we're not in Kansas anymore" *see* "I've a feeling …"
toys 80 note e, 82, 93, 98, 155 note j, 220
Tragedy of Miss Geneva Flowers, The (Babcock) 183
transcendent reality 93, 128, 132
transgender people 28, 115, 213
transmedia storytelling 36, 191 note t
traveling to Oz *see* going to Oz
trickster archetype 133
Trot (Baum character) 102, 120, 122
True Colors (CT youth conference) 182
true nature, one's *see* secrecy
truth 98, 127, 138
Tucker, Tim 62, 111
Tuerk, Catherine 57, 66
Turner Broadcasting 27
Turpen, Alan 83
twentieth century 30

"Ugly Duckling, The" (Andersen fairy tale) 124 note i
Uncle Henry (MGM character) 35, 93 note o, 94, 95, 106 note k
unconscious 86, 129, 132
　see also subconscious
Under the Rainbow (Kantrowitz) 138
uniqueness 7, 98, 126, 130
　see also acceptance; characters: celebrities
University of Connecticut Rainbow Center 182
University of Wisconsin 5
Utensia 88, 120, 134
utopia 12, 170, 187, 190
　as literary genre 90, 117
　Oz as 117, 137, 194

Velocity of Gary, The (film) 26
Velvet Rage, The (Downs) 66 note i
versions of Oz stories *see* Oz stories
villains, movie 25, 103, 184
　see also Wicked Witch
violence
　in gay lives 66, 92, 125, 188 note o
　in Oz stories 32, 33, 89, 90, 116

visual aspects of Oz *see* Emerald City; Kansas; MGM *Wizard*: CINEMATIC ASPECTS; Oz books; Ruby Slippers; Wicked Witch

Wainwright, Rufus 17, 20, 26, 154, 183
Was (Ryman) 32, 34, 49–50, 51 note n, 80 note e, 82, 146
Waters, John 20
Wausau, WI 21
weak males 93 note o 98, 106
websites *see* online information
West Hollywood, CA 18, 22, 24, 165
West Side Story (film) 46 note h
"What They Carried" (Currier short story) 146
What Time Is It, Mr. Fox? (singing group) 111, 184
Whatever Happened to Baby Jane? (film) 217
Where the Rainbow Ends (Currier) 149 note d
Whitaker, Anthony 83, 84
Whitcomb, Jim 76, 137–38
wholeness 131
Wicked 43 note b, 49–50, 103 note i
　Elphaba 103, 124–25, 184
　gay connection 102, 180–81, 182
　novel (Maguire) 32–33, 194
　objects for sale 51 note n, 182
　stage version 34, 191
Wicked: The Grimmerie (Cote) 181 note c
Wicked Witch 34, 88, 102, 120
　IN MGM FILM
　castle of 25, 44, 135
　as evil 101, 103, 119 note e, 133, 184
　magical objects of 36, 37, 92, 102, 135
　power of 92, 103, 105, 119 note e
　relationship to other characters 102, 104
　scariness of 37, 90–92, 89 note l, 128 note a
　visual aspects of 102, 135, 136
　FAN RESPONSE TO WICKED WITCH
　as camp 103–4, 152, 184
　dressing up as/performing 80, 82, 147, 183
　in gay film context 25, 26, 179
　positive feelings of fans 80 note f, 99 note f, 103–4, 184, 194, 209
　IN WORKS OTHER THAN MGM FILM
　Wicked 32–33, 103; *see also* Elphaba; *Wicked*
　other works 35, 37, 80 note e, 100
　see also Elphaba; Margaret Hamilton
Wicked Years books (Maguire) 181 note c
　see also individual titles, e.g., *Son of a Witch*

Winkies (Baum characters) 88, 110, 112, 119
    note e, 120
witches 80 note f, 92, 121 note f, 133, 148
    see also Elphaba; Glinda; Mombi; Wicked
        Witch
Wiz, The 17, 29 note f, 35
    compared with other versions 34, 124
        note j
    family/home in 102, 124, 130
    film 18, 37, 49, 113
    stage version 49, 83, 191
Wizard of A.I.D.S., The (musical) 34
Wizard of Oz (Oz character) 120, 132, 181
    as closet symbol 127, 130, 133
    learning magic 114, 131
    masculinity/as father figure 100–101,
        113–14, 138
Wizard of Oz, The (1900 Baum novel) *see*
    Wonderful Wizard of Oz
Wizard of Oz, The (1902 musical) 30, 33–34,
    114, 191
Wizard of Oz, The (1925 film) 34, 114
Wizard of Oz, The (1933 short film) 35
Wizard of Oz, The (1939 MGM film) *see*
    MGM *Wizard*
Wizard of Oz, The (2011 Andrew Lloyd
    Webber musical) 108 note n, 179
Wizard of Oz on Ice, The 34
Wizard's throne room (MGM film) 135
Wogglebug (Baum character) 112, 115
Women, The (film) 181 note f
Women in Love (film) 99 note e
wonder 50, 74, 90, 93, 133
    see also awe
Wonderful Wizard of Oz, The (Baum) 32,
    33–34, 38, 133, 191
    fan response to 18, 30, 47–48, 156, 184

illustrations 32, 37, 147
plot 90, 101, 120, 131
VERSIONS AND COMPARISONS
book versions 33, 51 note n, 52, 181 note c
film versions 34, 35, 114; *see also* MGM
    Wizard
MGM *Wizard* compared to 36–37, 43, 44,
    48 note i, 51
musical version (1902) 30, 33–34, 114, 191
see also Baum; Oz books
Wonderful Wizard of U.S., The (play) 163
Wonderland (Carroll's Alice books) 96 note t
Woolcott, Alexander 165
Woolf, Edgar Allen 46
Woozy (Baum character) 111 note s
work 122
world building 80, 88, 191 note t
World War II 166, 167
writers 6, 50, 117, 134, 162, 166, 183, 207, 220
    see also individuals, e.g., E. M. Forster; gay
        writers
writing about gay issues 7
writing about Oz (nonfiction) 7
writing letters/corresponding 87
Wynn, Bessie 114

yearning 132
    see also escape
Yellow Brick Road 44, 76, 82, 169
    in gay context 22, 24, 27, 148, 179, 180
young adult fiction 183, 187 note n
young adults 12, 86, 144, 149
    see also high school
younger generations 53, 182–84
Yranski, Joe 62, 125, 145, 147, 155, 159

Zen of Oz, The (Green) 107

www.ingramcontent.com/pod-product-compliance
Lightning Source LLC
Chambersburg PA
CBHW070909030426
42336CB00014BA/2346